Acceptable Risks

Politics, Policy, and Risky Technologies

C. F. LARRY HEIMANN

Ann Arbor

THE UNIVERSITY OF MICHIGAN PRESS

2000   1999   1998   4   3   2

A CIP catalog record for this book is available from the British Library.

Library of Congress Cataloging-in-Publication Data

Heimann, C. F. Larry (Clarence Fredrick)
    Acceptable risks :   politics, policy, and risky technologies   /   C. F. Larry
Heimann.
        p.   cm.
    Includes bibliographical references and index.
    ISBN 0-472-10813-1 (cloth)
    1. Technology—Risk assessment.   2. United States. Food and Drug
Administration.   3. United States. National Aeronautics and Space
Administration.   I. Title.
    T174.5.H44   1997
    353.9′9—dc21   97-27087
                                                                        CIP

To my parents, Marjorie and Charles,
who taught me to always learn from my mistakes.

Contents

Figures and Tables

Figures

Tables

Preface

Complex and risky technologies are an engine for economic growth in our society. Nonetheless, these new technologies also pose many problems for political leaders and the policymakers responsible for overseeing them. While some elements in our society may wish to turn back the clock to a simpler time, the truth of the matter is that technological progress and its associated risks are facts of life that we must to learn to live with. This book provides important insights on the nature of technological management by public agencies. While it provides no easy answers for avoiding catastrophic failure, this book can help guide political leaders and agency directors in making better choices for the management of these risky technologies.

In order to make this book accessible to a wide range of readers, I have tried to limit the use of mathematical expressions to modeling exercises within chapters 2, 4, and 5. Readers who do not have much interest or expertise in mathematics can skip over these modeling exercises without missing the general ideas found in this book. (Footnotes in the text will remind the reader of this fact.) Those who are willing to work through the modeling exercises will find greater support for these arguments and will be better prepared to apply these concepts to other policy areas. These exercises are interesting and informative, so I would urge the reader to work through them in order to maximize his or her benefit. In any case, there is plenty of material in this book that should be helpful to both scholars and public administrators wrestling with the management of risky technologies.

Acknowledgments

The process of seeing this book through from an idea to a published manuscript has been a long one indeed. I have many people to thank, starting with some of my professors in graduate school. Bill Lowry served as my adviser in graduate school and has continued to read my work and comment on it over the years. Not only is he an insightful professor, he is a good friend, and I am grateful for his help. John Gilmour and Jack Knight also served on my dissertation committee when these ideas were first being developed. Not only did they help get this project off the ground, but they encouraged me to pursue this matter further, knowing that there was still much to be done in order to turn this project into a first-rate piece of scholarship. During my years at Washington University, a number of other graduate students and professors commented on my work, and while I cannot list them all, I am particularly grateful to Craig Humphries, Charles Franklin, Ann Khademian, and Liane Kosaki for their constructive criticisms. Paul Wahlbeck (now of George Washington University) has been one of my best friends in graduate school and beyond. His help and support over the years have been tremendous.

I have been fortunate enough to work with some wonderful colleagues at Michigan State University. Tom Hammond and Jack Knott have read and commented on my work and have been tremendously supportive of this project. In addition, Paul Abramson and Paula Kearns have given me advice and encouragement at various stages of this project, for which I am grateful. I would also like to thank Michigan State University for awarding me an All-University Research Grant, which helped fund some of the travel and other expenses involved in this research.

In addition to my colleagues at Michigan State, a number of other scholars have offered constructive criticisms of my work at conferences and seminars. Among them are Jon Bendor, Don Chisholm, Gary Miller, Don Kettl, Martin Landau, Todd LaPorte, Scott Sagan, Lee Siegleman, and Jack Wright. Despite all the helpful comments I have received over the years, any errors that remain in this book fall squarely on my shoulders alone.

I am grateful to all the men and women at NASA and the FDA who took time from their busy schedules to talk with me and for sharing documentation that has aided my research. Without their cooperation, this project would not have been possible. I promised them anonymity as a condition of the interviews, and I have done my best to keep my word. I would like to extend particular thanks to the staff at the NASA History Office. They have been extremely helpful to me as I collected documents regarding the political and organizational changes that occurred at NASA; without their expertise, it is doubtful I would have been able to find as much pertinent information as I did regarding NASA.

Finally, I have many family and friends to thank for their encouragement and support over the years—far too many people to name in this brief section. I am particularly grateful to my brother John and his wife Sue for allowing me to stay with them while I was in D.C. and for building me an external hard drive that allowed me to do some of my work at home. I am especially thankful for my lovely wife, An, and our twin boys, Alex and Mark. They patiently listened to me talk about my work, tolerated my being absent from time to time, and freely gave me their love at the times I needed it most. Most important, An and the boys have reminded me that—in the grand scheme of things—there is more to life than getting books published. I thank God for blessing me with such a wonderful family.

CHAPTER 1

Understanding Agency Failure

On January 28, 1986, the entire nation focused on a single event. Seventy-three seconds after liftoff, the space shuttle *Challenger* was destroyed in a powerful explosion fifty thousand feet above the Kennedy Space Center. The losses resulting from this catastrophe were quite high. Seven astronauts, including Teacher-in-Space Christa McAuliffe, were killed as the shuttle broke apart and fell into the sea. The shuttle itself had to be replaced at a cost of over $2 billion. The launch of many important commercial and military satellites had to be delayed as American space policy ground to a complete halt. The accident had a profound impact on the National Aeronautics and Space Administration (NASA) as well. The agency's credibility and its reputation for flawless execution of complex technological tasks were lost along with the *Challenger*. To this day, the legacy of *Challenger* haunts the decisions of both the agency and its political superiors in Congress and the White House.

An examination of the shuttle remnants and other launch data revealed the technical cause of the accident. The shuttle was destroyed when an O-ring seal on the right solid rocket motor failed, allowing the escaping hot gases to burn through and ignite the main fuel tank of liquid hydrogen and liquid oxygen. Although identifying the technical cause of this disaster is important, it represents only one aspect of the problem. Perrow (1984) has argued that organizational and technological failures have become intimately linked so that to fully understand the cause of most major accidents, we must analyze both the administrative and technical aspects of the situation. While there have been some administrative critiques of NASA in the wake of this disaster, almost all have centered on issues of bureaucratic culture, such as the agency's propensity to ignore key evidence and the myopic view of its mission. Surprisingly little has been done on a systematic analysis of the NASA organization structure and how it may or may not have contributed to the loss of *Challenger*.

Understanding how organizational structure and behavior can affect the likelihood of agency failure is a concern not only to NASA; it is an issue that is becoming relevant to a wide array of public agencies. The development of new technologies is occurring in all sectors of the economy and is taking place at an accelerating rate. Policymakers have generally applauded these changes because of the economic growth that usually follows technological advances As more complex technologies are created, however, the potential for major accidents increases as well. This concern for failure is augmented by the fact that mishaps with many types of new technologies have catastrophic consequences. The net result is that while we are eager to acquire the benefits of technologies advances, we are also reluctant to accept all the potential consequences of this policy.

These cross pressures bind administrative agencies responsible for managing and/or regulating these new technologies. On the one hand, agencies are told by political superiors not to inhibit important technological advances and may even be charged with promoting such development. On the other hand, agencies must provide enough monitors and guidance to ensure that no major accidents will occur under their watch. Consider the example of the Food and Drug Administration (FDA) and its review and approval of new pharmaceuticals. If the FDA were to wrongly give its approval for a new drug, many people could be seriously harmed or killed as a result. At the same time, both industry officials and public-interest groups have accused the FDA of raising the costs of producing new drugs—which increases the price of current drugs and inhibits the development of new ones—and have claimed that the agency has denied or significantly delayed the approval of important new pharmaceuticals. Similar cross pressures are felt by the Environmental Protection Agency with regard to pollution control, the Nuclear Regulatory Commission in response to nuclear safety standards, the Federal Aviation Administration in the area of airline safety, and many other agencies. Thus, it is clear that the issue of reliability in organizational performance has been a steadily growing concern for modern bureaucracy.

The reliable management of new technologies provides further challenges to the traditional approach to bureaucratic policy-making. It is well known that bureaucrats typically "muddle through" problems, relying on a trial-and-error process to achieve the desired results (Lindblom 1959; Braybrooke and Lindblom 1963; Jones 1984; Hayes 1992; but see Bendor 1985). Given the large costs associated with catastrophic accidents, however, the general public and its elected officials often demand failure-free management of these technologies. How viable can a policy strategy of trial and error be when the responsible agencies are prohibited from committing any errors? Clearly there are limitations to using the typical incremental approach when dealing with the management of hazardous technologies.

In the same manner, presidential appointees and legislators who are charged with overseeing the operations of these agencies also face difficulties. Knowing the concern for catastrophic failure, bureaucrats are sure to publicly state that safety and reliability are the agency's top priorities when asked by inquiring political superiors. Yet that alone cannot be satisfactory since it is clear that simply stating an objective is no guarantee that the agency will take the necessary action to realize that objective. At the same time, these political superiors cannot utilize objective statistical methods in trying to determine whether an agency's performance is satisfactory. Such methods involve, at one level or another, counting the number of accidents that have occurred—which is antithetical to the goal of preventing accidents from occurring in the first place. What both career bureaucrats and political superiors need is to understand how to reduce the probability of failure before it occurs, not after the fact.

Theory to the Rescue?

Public administration theory could be particularly instructive here. If we had a strong theoretical understanding for the factors that contribute to greater organizational reliability, we could use this knowledge to derive principles for the sound management of hazardous technologies. Unfortunately, there are a number of shortcomings with the public administration research in this area. The first is simply the lack of work done with regard to organizational reliability. The traditional public administration focus on organizational design has involved the pursuit of efficiency, in the sense of minimizing costs for a given level of output. Implicit in this traditional analysis is that the reliable performance of the organization was constant. The critical question therefore is usually how one might achieve same level of services at a lower cost. As a result, the policy recommendations from this traditional line of thinking have been to streamline administrative systems and reduce organizational redundancy as much as possible.

The work of Martin Landau on redundancy in organizations was a particularly important contribution to this debate inasmuch as he recognized that administrative reliability is dependent on structural factors. In breaking with conventional wisdom, Landau's landmark 1969 essay, "Redundancy, Rationality, and the Problem of Duplication and Overlap," asserted that the critical question was not how to cut the costs of administrative performance, but rather how to insure the organization's effectiveness. Landau began by noting, "No matter how much a part is perfected, there is always the chance that it will fail" (1969, 350). As he observed, a streamlined system requires only that one part fail for the entire system to fail. Drawing on concepts from engineering reliability theory, Landau argued that redundancy built into the system can make an organization more reliable than any of its parts. Therefore, Landau concluded, administrative redundancy and duplication can be an important part of effective government.

Some work has been done to extend Landau's initial insights regarding organizational redundancy and administrative reliability, primarily by students and colleagues of Landau. Jon Bendor's book, *Parallel Systems* (1985), originally written as a dissertation under Landau, was the most comprehensive effort to follow up on these ideas. Bendor formalized many of Landau's concepts and was the first to conduct empirical testing of these propositions, focusing on transportation planning and operations in three American metropolitan areas. Donald Chisholm's book *Coordination without Hierarchy* (1989), also written originally as a dissertation under Landau, discussed the notion of reliability and redundancy as it exists in informal organizational structures. LaPorte and Consolini (1991) and Rochlin, LaPorte, and Roberts (1987) have also extended some of Landau's concepts of reliability to the operations of air traffic controllers and aircraft carrier battle groups.

The policy prescriptions that follow from these two positions are thus quite different. The traditionalist argument tells us to reduce redundancy and streamline administrative systems whenever possible. On the other hand, Landau advocates the opposing view of increasing redundancy by adding parallel units to the system. Most interesting, however, is the fact that an analysis of the organizational changes at NASA reveals that neither the traditionalists nor Landau are fully correct. Certain parts of the space agency followed a traditionalist policy of streamlining while other segments of NASA adopted the Landau perspective by generating new parallel linkages. Yet, as I will show in a later chapter, both these decisions were wrong and contributed to the untimely destruction of *Challenger.*

How can this be? The reason is due to a fundamental limitation in the current framework for discussing organizational reliability. Most work in this area has implicitly assumed that there was only one kind of institutional failure and thus only two possible states for organizational performance: the agency either adopted the proper policy or did not. But it should be recognized that the latter possibility conceals two problems: the agency can simply fail to act, or it can adopt an improper policy. Considering the impact of both forms of error is important because it leads us to a different set of policy prescriptions. An organizational structure that is effective at preventing one type of error may not be equally effective at preventing the other type of error. Unfortunately, apart from a brief discussion of this issue in Bendor 1985 (49–52) there has been little discussion of this problem in the organizational reliability literature.

Another problem with the research done in this area is that a schism has developed between public administration scholars studying organizational reliability and technological management. The debate between "high reliability" theorists and "normal accident" proponents calls into question whether it is even possible to develop principles for sound management of hazardous technologies. Advocates of high reliability theory argue that nearly error-free operations of hazardous technologies are possible if an appropriate organizational design is established and proper management techniques are utilized. In contrast, normal accident theorists claim that major systems failures are inevitable regardless of the effort made to protect against them. Essentially, normal accident theorists are telling us that the goal of highly reliable management is not attainable in the long run, so any discussion about how to pursue this objective is of limited value. In order to discuss how to manage these new and complex technologies, we must first resolve the issue of whether or not the feat is actually possible.

Let us consider each of these theoretical challenges in more detail.

Types of Administrative Failure

There is an old adage that says that failures are divided into two categories—those who thought and never did, and those who did and never thought. In much the same way, administrative problems often have a richer structure than the simple two-state (operating   failed) model can incorporate. In particular, bureaucracies are often in the position to commit two types of errors: (1) implementation of the wrong policy, an error of commission; and (2) failure to act when action is warranted, an error of omission. If we consider the agency's decision to take action to be comparable to the acceptance of a hypothesis, we can relate these two kinds of failures to the more familiar type I and type II errors often studied in statistics.

To establish this link, we must first define the null and alternative hypothesis in terms of potential bureaucratic action. Since presumption often favors the status quo, let us consider the null hypothesis to be that the agency should not take any new action and the alternative hypothesis to be that the bureau should take such action. Therefore, if the agency chooses to act when it is improper to do so (rejects the null hypothesis when it is true), a type I error has been committed. Likewise, if the bureau fails to act in a situation where it should (accepts the null hypothesis when it is false), then a type II error has been committed.

To illustrate the concept of type I and type II errors in organizational systems, let us consider the example of NASA and its decision to launch the space shuttle. The space agency traditionally approaches the launch decision with the assumption that a mission is not safe to fly. Subordinates are then required to prove that such is not the case before the launch is permitted. The null hypothesis, therefore, is that the mission should be aborted. If NASA were to reject the null hypothesis by launching a mission that is actually unsafe, it would be committing a type I error. On the other hand, if NASA decides not to launch a mission that is technologically sound, then it has committed a type II error. The agency's choices and consequences are summarized in figure 1.1.

The proper course of action:

		Launch	Abort
NASA decides to:	**Launch**	Correct Decision Mission successful	Type I Error Accident occurs; Possible loss of life and/or equipment
	Abort	Type II Error Missed opportunity; wasted resources	Correct Decision Accident avoided

Fig. 1.1. Summary of NASA responses and possible errors regarding launch decisions. (Null hypothesis: the mission should be aborted.)

Each form of failure is associated with a different set of costs. By committing a type II error, NASA loses the opportunity to achieve its objectives and wastes time, effort, and materials that could have been usefully employed elsewhere. For example, the shuttle's propellants in the external tank, liquid hydrogen and liquid oxygen, are lost if the mission is scrubbed, and they alone have been valued at approximately $500,000. Furthermore, the agency may forfeit the opportunity to carry out rare scientific research, as was the case when NASA missed the launch date for its Astro mission to study Halley's Comet. The *Challenger* accident clearly demonstrated, however, that a type I failure may be far more costly. As noted earlier, the destroyed shuttle has been replaced by the *Endeavor* at an expense of more than $2 billion, and the death of the seven astronauts represents an incalculable loss. Certainly in the case of NASA, type I errors are associated with greater costs than type II failures.

Of course, there are instances where type II errors are as costly as, or even more expensive than, type I failures. Consider again the example of the FDA's drug approval process, as illustrated in figure 1.2. The FDA traditionally evaluates new drug applications with the assumption that the phar-

The proper course of action:

		Approve	Reject
FDA decides to:	**Approve**	Correct Decision Helpful drug in the marketplace	Type I Error Accident occurs; Medical impact includes possible loss of life
	Reject	Type II Error Needed drug denied to patients; may result in loss of life	Correct Decision Potential medical catastrophe avoided

Fig. 1.2. Summary of FDA responses and possible errors with regard to drug approval decisions. (Null hypothesis: the new drug should be rejected.)

maceutical is unsafe. The petitioning company is then required to demonstrate through clinical trials that such is not the case before the application is approved. The null hypothesis, therefore, is that the drug should be rejected. If the FDA were to reject the null hypothesis by approving a new drug that is actually unsafe, it would be committing a type I error. Such an error might have severe medical repercussions for patients using the drug, including the possible loss of life.

On the other hand, the agency may accept the null hypothesis even when it is not true, resulting in a type II failure. If the FDA decides not to approve a drug that is actually safe and effective, then it has committed such an error. The costs of this failure may be equally grave. By committing a type II error, the FDA denies patients the opportunity to use a new drug that could be instrumental in their timely recovery. This issue may be particularly important in cases where existing therapy is minimal and/or the illness is considered terminal. What is important to recognize is that in the case of the FDA, each type of error has similar and serious potential costs associated with it.

The exact cost trade-off between these types of failure would vary, of course, for different agencies and according to the individual circumstances prevailing at the time of each decision. For this reason, it is important to develop a general approach to the study of organizational reliability that recognizes both types of errors and identifies the consequences associated with them.

By recognizing both forms of potential failure, we are also better able to understand the nature of the trade-offs demanded. In hypothesis testing, gains in type I reliability often come at the expense of type II reliability. In much the same way, we will see throughout the course of this book that measures that serve to limit type I errors often lead to a greater number of type II failures. For example, it will be shown in chapter 4 that organizational structures that reduce the likelihood of type I errors are susceptible to more type II failures. However, just as it is conceivable to reduce both α and β in hypothesis testing by increasing the sample size, it is possible to increase both type I and type II reliability by raising an agency's resource levels. But because of resource limitations in the real world, it is inevitable that bureaucrats and their political superiors will have to strike a balance between each type of reliability. Not only would a multiple error framework provide more theoretical richness to a study of organizational reliability and decision making, but it is more empirically relevant to any policy discussion of agency behavior.

High Reliability or Normal Accidents?

A general theory of organizational reliability must not only incorporate the possibility of multiple types of error, but it must also speak to the current debate between high reliability theorists and normal accident scholars. In making a distinction between high reliability and normal accident theory, it should be noted that the boundaries of these two theories are not precisely drawn. Scholars from each group do not always agree on all the details, and some may not even agree that such a dichotomy exists (LaPorte 1994). Nonetheless, as Sagan (1993) observes, proponents from each of these schools of thought do agree on a number of fundamental principles. In order to comment on the debate between these two camps, we must first outline the major tenets of each theory.

Our examination begins with a review of high reliability theory. According to this school of thought, there are four axioms that must be adhered to in order to ensure reliable management of risky technologies. The first is a commitment by political and organizational leaders to make safety a very high priority (LaPorte 1988; Roberts 1990; LaPorte and Consolini 1991). Such a commitment is important in part because reliable management is an expensive and perpetual goal. Unless political and organizational leaders actively make safety a very high priority, they may be motivated to shift funds to other purposes and thus undermine the resource base that is so critical to maintaining reliable performance (Wildavsky 1988). In addition, such a commitment by organizational leaders is important in order to communicate this message clearly and effectively through the rest of the organization. As Miller (1992) has noted, hierarchical control is less effective in the absence of a credible commitment by upper-level management to the goals of the agency. Making such a commitment to safety is an important step toward ensuring reliable management of hazardous technologies.

A second important element of high reliability theory is the need for redundancy within and between organizations. Earlier it was noted that individuals within an organization are less than perfect, but when operating in a redundant organizational structure, the system as a whole can limit the failings of the people within it. As Bendor succinctly stated, "duplication is a substitute for perfect parts." (1985, 291) Thus, high reliability theorists hold that utilizing redundant organizational designs is an appropriate means toward reducing the likelihood of agency failure.

A third tenet of high reliability theory is the creation of a "culture of reliability" within an organization. Proper socialization of subordinates can enhance safety by encouraging uniform and appropriate responses by field-level operators (Weick 1987). This socialization in turn allows the agency to decentralize authority to lower levels with confidence that subordinates will take appropriate action with regard to safety issues. As a consequence of such decentralization, the organization will have greater flexibility in responding to any anomalies that occur with new technologies. This flexibility can be important in containing the damage caused by technical failures and preventing these mishaps from becoming major accidents.

In a related manner, the final element of high reliability theory is the value of organizational learning. The small-scale failures that result from technological anomalies can provide the agency with valuable information about the potential dangers. By running controlled simulations of potential failures and extensive testing, an agency may engage in a learning process of "sophisticated trial and error" (Morone and Woodhouse 1986; Woodhouse 1988). The drug testing requirements of the FDA are a prime example of this learning. By first requiring animal testing of all new pharmaceuticals and then limiting the number of human participants in Phase I clinical trials, the FDA hopes to weed out most dangerous drugs early in the process, thus minimizing the risk new drugs pose to the population. Of course, not every agency has the opportunity to engage in such learning or to apply the other strategies mentioned earlier. Still, scholars have found that highly reliable agencies utilize some mix of these principles in order to ensure that the likelihood of catastrophic failure is minimal.

Normal accident theory stands in stark contrast to high reliability theory. Charles Perrow laid the theoretical foundation for this school of thought in his influential book *Normal Accidents* (1984), a work he began as a member of the presidential commission investigating the accident at the Three Mile Island nuclear power plant. The term *normal accidents,* Perrow states, was chosen to convey the idea that "given the system characteristics, multiple and unexpected interactions of failures are inevitable. This is an expression of an integral characteristic of the system, not a statement of frequency" (1984, 5). Normal accident theory, in its original form, is applicable only to select technologies and not meant to cover all types of high-risk technology.

According to Perrow, the two system characteristics that inevitably result in normal accidents are complex interactions and tight coupling. Perrow describes these of these factors concisely by stating:

> Complexly interactive systems can have independent failures, each insignificant in itself, that interact in unexpected and even incomprehensible ways such as to evade or even defeat the safety devices set up to respond to the individual failures. If the system is also "tightly coupled" the initial failures cannot be contained or isolated and the system stopped; failures will cascade until a major part of the system or all of it will fail. (1994, 216)

It should be noted that loosely coupled systems are able to avoid normal accidents because they have the slack needed to absorb any disturbances that arise. Similarly, linear system interactions reduce the likelihood of major accidents because small anomalies can be easily seen and quickly resolved. Normal accidents, then, are a danger only when complexly interactive systems are combined with tight coupling.

In these cases, normal accident theorists would dispute the value of redundancy in a system. In fact, these scholars claim that additional redundancy may actually contribute to failure in two ways. One problem with increasing redundancy is that it makes the system more opaque, and thus it can obscure the true source of error. In such an organizational design, problems may go unnoticed for extended periods of time since overall performance is maintained by backup units. Over time these initial errors may cascade into major failures simply because it is difficult to contain or isolate errors that cannot be clearly identified. A second potential problem with redundancy is that its value is thought to hinge on the fact that it provides independent checks on system performance. The existence of complexly interactive systems, however, belies the claim of independence. In these cases, not only is redundancy useless as a check on system reliability, but the interactive failure of redundant units may lead to unanticipated problems that cannot be easily contained.

Complex interactions and tight coupling provide an additional challenge to the goal of reliable management—the appropriate organizational response to one factor is inappropriate for the other. Agreeing with the high reliability theorists, Perrow notes that the potential harm of complex interactions can be mitigated by the decentralization of decision-making authority. Tightly coupled systems, however, require increased centralization in order to enhance the coordination needed to operate such systems effectively. Since it is difficult for agencies to centralize and decentralize at the same time, it is clear that the demands that complex interactions and tight couplings place on organizations are incompatible and that such systems cannot be made "fail-safe" regardless of the effort and resources devoted to them.

Additional work by normal accident theorists calls into question some of the other claims of high reliability theory. Safety may reportedly be a major objective, but it is only one of many competing goals that agencies seek to satisfy (Vaughan 1990; Sagan 1993). Organizational learning from past mistakes or "sophisticated trial and error" is often inhibited by the desire to avoid blame and cover over errors. A "culture of reliability" requires intense military style discipline and socialization, which are incompatible with the democratic values of civilian-sector organizations (Perrow 1984; Sagan 1993). Scott Sagan, whose own work in this area has helped clarify the differences between the two schools of thought, has argued that essentially normal accident theory is "pessimistic" and high reliability theory is "optimistic" in nature because the latter claims that there are ways to safely manage hazardous technologies while the former challenges the notion that reliable management over the long term is possible (Sagan 1993).

Although high reliability theorists and normal accident scholars seem to take divergent positions on so many issues, one has to wonder if the current exchange is not generating more heat than light. Part of the problem with the debate is that terminology is sometimes applied in an inconsistent manner and the predictions of each group are imprecise. Sagan (1993) acknowledged this problem in his review of the literature at the beginning of *Limits of Safety*. One problem is that most of these scholars fail to explicitly recognize the existence of multiple types of errors, which in itself can cause some confusion in the debate. Moreover, with some notable exceptions, most authors on each side of the debate are careful not claim any absolutes. The result is that the debate sometimes seems like an argument over whether the cup is mostly full or partially empty. In spite of potential ambiguities in language, it is evident that we have some clear differences in the positions taken between these two camps. As Karlene Roberts—a principal member of Berkeley's High Reliability Organizations group—stated in her 1990 essay:

[Perrow's] message is that if these characteristics exist in hazardous technologies, catastrophes will occur no matter how low the probability. Our observations of three nuclear aircraft carriers show that . . . the organizations have developed strategies for avoiding these negative characteristics. (1990, 173)

In an earlier article, Roberts also conceded that while "parts of these systems fail . . . it is not really clear that all high-risk technologies will fail" (Roberts 1989, 287). While some linguistic ambiguities make it difficult to sort through this debate, there is no doubt that there are important differences between these groups of scholars.

Even if the miscommunication issues could be fully resolved, there would still remain a serious obstacle to resolving the current debate. Part of the reason for the conflict between these two schools of thought is that the foundation for a general theory of organizational reliability is not complete. By allowing for multiple types of failure and developing a more formal approach to modeling the subject, it may be that some common ground between the two schools of thought can be reached. A more thorough analysis of organizational reliability may indeed show that these camps are not as far apart as the current debate portends.

Moving toward a Theory of Organizational Reliability

The purpose of this book is to lay the groundwork for a general theory of organizational reliability and agency decision making. The first step in this process is to specify the types of decisions I will be considering. This specification is important because, in addition to the difficulties already mentioned, one problem in the current debate between high reliability theorists and normal accident scholars is that the level of decision making under investigation is often not clearly identified. Students of decision theory recognize that organizations are engaged in three levels of decisions: strategic planning, tactical planning, and operations control (Anthony 1965). Each of theses types of decisions presents its own set of challenges and will be considered in turn.

Strategic planning is concerned mainly with prioritizing agency objectives and establishing managerial policies and developing the necessary resources needed to satisfy these objectives. In the context of the NASA example, illustrations of strategic planning would include securing budgetary resources, determining the mix of missions with and without astronauts, and establishing how much and what types of errors will be tolerated by the agency. These types of decisions are important because they are, by and large, responsible for maintaining the capabilities of the agency, determining its rate of growth, and ultimately defining its success or failure.

Tactical planning deals with the effective allocation of resources to satisfy agency demands and technological requirements. Again, with regard to NASA, some examples of tactical planning would include deciding which field centers and contractors will be involved in each mission, scheduling and launching space missions, and determining the number and types of astronauts and other personnel needed to execute these missions. One difference between tactical and strategic planning is the level at which the decision is made. Strategic decisions are generally resolved by the upper management of an organization, while tactical decisions are predominantly the responsibility of middle management.

Operational control relates to the actual execution of agency policy in a manner consistent with the strategic and tactical decisions made at upper levels of the organization. To illustrate this, consider for a moment the launching of the shuttle. Decisions regarding when, where, and whether to launch shuttle missions are tactical decisions. Following them, technical decisions regarding the actual launch, the space operations, and the eventual landing of the shuttle would be classified as operational control matters.

One important difference between these types of decisions is the amount of risk and uncertainty associated with them. Strategic planning generally involves the use of long-range planning horizons, and such decisions are thus made under high levels of uncertainty and with large amounts of risk to be considered. Tactical decisions are employed with medium-range time horizons, resulting in moderate levels of uncertainty. Operations control tends to deal with more immediate concerns and lower levels of risk. The question I address in this book is how agencies manage the uncertainties produced by new and risky technologies. As a result, I will concentrate my analysis on an agency's strategic and tactical decisions. This is not to say that the principles developed here are inapplicable to operations control, but I will make little effort to draw such parallels in the course of this work.

To test the validity of the theory and to provide real-world insight on the issue of organizational reliability, I will focus my attention on the behavior of two agencies. It should come as little surprise that the first case I investigate is NASA's effort to explore outer space. Understanding NASA policy-making is important because of the large number of interests linked with space exploration. Outer space is associated with great military interests. Indeed, American space policy began under the auspices of the military and has been associated with defense, in one form or another, throughout most of its history. Space exploration is also associated with great commercial interests. Through the development of satellite and communications technology and with the possibility of precision manufacturing in a weightless environment, there is a great deal of money to be made in expanding access to outer space. Finally, space exploration is associated with great human interests. For centuries people have looked toward the heavens with a sense of awe and wonder. Today, space probes provide scientists with new insights about the universe while space exploration by astronauts provides the public with spectacular drama and heroism. As a consequence, Americans have been willing to invest large amounts of money and accept great risks for space exploration.

For several reasons, the management changes at NASA represent good material for a case study in organizational reliability. First, NASA is an agency that must carry out its mission while lacking a good deal of information about the technology it employs and the environment in which it must operate. Unable to eliminate risk altogether, the agency must devise a strategy to minimize risks and contain potential errors. This strategy development would certainly be valuable in a study of organizational reliability.

Second, because of the scope of uncertainty and the massive size of its projects, the space program is something that, if it is to be successful, is dependent on an organization. While putting a man on the moon was a marvelous engineering feat, it was also an amazing administrative achievement. Without large-scale cooperation within NASA and between other agencies and contractors, reaching this goal would have taken many more years than it did.

Third, NASA had clearly developed a reputation for reliability and safety in its Apollo years and had evidently undergone changes in its priorities in the 1980s, experiencing trouble in a number of programs such as the shuttle and the space telescope. Thus, it can illustrate features of a reliable organization as well as illuminate the political factors that hamper the pursuit of reliability.

The second case I consider is the regulation of pharmaceuticals at the FDA. For more than fifty years, the Food and Drug Administration has served as guardian of the nation's food supply, pharmaceuticals, cosmetics, and medical devices. The regulatory reach of the FDA is quite broad; it has been estimated that 25 cents of every consumer dollar falls under the agency's jurisdiction. While the FDA has generally earned high marks for its actions and praise from its superiors, it has come under increasing fire in the past decade. Most visibly, gay activists have demonstrated against the agency in order to force the FDA to release more AIDS medication into the marketplace.

As was the case with NASA, a case study of the FDA offers several advantages. First, the FDA must accept some level of risk while approving pharmaceuticals. The amount of testing needed to prove conclusively that a new drug is safe would be cost-prohibitive to the industry. At the same time, releasing bad drugs could severely hurt the general public and result in a major political fallout for the agency. Clearly, the FDA must develop some strategy to strike a balance between these two types of errors.

Second, to successfully meet its demands, the FDA must depend on sound management techniques and a proper organizational structure to effectively process new drug applications. The sheer number of new pharmaceuticals introduced each year necessitates such management. Furthermore, by dividing the labor of new drug approval between specialists, the FDA illustrates some of the classic advantages of bureaucracy. In this regard, it makes a good subject for a study of bureaucratic reliability.

Third, like NASA, the FDA had previously established a reputation as a reliable agency. Perhaps the FDA's proudest moment was in the 1960s when it was lauded for its decision to keep thalidomide off the market, thereby preventing some of the birth defects that followed the drug's use in Europe. Starting in the late 1970s and into the 1980s, however, the agency's political atmosphere changed. Increasingly, the FDA has been under pressure from members of Congress and others to move new and cheaper drugs into the marketplace at a faster pace. TPA (a treatment for coronary heart disease) and AZT (an anti-AIDS drug) are prime examples of drugs whose surrounding hoopla caused the FDA to reevaluate and alter its approval process. Even the once-notorious thalidomide has been targeted by special-interest groups for FDA reevaluation as a possible treatment for AIDS patients.

These case studies rely on interview data gathered from both agencies between 1990 and 1993 as well as documentation collected between 1990 and 1995. At NASA, most interviews were conducted at the Office of Safety and Mission Quality because of its responsibility for the agency's reliability policy, although later interviews branched out to other departments in the agency. Additional material on organizational changes at NASA were made available through the archives at the NASA History Office. At the FDA, most interviews focused on the drug approval process and thus were carried out with people in the Center for Drug Evaluation and Research, the AIDS Coordination Staff, and the Center for Biologics. These case studies also benefited by documentation, such as memos and reports, provided by personnel in both agencies.

Before we can delve into these cases, however, we must first construct some theoretical guidelines to inform this effort. I begin with a discussion of the incentives and choices an agency faces when trying to strike a balance between type I and type II errors.

CHAPTER 2

Reliable Decision Making and the Influence of Political Incentives

In the months that followed the *Challenger* disaster, it was revealed that NASA had known about the problem of the eroding O-rings well in advance of the accident. Many commentators portrayed the decision to launch the ill-fated mission in light of such information as an irrational one. Performing a simple cost-benefit analysis would seem to support this notion. Given the high costs of a major failure—loss of shuttle and crew—and the relatively low opportunity costs involved in aborting the launch, the probability of mission failure need not be very high to justify postponing the mission. Are we left to conclude that one of the most technologically sophisticated agencies in the federal government was simply acting in an irrational manner at the time of the *Challenger* disaster?

Part of the difficulty here is that in deciding how to allocate its efforts and resources, a bureau must consider many different factors. In most cases, agency decisions need to be sensitive to both the economic costs and the political incentives that form the organizational environment. Economic costs are the portion of the damage that can be measured directly in monetary terms or represent physical losses. For example, when NASA launched the unsuccessful *Challenger* mission in 1986, billions of dollars of equipment was destroyed. Even more important was the loss of life for the seven astronauts. Government cost-benefit analysis treats a human life as worth $2.6 million, while others argue that the value of life is incalculable and priceless; in either case, we can broadly agree that loss of life or limb represents an economic or physical cost of failure. These economic losses are a function of many variables, including the nature of the technology and the type of failure. It is important to note that these costs are not usually borne by the agency directly, but by its constituency.

The agency does not remain unscathed, however, for there are often political costs associated with failure. These political losses—such as damage to reputation and influence—are the primary motivation for agency decisions. Although these losses are not directly measured in terms of dollars, political costs may have economic consequences, such as budget cuts. Furthermore, political costs are often correlated with the level of economic damage caused by agency failure. When there are large economic costs associated with a failure, then the agency can expect greater political repercussions from its actions. Likewise, if the economic damage is minimal, then the agency generally receives little fallout from its erroneous decisions. There are a number of factors, however, that either moderate or intensify the political losses resulting from economic harm. Since political losses affect the agency directly, it is reasonable to assume that the bureau's activities are directed at minimizing these costs.

It is important that we understand the political incentives that influence agency decision making. As noted in chapter 1, resource limitations dictate that an agency strikes a balance between acceptable levels of type I and type II errors. How the agency allocates effort and resources to reduce each form of error is dependent largely on the political incentives an agency faces. This chapter provides a general discussion of the political factors that influence agency decision making. In the following chapter we will apply the lessons of this chapter by examining how political factors have influenced decision making at NASA and the FDA.

An Agency's Cardinal Rule

It is without question that bureaucratic decisions often have political implications. When an agency chooses to pursue a certain course of action, it tends to benefit some group of people while placing others at a relative disadvantage. As a result, there are many factors that bureaucrats must consider as they seek to make politically acceptable choices. But there is one decision-making principle that most agencies consider paramount: the agency should not be seen committing any visible failure. If we recognize the power and the implications of this simple cardinal rule, we gain immense understanding as to why agencies make many of the choices they do.

This rule is not limited to a handful of public organizations; rather, it is applied by a wide variety of agencies. Social service agencies do not want to be found wasting large sums of money, nor do they wish to be seen as unresponsive to the needs of those who are in their charge. The National Park Service would suffer if it were revealed that our natural treasures were being neglected. Parole boards cringe when it is reported that a recent parolee has committed another heinous crime. The desire to avoid visible failures is especially strong among agencies that manage or regulate risky technologies. As noted in the previous chapter, failure in these cases can be accompanied by catastrophic consequences that are plainly evident. The high costs of failure compounded by the intense media attention generated by disaster is a combination that agencies surely wish to avoid. Thus a great deal of effort is taken by agencies to avoid committing any visible errors.

If it is true that the economic costs of failure are borne primarily by the agency's constituency and not the agency itself, then why is the desire to avoid visible failure so strong? One reason is that visible failures are almost always followed by increased oversight from an agency's political superiors. Agencies find oversight distasteful for a number of reasons. To begin with, oversight usually involves some degree of harassment and scolding of the agency, which might occur during legislative hearings, through written communications with the agency, or even in political statements released to the press. Furthermore, oversight creates uncertainty for the agency inasmuch as it opens the door for political superiors to impose new rules on the agency. Likewise, increased oversight may place agency resources at risk if political superiors believe that the agency either needs or deserves a smaller budget or fewer personnel.

In addition to the tangible costs of oversight, most bureaucrats view increased supervision by political superiors as an affront to the professionalism of the agency. This tendency is especially true for agencies regulating risky technologies. The primary reason these agencies exist is to bring needed expertise to difficult policy decisions. As professionals, these bureaucrats rarely appreciate being second-guessed or overruled by politicians who have less training and expertise. Furthermore, as the value of their expertise diminishes in the political arena, the ability of an agency to promote its agenda decreases as well. Because oversight proceedings often become venues in which the agency's decision making and professionalism are publicly challenged, bureaucrats seek to avoid actions that will encourage political oversight and loss of autonomy that follows it.

The good news for bureaucrats is that oversight proceedings are not the norm in our political system. Indeed, oversight rarely occurs apart from the detection of an agency failure. As McCubbins and Schwartz (1984) point out, there are few incentives for politicians to scrutinize agencies apart from a known failure. The reason is pretty straightforward. Politicians who expend the time and energy to investigate a successful agency not only gain few political rewards, but also pass up the opportunity to engage in more productive activities that will enhance their electoral advantage. On the other hand, if agency failure sets off a "fire alarm" with some affected interest group, then politicians who take corrective action against the agency gain the favor of the interest group and the opportunity for greater media exposure. Hence, McCubbins and Schwartz argue that it is in a politician's interest to investigate only agencies that have set off a fire alarm by failing in some visible way.

On the flip side, it is almost always in the interest of some politician to begin oversight proceedings against any agency that has failed. The intensity of this oversight, however, tends to be correlated with two factors. First, as the economic cost of failure increases, the political cost to the agency (via over-sight) rises. A costly failure has either affected a broad segment of the popula-tion or impacted a smaller group in an intense manner. In either case, we would expect that there would be significant rewards for politicians who come down hard on the agency. Second, as effort increases to prevent failure, the punishment associated with failure tends to decline. An agency that expended a great deal of effort to prevent a failure that occurred anyway can be seen as a victim of unfortunate circumstances and random chance. In contrast, an agency that has been less diligent is its effort to prevent failure can be chas-tised for its idleness. Thus, as an agency decreases its efforts to ensure reliable performance, it will not only increase the likelihood of failure, but the political costs associated with such failure will rise as well.

Certainly there are strong political incentives for an agency to adopt the cardinal rule mentioned earlier—the agency should not be seen committing any visible failure. The next question we must ask is this: How does this rule actually affect agency decisions? To answer it, we must remember that agen-cies operate in a world of limited resources; trade-offs are necessary. As the agency allocates more resources toward limiting type I error, the probability of that type of failure declines while the likelihood of a type II failure rises. Therefore, if all else were equal, we would expect an agency to evenly divide its resources between type I and type II reliability. Rarely, however, is all else equal. For instance, in the previous chapter it was noted that there are often differences in the economic costs of each type of failure. In such cases, we would expect an agency to shift its effort so as to reduce the probability of the more costly error occurring. Not only would such a strategy reduce the likeli-hood of heightened oversight, it would also lessen the intensity of such over-sight inasmuch as the agency has made good-faith efforts to avoid the failure. In a similar manner, agencies will allocate greater effort to reducing the more probable failure. If one type of failure is more likely to occur naturally, then agency efforts to bolster performance in this area will not only reduce the prospect of political oversight, but will also limit the penalties incurred if such a failure still occurs.

Differences may also exist in regard to the visibility of each form of error. For example, it may be that a type I error would be plainly visible while a type II failure would be much harder to detect. The cardinal rule says that agencies seek to avoid visible errors since the "fire alarms" that trigger over-sight can be set off only when an error has been detected. The problem with this visibility clause is that it may lead to decisions that are politically smart but not policy wise. One reason is that the most visible failure is not always the worst failure. If one type of error were more visible than the other—leading to a higher probability of punishment—it makes sense for the agency to devote more effort to lowering the probability of occurrence. That is a politically smart choice for the agency. If the more visible error, however, is not the more costly one in an economic sense, the agency may be shifting its effort away from preventing errors that are more damaging to its constituency in order to reduce the probability that the organization suffers political losses. In this regard, such choices may not prove to be policy wise.

A further result of the agency's desire to avoid visible errors is that it will seek to minimize failures that affect smaller or more organized groups. Olson (1982) argued that information is a collective good and is more likely to be obtained by smaller and more organized interest groups. In this case, the critical information is with regard to the existence of a particular type of failure. These smaller groups are better able to organize a monitoring system that would heighten the visibility of the errors they are most concerned with. If bureaucrats know these groups are more aware of potential failure, they are more likely to cater to the groups' interest in order to minimize the political costs. Such behavior, however, raises concerns about equitable policy as well as responsiveness to the needs of the majority.

Up to this point, this analysis has focused on the agency's desire to avoid the political consequences of failure. While the desire to escape negative sanctions provides powerful incentives for agency action, it must also be noted that organizational decisions are often based in part on the policy preferences of the agency. There may be times, for example, when an agency has an internal preference for either reducing type I failures or lessening type II errors. This preference could arise as a response of the perceived values of legislators, presidents, and other political officials. For example, in chapter 1 we noted that type II errors often lead to missed opportunities and wasted resources. Thus, when politicians emphasize the importance of cost-effectiveness in legislative hearings and public statements, they are revealing to the agency their preference for lowering the amount of type II error committed. Agencies wishing to be responsive to the perceived values of political superiors would reallocate their resources accordingly.

It may also be that an agency's "bureaucratic culture" leads it to allocate additional resources and effort to reduce certain types of errors at the expense of others. In his work on organizational culture, Schein (1985) defines culture as a pattern of basic assumptions that are taught to new organizational members as the correct way to perceive and think about problems. Such culture may arise as a result of past agency experience, common educational training of employees, or the vision of organizational leaders. In our context, it is important to recognize that cultural preferences and politically favored choices are not always optimal in an economic sense. For example, an agency's culture may lead the organization to avoid type I errors regardless of costs associated with type II errors. Thus, these intrinsic preferences of agencies may also lead bureaucrats to act in a nonoptimal manner.

In principle, the agency's responses to visibility and perceived political demands imply that political officials have the potential to either offset agency biases or attenuate them by monitoring the agency. Consider the following scenario. If the official exerts more effort to monitor the agency with regard to type I failure, the likelihood of failure detection will increase and, consequently, effort will be shifted toward preventing that type of error. It is clear that there is some level of monitoring that could offset other political considerations such that the end result is an allocation no different from the one in which only economic costs of failure were considered.

The political superior's ability to affect agency behavior through monitoring depends on three assumptions. First, it assumes that the official finds it worthwhile to get involved in the process. Ripley and Franklin (1976) note that for legislators, the opportunity costs involved in oversight usually outweigh the benefits. Indeed, the whole point of "fire alarm" oversight is that it would minimize the opportunity costs of oversight while allowing the politician to still reap most of the benefits. Second, it assumes that the superior knows the true cost ratio and other relevant information. But, as noted earlier, one reason for bureaucratic discretion is that the superior simply does not know this information. Third, such behavior is predicated on the assumption that the political official does not have her or his own policy preferences apart from cost factors. If the superior has preferences between types of reliability, she or he might use monitoring and oversight to push the agency to do her or his bidding in spite of cost factors as noted earlier in this discussion. Thus, monitoring by the superior may not be a cure-all for the potential mischief of the agency.

Government agencies are public creatures that respond to political stimuli. In this section we have seen how the cardinal rule of public agencies—do not be found committing any visible failure—leads to the following behaviors:

All else being equal, the agency will choose to divide its efforts and resources evenly between type I and type II reliability.

Given different costs of type I and type II failure, the agency will divide its efforts and resources in such a way as to reduce the probability that the more costly error will occur.

If the state of technology makes one type of failure more likely, the agency will divide its efforts and resources in such a way as to reduce the likelihood that the more probable error will occur.

If political officials and the public are less likely to be aware of a particular type of error, then the agency will divide its efforts and resources between type I and type II reliability in such a way as to reduce the probability of committing the more visible error.

Policy preferences induced from political incentives may lead the agency to divide its efforts and resources between type I and type II reliability in a non-cost-effective manner.

Although each of these principles seems reasonable in light of the discussion in this section, these hypotheses can be further substantiated through the use of mathematical modeling. Developing such a model is the focus of the next section of this chapter.[1]

Modeling Agency Incentives

We begin the discussion of an agency's political incentives by developing a basic formal model of the situation. Using a formal model offers two advantages in this case. First, it allows us to incorporate probability into our discussion in a direct and natural manner. This is important since an agency's decisions are dependent on the probability of each type of failure. Another advantage to formal models is that they require explication of assumptions and add clarity to our discussion. The purpose of this modeling exercise will be to confirm the properties mentioned at the end of the previous section.

The focus of our inquiry is the amount of effort and resources bureaucrats allocate to reducing the two types of error. Let us define e_1 and e_2 as the effort or resource level allocated to reducing type I error and type II error, respectively. Working with the assumption of limited resources, we impose the constraint that $e_1 + e_2 = 1$. This is to say that the agency's efforts and resources are divided entirely between those aimed at preventing type I and type II errors.

The probability that a particular type of error will occur is: f_j, $j = 1, 2$. The probability f_j is a function of both the agency's efforts to increase type-j reliability and the state of nature, θ_j, formally stated as $f_j = f(e_j, \theta_j)$. Throughout the chapter, we will assume that the agency does not know θ_j, and therefore cannot know f_j exactly. This assumption serves a twofold purpose. First, it inserts a level of uncertainty into our model that exists in the real world. Second, it also means that even if the agency were to allocate 100 percent of its effort to reducing a certain type of error, there is still a chance that failure will occur. While the agency does not know the exact probability of failure, it does know that increasing the level of effort devoted to type-j reliability will reduce the probability that this type of error occurs. In more formal terms, the agency knows that $f(e_j^*) \leq f(e_j)$ when $e_j^* > e_j$, $\forall j$. Restated, this condition holds that

---

1. This modeling exercise can be skipped over by the reader without loss of continuity.

$$\frac{\partial f_j}{\partial e_j} < 0, \ \forall j.$$

In this model, the types of failure are interconnected via the effort mechanism and resource constraint. While f_1 is a function of e_1, it is also a function of e_2 since $e_1 = 1 - e_2$. As a result, shifting effort to increase type I reliability will decrease the probability of a type I failure; at the same time such behavior lowers the effort level devoted to type II reliability and thus increases the chance of a type II failure. For ease of analysis, we will assume that any increase in the reliability of one type decreases the reliability of the other type by the same magnitude, so that

$$\frac{\partial f_j}{\partial e_j} = -\frac{\partial f_{\bar{j}}}{\partial e_{\bar{j}}}, \ \forall j, \bar{j}.$$

The agent's payoff function consists of two parts. First, the agency receives a positive reward for implementing reliable policy, termed u_r. This term might be thought of as the job satisfaction the agency feels when it knows it is implementing sound public policy. Achieving success in accord with the desire of its political superiors, u_r could also represent the utility an agency gains from larger budgets or increased influence in the policy arena. We will begin be assuming that the utility the agency receives for type I reliable policy is the same as the utility the agency receives for type II reliable policy ($u_{r1} = u_{r2} = u_r$). Later in this section, however, we will relax this assumption and discuss possible changes in agency effort when bureaucratic culture and other political incentives lead to policy preferences between u_{r1} and u_{r2}.

Just as policy success garners political rewards, the detection of an error results in political costs to the agency. This part of the payoff is represented by the term, $u_{\Omega j}$. These political costs may result from heightened congressional oversight or greater infringement on an agency's autonomy. Such losses may also come from media scrutiny, which can diminish a bureau's influence and prestige. In any case, the amount of disutility from these political losses is itself a function of two variables: cost of error (c_j) and agency effort [$u_{\Omega j} = f(c_j, e_j)$].

By cost of errors, we mean the economic damage caused by a type-j failure. In addition to the cost per unit of error, we also need to consider the number of people affected by the error. The broader the population affected by a type-j failure, the larger the costs associated with it. As noted earlier, it is reasonable to expect that when there are large economic costs associated with a failure, then the agency can expect greater political losses. At the same time, if the economic damage is minor, then the political consequences suffered by the agency are generally negligible. In every case, we assume that increasing costs of errors increases the penalty associated with failure

$$\left(\frac{\partial u_{\Omega j}}{\partial c_j} > 0, \forall j \right).$$

For ease of analysis, we will also assume that the rate at which the penalty increases is independent of the type of error that occurred, so that

$$\frac{\partial u_{\Omega 1}}{\partial c_1} = \frac{\partial u_{\Omega 2}}{\partial c_2} = \frac{\partial u_{\Omega}}{\partial c}.$$

Effort is also an important factor in determining the oversight penalty. As a failure becomes known to political officials, information is usually received about the costs of failure and the agency's efforts to guard against each form of error. Information regarding agency effort is important because it is generally recognized that the agency does not have complete control over reliability—that is, nature provides exogenous shocks that affect performance (which we have modeled θ_j). When a failure occurred, politicians and the public would be more tolerant of an agency that devoted all its resources to reducing the probability of error than the one that committed only minimal resources to the type of error that occurred. Therefore, we will assume that

$$\frac{\partial u_{\Omega j}}{\partial e_j} < 0, \forall j.$$

Again, we will also assume that the rate at which the penalty decreases is independent of the type of error that occurred, so that

$$\frac{\partial u_{\Omega 1}}{\partial e_1} = \frac{\partial u_{\Omega 2}}{\partial e_2} = \frac{\partial u_{\Omega}}{\partial e}.$$

To summarize, we have made the following assumptions:

1. $e_1 + e_2 = 1$.
2. $f_j = f(e_j, \theta_j)$.
3. $f(e_j') \leq f(e_j)$ when $e_j' > e_j$, $\forall j$. Restated, this condition holds that
$$\frac{\partial f_j}{\partial e_j} < 0, \forall j.$$
4. $\frac{\partial f_j}{\partial e_j} = -\frac{\partial f_{\bar{j}}}{\partial e_j}$, $\forall j, \bar{j}$.
5. $u_{r1} = u_{r2} = u_r$ (this assumption is relaxed later).

6. $u_{\Omega j} = f(c_j, e_j)$.

7. $\dfrac{\partial u_{\Omega j}}{\partial c_j} > 0, \forall j; \dfrac{\partial u_{\Omega 1}}{\partial c_1} = \dfrac{\partial u_{\Omega 2}}{\partial c_2} = \dfrac{\partial u_{\Omega}}{\partial c}$.

8. $\dfrac{\partial u_{\Omega j}}{\partial e_j} < 0, \forall j; \dfrac{\partial u_{\Omega 1}}{\partial e_1} = \dfrac{\partial u_{\Omega 2}}{\partial e_2} = \dfrac{\partial u_{\Omega}}{\partial e}$.

Furthermore, formalization of the agency's payoff function is as follows:

$$\pi_a = u_r - u_{\Omega 1} - u_{\Omega 2}$$

where u_r is the utility the agent derives from reliable performance in a given period and $u_{\Omega 1}$ and $u_{\Omega 2}$ are the levels of disutility an agent receives following a failure. Consequently, the agency's expected payoff function is simply these terms multiplied by the probability of each occurring, as noted below.[2]

$$E\pi_a = (1 - f_1 - f_2)u_r - f_1 u_{\Omega 1} - f_2 u_{\Omega 2}$$

The agency's objective is to choose levels of e_1 and e_2 such that the expected payoff is maximized. Having defined the parameters of the model, we can now move on to discuss how agency incentives affect the choices made with regard to reliable performance. Specifically, we will investigate four properties of agency behavior under these conditions. In doing so, we will illustrate ways in which bureaucratic expertise and political incentives may be at odds with each other.

PROPERTY 1. *All other things being equal, the agency will divide its efforts and resources evenly between type I and type II reliability.*

The formal proof for this property is as follows:

As previously stated, the expected payoff function for the agency is:

$$E\pi_a = (1 - f_1 - f_2)u_r - f_1 u_{\Omega 1} - f_2 u_{\Omega 2}.$$

Differentiating this equation by e_1 and setting the result equal to zero yields the following expression:

$$\frac{dE\pi_a}{de_1} = -\frac{\partial f_1}{\partial e_1}u_r - \frac{\partial f_2}{\partial e_1}u_r - \frac{\partial f_1}{\partial e_1}u_{\Omega 1} - \frac{\partial f_2}{\partial e_1}u_{\Omega 2} = 0.$$

---

2. Note that there is no interaction term in the expected payoff function. In chapter 4 I will demonstrate the mutual exclusivity of type I and type II errors for any given policy decision.

Grouping the u_r terms gives us the equation:

$$-u_r \left(\frac{\partial f_1}{\partial e_1} + \frac{\partial f_2}{\partial e_1} \right) - \frac{\partial f_1}{\partial e_1} u_{\Omega 1} - \frac{\partial f_2}{\partial e_1} u_{\Omega 2} = 0.$$

By previous assumption,

$$\frac{\partial f_1}{\partial e_1} + \frac{\partial f_2}{\partial e_1} = 0.$$

Therefore, the expression simplifies to

$$-\frac{\partial f_1}{\partial e_1} u_{\Omega 1} = \frac{\partial f_2}{\partial e_1} u_{\Omega 2},$$

which by the same assumption can be reduced to: $u_{\Omega 1} = u_{\Omega 2}$. Total differentiation of this expression yields:

$$\frac{\partial u}{\partial e} de_1 + \frac{\partial u}{\partial c} dc_1 = \frac{\partial u}{\partial e} de_2 + \frac{\partial u}{\partial c} dc_2.$$

Since we are assuming that costs are equal at this time, the equation reduces to $de_1 = de_2$. Integrating both sides gives us the result that the agency's payoff is maximized when $e_1 = e_2$.

The intuition behind this property is relatively straightforward. Given fixed resources, we recognize that an increase in one type of reliability translates into a decline in another form of reliability. As a result of this trade-off, u_r becomes a nonfactor since the utility gained from increasing one form of reliability is offset by the decline in the other form of reliability. To maximize their payoff, therefore, the agency attempts to control the political losses associated with failure. At this stage, we assume that the agency treats costs equally.[3] The only thing left for the agency to do is to adjust its effort levels, which are set so that expected punishment from each type of failure is equal. The end result is that the agency allocates effort evenly between type I and type II reliability.

The economic costs associated with different types of failure, however, are rarely equal. To understand how these cost factors lead to adjustments in the agency's effort levels, we consider the following property:

---

3. This treatment may be either because the economic costs really are equal or because the agency is unable to determine the true costs. If the agency cannot determine the costs of potential errors, then it would be rational for the agency to assume that the costs are equal.

PROPERTY 2. *Given different costs of type I and type II failure, the agency will divide its efforts and resources in such a way as to reduce the probability that the more costly error will occur.*

The formal proof for this property is as follows:

As noted in the previous proof, the agency's payoff is maximized when $u_{\Omega1}(c_1, e_1) = u_{\Omega2}(c_2, e_2)$. Total differentiation of this equation yields:

$$\frac{\partial u}{\partial e} \, de_1 + \frac{\partial u}{\partial c} \, dc_1 = \frac{\partial u}{\partial e} \, de_2 + \frac{\partial u}{\partial c} \, dc_2 \text{ or } \frac{\partial u}{\partial e}(de_1 - de_2) = \frac{\partial u}{\partial c} \, (dc_2 - dc_1).$$

Previously, we assumed that $\partial u/\partial e < 0$ while $\partial u/\partial c > 0$. It is clear, therefore, that under these conditions, if $(c_1 - c_2) > 0$, then $(e_1 - e_2) > 0$. Thus, when the agency recognizes that one type of error is more costly than another, the allocation of effort will be shifted toward preventing the more expensive error.

Again, this property seems to support our intuition. If one type of error is more costly, the agency will allocate more effort toward preventing it, for two reasons. First, devoting more effort to the costly error reduces the probability that the error (and the negative consequences that would accompany it) will occur. Second, if the error were to occur, the agency would be punished less in the oversight process or in the media because the agency expended greater effort to prevent it.

For the most part, these two properties are reassuring. Property 1 tells us that when the agency has reason to believe that the costs are equal, then they will treat each type of potential error equally. This property satisfies our desire for a bureaucracy that is objective and equitable in its actions. Likewise, property 2 tells us that if the bureaucracy knows one type of error is more costly, then it will shift its effort in such a way as to reduce the probability that the more costly error occurs. This behavior ties in well with the notion of bureaucratic expertise. For each individual policy decision, political superiors do not know the true cost ratio and therefore give the agency, which has greater knowledge of the cost ratio, discretion to act on the issue. Under the conditions of property 2, bureaucratic experts use their information and authority to minimize the expected costs of failure.

To this point, we have assumed that if an error were to occur, it would be automatically detected—either by affected interest groups or by political officials directly—with oversight and appropriate punishment commencing.[4]

---

4. McCubbins and Schwartz (1984) emphasize the role of interest groups in sounding off the "fire alarm" to the political superior. However, other research on oversight makes it clear

There are many circumstances, however, in which political superiors, affected interest groups, and the broader public simply do not know if an error has occurred. Furthermore, if an error cannot be detected, then the agency cannot be held accountable via oversight. This asymmetry of information may lead agencies to shift their effort allocation in ways that may not be cost-effective.

PROPERTY 3. *If political officials and/or the public is less likely to be aware of a particular type of error, then the agency will divide its efforts and resources between type I and type II reliability in such a way as to reduce the probability of committing the more visible error.*

The formal proof for this property is as follows:

Let k_j be the probability that the superior would be aware of an error occurrence. The agency's expected payoff function is now changed to: $E\pi_a = (1 - f_1 - f_2)u_r - k_1 f_1 u_{\Omega 1} - k_2 f_2 u_{\Omega 2}$ since oversight depends both on the probability of an error occurring and the probability it is detected. Following the logic of the previous proofs, we find that the agency's payoff is maximized when $k_1 u_{\Omega 1} = k_2 u_{\Omega 2}$ or $k_1/k_2 = u_{\Omega 2}/u_{\Omega 1}$. At this point, we recognize that if there is greater knowledge of a type I error, $k_1/k_2 > 1$, the agency will shift effort toward type I reliability in order to avoid the penalty associated with it.

Again in this case the agency is seeking to minimize the expected losses that could come when a failure is known to have occurred. If one type of error were more visible than the other—leading to a higher probability of punishment—it makes sense for the agency to devote more effort to lowering the probability of occurrence. The downfall is that the more visible error is not necessarily the more costly one. Thus, it could well be that the agency shifts effort away from preventing errors that are more damaging to its constituency in order to reduce the probability that the organization suffers political losses.

So far in our analysis the agency has been indifferent toward the rewards received, $u_{r1} = u_{r2} = u_r$. There are times, however, when an agency has preferences between reducing type I failures and lessening type II errors. This preference could arise as a result of the perceived values of legislators, presidents, and other political officials, or it might be the result of an agency's culture. In these cases, we note the following:

---

that political superiors can, and do, initiate oversight with little prodding from interest groups (Foreman 1988). Indeed, some errors are so obvious that it would be difficult for political superiors to ignore them. The explosion of the space shuttle *Challenger* is a good example of this.

PROPERTY 4. *Policy preferences induced from political incentives may lead the agency to divide its efforts and resources between type I and type II reliability in a non-cost-effective manner.*

The formal proof for this property is as follows:

Relaxing assumption 5, the expected payoff function for the agency is now changed to:

$$E\pi_a = (1 - f_1)u_{r1} - (1 - f_2)u_{r2} - f_1 u_{\Omega 1} - f_2 u_{\Omega 2}.$$

Differentiating this equation by e_1 and setting the result equal to zero yields the following expression:

$$\frac{dE\pi_a}{de_1} = -\frac{\partial f_1}{\partial e_1} u_{r1} - \frac{\partial f_2}{\partial e_1} u_{r2} - \frac{\partial f_1}{\partial e_1} u_{\Omega 1} - \frac{\partial f_1}{\partial e_1} u_{\Omega 2} = 0.$$

By assumption,

$$\frac{\partial f_1}{\partial e_1} + \frac{\partial f_2}{\partial e_1} = 0,$$

therefore the result reduces to: $u_{r1} - u_{r2} = u_{\Omega 2} - u_{\Omega 1}$. If $(c_2 - c_1, > 0)$, then we would expect (because of property 2) that if the agency were policy neutral, it would adjust its effort level toward e_2 until $u_{\Omega 2} - u_{\Omega 1} = 0$. By the result obtained above, however, the agency will not make the full adjustment to the point where $u_{\Omega 2} - u_{\Omega 1} = 0$, but only to the point $u_{\Omega 2} - u_{\Omega 1} = u_{r1} - u_{r2}$. If $u_{r1} > u_{r2}$, then the agency will allocate less effort to preventing type II errors than would be warranted by economic costs; if $u_{r2} > u_{r1}$, then the agency is allocating more effort to type II failures than economic conditions alone dictate. It is clear that bureaucratic preferences lead the agency to choose an effort allocation that, based on cost considerations alone, is unwarranted. Of course, this property is true because politically favored choices are not always optimal in an economic sense.

Although the first two properties were reassuring, these last two seem to be less so. Rather than allocating effort in such a way as to minimize the economic costs of errors, these factors work to shift effort toward minimizing the political costs of failure. Those who promote neutral bureaucratic expertise as an advantage in policy formulation and implementation would be displeased by the implications of properties 3 and 4. These properties question whether such expertise is neutral and note that agency choices can be made to veer from ones that a strict economic analysis would indicate are better. On the other hand, those who are concerned about the responsiveness of bureaucracy should applaud the fact that agencies can be sensitive to changes in their political environment. Political leaders and active interest groups clearly have the ability to alter the decisions of an agency in determining how to allocate effort and resources.

The objective of this exercise was to better understand the incentives that motivate agency choices to pursue greater type I or type II reliability. But up to this point, we have assumed that agencies make a one-time decision regarding the allocation of resources. Is it possible that agencies may choose to shift resources from type I to type II reliability over time? If so, how might political factors influence their judgment? To answer these questions, we move on to the next section.

Are Agency Beliefs Static?

In the previous section, I argued that agency failure is a function of two variables: (1) effort and resources and (2) the state of technology. The amount of effort and resources applied toward preventing a particular sort of error is known with regard to the total amount allotted and its marginal impact on the likelihood of failure. The state of technology, on the other hand, is much more uncertain. The best an agency can do is estimate this state and then allocate resources in order to bring the probability of each type of failure down to the appropriate levels. If there is uncertainty over the state of the technology and this uncertainty affects an agency's allocation decision and its overall likelihood of failing, does it make sense for the agency to revise its beliefs about the state of the technology as new information becomes available?

Those who do research in Bayesian decision analysis would argue that it is rational for an agency to update its assessments in light of new information. In a Bayesian schema, the decision maker begins by choosing some probability distribution to model an uncertain outcome; in this case, it is the probability of experiencing a certain form of failure. This distribution is a function of the state of nature or, in our case, the state of technology. Having run n trials with the technology, the decision maker observes x number of successes. The decision maker can then use these observations to revise his or her beliefs about the state of technology using Bayes' theorem. The process—illustrated in figure 2.1—can be reiterated as long as the decision maker chooses to do so.

Some researchers would argue that the Bayesian process places too many demands on the analytical skills of the decision maker. In response, some have suggested a cybernetic theory of decision making (Steinbruner 1974). The cybernetic theory basically states that decision makers monitor a few key

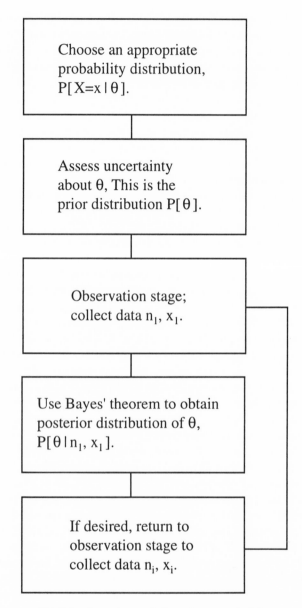

Fig. 2.1. Bayesian updating of agency beliefs

variables, make incremental changes based on the state of these variables, and then monitor the results via feedback loops. The debate between Bayesian and cybernetic theorists revolves in part around normative issues. Bayesian theorists argue that decision makers ought to behave as Bayesians because their expected payoffs in the long run would higher than any alternative method. Cybernetic theorists would respond be saying that this is all well and good, but studies seem to indicate that a large percentage of the population actually chooses to behave in ways that are closer to the cybernetic paradigm. For our purposes here, it is sufficient to say that many decision makers will update their assessment of the state of technology in some manner as new information becomes available.

Of course, we should not be too quick to dismiss the cybernetic view of decision making. In arguing for a cybernetic model of decision making, Steinbruner (1974) also posits that "the two [competing] values of a complex problem will not be related to one another in the mind of the decision maker, but divided and pursued separately, as if they were independent considerations" (108). Steinbruner does concede that the assumption of value separation may not apply to some managers who are specifically trained to weigh competing demands; in fact, it is reasonable to think that most technological managers are aware of the inherent trade-offs between type I and type II errors. But are public managers immune from the value separation problem? I would argue that some value separation does occur since for any point in time, there is one type of error that is of greater concern to the public and on which bureaucrats feel a need to focus first. After achieving some acceptable level of reliability in this area, the agency is then free to pour its remaining resources into limiting the other form of failure. Doing so ensures that at a minimum the agency is meeting its most pressing political demand while still recognizing the trade-offs involved.

What consequence does this behavior have when combined with the fact that agencies are constantly updating their beliefs about the state of technology? After an agency observes one or more successes and uses that information to update its assessment of the technology and the likelihood of failure, it can now justify transferring resources employed to prevent one form of error to other areas. In doing so, it is still meeting the political demand to limit the failure that is currently of greater concern for the majority of politicians, while trying to do all that it can to minimize the other form of failure. Why is this latter objective so important? Most agencies seek to appease as broad an audience as possible because political uncertainty is an inherent part of our system of government. Groups or individuals in power at one point in time cannot remain in power indefinitely; they are eventually put out in favor of some other set of interests. Hence, by shifting resources to other areas, the agency is able to hedge its bets in light of such uncertainty by pacifying those interests that are not in power today but could be tomorrow.

Interestingly, this type of behavior becomes problematic when the technology itself is highly reliable. In such cases, the agency is likely to observe a longer string of successes without experiencing any failures. Instead of seeing such an outcome as validation of its initial assessment, the agency has a political incentive to revise its judgment of the state of technology. Having revised the probability of failure downward, the agency can now justify shifting resources toward other activities. Unfortunately, transferring resources can backfire and actually increase the likelihood of failure down the road. The first few successes cause the agency to revise its appraisal of the state of technology, which in turn leads the agency to shift the balance of resources. If the next few trials are also successful, the agency repeats the pattern. This behavior continues until the agency's estimates of reliability are so high and resources allocated to guarding against failure so low that it is almost inevitable that a failure occurs. The failure might cause a dramatic reassessment by the agency, but in most cases it is only a matter of time before this cycle begins again.

The decision to revise assessments and shift resources ought to include the possibility that the initial judgment was correct and that shifting resources in other directions will actually increase the chances of failure later on. Unfortunately, this calculation is rarely considered by public agencies. Why is that the case? In part, the answer is because bureaucrats—like most people—are risk averse and wish to minimize uncertainty. Remember that the motivation to revise and shift is driven for the most part by political uncertainty. As mentioned earlier, and will be discussed in more depth toward the end of this book, changes in the political winds are inevitable, and the uncertainty they create will always remain a powerful motivator of risk-averse agents. Thus, it seems likely that cycles of failure are inevitable for public agencies.

Conclusions

It should be noted that these decision-making principles may be employed by subunits within organization as well as by the parent agency itself. As Cyert and March (1963) have noted, organizational subunits can sometimes have operational objectives that are different from other subunits or from the central management of the organization. This possibility increases for subunits that operate within a more decentralized environment or are granted a greater measure of autonomy over subunit decisions. For this reason, it is quite possible that the agency headquarters favors greater emphasis on limiting type I errors while a subunit within the agency is more concerned with preventing type II failures. These possibilities must also be considered in any political analysis of organizational incentives.

This chapter has discussed how political incentives affect an agency's decision about how much effort and resources should be allocated toward preventing each type of error. Although the principles laid out here are sensible, the question remains whether agencies actually behave in this fashion. Do technologically oriented agencies allow themselves to be swayed by political factors, or do they rely solely on their technical expertise to make these decisions? The rest of this book is dedicated to answering this question. In the next chapter, we will see that these factors existed at both NASA and the FDA. In later chapters, I will show how these incentives affected organizational behavior and the policies that came out of these two agencies.

CHAPTER 3

Shifting Political Incentives at NASA and the FDA

Unfortunately, it is difficult to eliminate type I and type II errors at the same time. Allocating resources or employing personnel in such a way as to reduce the incidence of one type of failure often serves to increase the probability that the other form of failure will occur. For example, it will be shown in the next chapter that organizational structures that limit type I errors are more vulnerable to type II failures. In the previous chapter, I have argued that the decision of where an appropriate balance should be struck is a function of both technological performance and political factors. As a first step in the process of verifying these claims, we now focus on the behavior of two agencies—the National Aeronautics and Space Administration (NASA) and the Food and Drug Administration (FDA)—to see how political incentives may have affected their decision making.

Political Incentives and NASA Behavior

Understanding NASA's organizational changes requires that we first focus on the political factors that influence the agency. Our objective here is not to provide a comprehensive political history of NASA; it would take an entire volume to do so. Rather, the focus will be on how political factors affected NASA's balance between type I and type II reliability. To facilitate such an analysis, I broadly divide the discussion of NASA's history into four major periods: the creation of NASA, the Apollo era, the space shuttle era, and the post-*Challenger* era. The political history of the agency in each of these periods is presented and then followed by a brief discussion based on the principles mentioned in the previous chapter.

The Creation of NASA

The United States had been active in rocketry long before NASA was established. After World War II, the United States was able to acquire Germany's major rocket team, led by Wernher von Braun. The U.S. Army put von Braun to work on missile and rocket development, while other branches of the military also found ways of getting involved in rocketry. The services competed with each other while a civilian organization, the National Advisory Committee for Aeronautics (NACA), worked on the sidelines producing research on aerospace issues.

The Soviet Union's launch of the satellite *Sputnik 1* was accompanied by a large public outcry in the United States for more concerted and intensive action in the area of space. While President Eisenhower agreed to develop a more rigorous space policy, he was not convinced that such action was the best response to the situation. The success of *Sputnik* was certainly a propaganda advantage for the Soviets. But in regard to national security, Eisenhower did not believe that the Soviet launches represented a major disruption in the balance between the superpowers.[1]

Furthermore, Eisenhower generally wanted to conserve the nation's resources and reduce the size of the federal government. As a result, he was not eager to expand government efforts in the area of space policy. Some supporters in Congress agreed with the president on this issue, but many more legislators were moved by the public's demand for action. In particular, Senate Majority Leader Lyndon Johnson took aim at the president on the space issue. Johnson formed a special committee on space and held hearings about the administration's lack of effort on space policy. These rising political pressures eventually forced the administration's hand in expanding American space policy.[2]

President Eisenhower chose to respond to this issue by transforming the NACA into the National Aeronautics and Space Administration (NASA) in 1958. In doing so, Eisenhower emphasized the civilian nature of space exploration over its military applications. There were a number of reasons why the president chose this option over the acceleration of one of the military's rocketry programs. First, an essentially new agency would be easier to control and maintain within the fiscal limits the administration wanted to set. Second, previous experience had shown that it would be difficult to choose one branch's program over the others without resulting in a great deal of political turmoil. Finally, Eisenhower was also concerned about the rising influence of the military-industrial complex and did not wish to fuel that relationship with the infusion of new space program funds.[3]

Moreover, Eisenhower was able to take advantage of the situation by transferring some of the military's resources to the new civilian space program. Among some of the military projects transferred to NASA were the navy's Project Vanguard, the army's Jet Propulsion Laboratory, two lunar probes and three other satellite projects from the air force, and the Army

---

1. McDougall 1985, 146, 158.
2. Ibid., 149.
3. Ibid., 8, 172–74.

Ballistic Missile Agency in Huntsville, Alabama, where von Braun's team worked.[4] Additionally, a large number of personnel from the Defense Department and other sectors of the federal government were transferred to NASA. These transfers served the dual purpose of accelerating the civilian space effort while preventing such an expansion from having an adverse effect on the administration's fiscal policy.

Although a technologically oriented agency, NASA was born of political circumstances and continually influenced by political factors. While many in Congress were eager to promote the agency and expand its budgetary authority, the president was able to keep NASA expenditures under control. Further, the transfer of personnel and programs from Defense to NASA cemented a relationship between military and civilian space organizations that remains strong today. The transfers affected NASA in other ways as well. The first program transferred to NASA, Project Vanguard, brought with it the experience of failure and affected the bureaucratic culture at NASA. To understand the impact of this transfer better, we should consider briefly the history of Project Vanguard.[5]

The Eisenhower administration had discussed the possibility of putting a U.S. satellite in orbit long before *Sputnik.* It was decided for political reasons to give the honor of launching the first American satellite to the navy's Project Vanguard.[6] In December 1957, project engineers announced they were ready to attempt the first launch of an American satellite with the Vanguard TV-3 rocket. The White House, hoping to allay concern over the Soviet launches, publicized the event and invited reporters from around the world to attend. The launch proceeded on December 6, 1957, after two days of weather delays. The rocket rose four feet and then fell back onto the pad and exploded in dramatic fashion.

The bold headlines of the next day's *New York Times* announced, "Failure to launch test satellite assailed as a blow to U.S. prestige." Others in the media

---

4. Rosholt 1966, 44–47, 117.

5. The following information on Project Vanguard comes primarily from Green and Lomask 1970.

6. In terms of technological development, the Army Ballistic Missile Agency was the most likely candidate to launch the first satellite. Its Redstone rocket was already considered capable of the feat. In fact, after hearing about the Soviet launch of *Sputnik 1,* the Redstone's creator, Wernher von Braun, told Secretary of Defense Neil McElroy, "We knew they were going to do it! Vanguard will never make it. We have the hardware on the shelf. For God's sake, turn us loose and let us do something. We can put up a satellite in sixty days, Mr. McElroy! Just give us the green light and sixty days!" However, von Braun's team had previously designed the V-2 missile, and some administration officials were uncomfortable with the idea that the first American satellite would ride on the descendant of a Nazi rocket. To insure, therefore, that von Braun did not "accidentally" launch a satellite into orbit before Vanguard, the army sent inspectors to the launch site to monitor all activities (McDougall 1985).

were less kind, calling Vanguard names such as "Kaputnik," "Stayputnik," and "Flopnik." Senator Johnson spoke for many Americans when he called the situation "most humiliating." At the UN meeting hall in New York, the situation was worse. The Soviet delegation to the United Nations publicly asked the United States if it was interested in receiving aid under the Soviet program of technical assistance to backward nations. To be sure, Vanguard was a technical failure, but it was also a political humiliation.[7]

The experience of Vanguard can be put into the framework of type I and type II failures. The Vanguard TV-3 incident was unmistakably a mission that should have been aborted—a clear example of type I error. While Project Vanguard did have some measure of success in later launches, this initial failure would brand the project in an enduring fashion.

The fact that NASA later inherited Project Vanguard from the navy certainly affected the bureaucratic culture at the space agency. Employees who once worked on Vanguard had been stigmatized by the experience, and they reminded their new colleagues at NASA of the potential scorn associated with this type of failure. Having seen or experienced the fallout that accompanied such an error, it is not at all surprising that NASA showed great concern about avoiding type I error.

The example of Vanguard also demonstrates another reason why we would expect NASA in this period to favor type I reliability. When a rocket explodes on the pad, it does not take a rocket scientist to figure out that a failure has occurred. On the other hand, it would take a rocket scientist to know if NASA aborted a mission it could have safely launched. At the time, however, there was not a large group of outside experts in this field available. Most rocketry experts were either transferred to NASA or under contract with the agency. As a result, NASA had a near monopoly over information on type II launch errors. This difference in visibility should have driven NASA to allocate more of its effort and resources toward preventing the more visible type I error.

NASA in the Apollo Era

Eisenhower would not support a major space initiative throughout his term. At the end of his term, even NASA administrator Keith Glennan, appointed because he shared Eisenhower's general perspective on space policy, felt that the White House had not given NASA the support it deserved.[8] Democratic candidate John F. Kennedy used the administration's inaction against his

---

7. To make matters worse for the navy, the army was finally given the green light. On January 31, 1958, only fifty-six days after the failure of Vanguard, von Braun's team successfully placed the first American satellite, *Explorer 1,* into orbit.

8. Rosholt 1966, 185.

opponent, Vice President Richard Nixon, in the 1960 presidential election. Kennedy's statements, however, were often aimed at the military ramifications of rocketry and space, leaving many people unsure of what his position would be on the civilian space program. Once in office, Kennedy ordered the Budget Bureau to review the final Eisenhower budget. At that time, NASA pushed for a 28 percent increase in funding, but the new administration decided to make little change in Eisenhower's minimal space budget.[9]

On April 12, 1961, the United States was again shaken by the news of another Soviet space achievement. Cosmonaut Yuri Gagarin had orbited Earth and become the first person in space. As a technical achievement, this event surpassed the United States's current and planned activities in space. As was the case with *Sputnik* four years earlier, the news of the Soviet advance did not bode well with the American public.

The House Astronautics Committee wasted no time in responding to the Gagarin flight. Legislators were anxious for an American "space first" and looked to NASA to provide it. Representative James Fulton (R-PA) said to the new NASA administrator, James Webb, "Tell me how much money you need and this committee will authorize all you need."[10] Chairman Overton Brooks demanded that the Kennedy administration take any steps necessary to regain the American advantage in space. Webb later remarked that "the committee is clearly in a runaway mood."[11] Congress was more than ready for an acceleration of NASA's mission.

Two days later, Kennedy met with his top advisers to find a way to beat the Soviets in space. The president asked about "leapfrogging" the Soviets by either going around or landing on the moon first. During the meeting, however, science adviser Jerome Weisner warned that "now is not the time to make mistakes."[12] Kennedy clearly recognized, as did both Weisner and Webb, that a type I failure, such as Vanguard, could easily turn out to be a far worse blow for U.S. technological prestige.

There were other motives for Kennedy to support a lunar landing. Only five days after the Gagarin flight, the administration suffered another embarrassment during the attempted coup at the Bay of Pigs in Cuba. Historian John Logsdon notes that while there was never an explicit link between the Bay of Pigs fiasco and the lunar landing decision, it was nonetheless a factor.[13] As presidential aide Ted Sorenson noted, Kennedy's decision was influenced by

---

9. Ibid., 190.
10. U.S. House 1961, 7.
11. McDougall 1985, 317.
12. Ibid., 318.
13. Logsdon 1970, 111–12.

the fact that the Soviets had gained tremendous world-wide prestige from the Gagarin flight at the same time we had suffered a loss of prestige from the Bay of Pigs. It pointed up the fact that the prestige was real, not simply a public relations, factor in world affairs.[14]

In the end, Kennedy chose to support the space agency and its efforts to get to the moon.[15]

On May 25, 1961, Kennedy made his dramatic call for landing a man on the moon by the end of the decade. The president stated that such an expansion would require a budgetary increase of $531 million in fiscal year 1962 and a five-year increase of $7 to $9 billion.[16] After delivering the speech, Kennedy first thought that the congressional response was somewhat "less than enthusiastic."[17] Actually, many legislators were annoyed at the fact they did not have a larger role in the decision, but they were generally supportive of the administration initiative.[18] It was agreed that the United States would try to beat the Soviets on its way to the moon.

In the immediate aftermath of the Gagarin flight and Kennedy's call for a lunar landing, NASA was given a large budget and plenty of autonomy. As the space budgets began to increase at astronomical rates, however, so did opposition in Congress. Fiscal conservatives became more energized as the NASA budget expanded, claiming that the space program was filled with "unnecessary boondoggles."[19] Many moderates began to get the feeling that continued geometric increases in the budget were the signs of a loose and wasteful program.[20] In 1963, the first serious debate over NASA's mission occurred in Congress.

Dissension was not limited to the conservatives. Many liberals in Congress supported the concept of a national space program but wished aloud for some of the money to be diverted to social programs on earth.[21] Some of these

---

14. Ibid., 112.

15. Given the hawkish tone of Kennedy's campaign, one might wonder why the president did not implement his "moon race" through the Defense Department. Kennedy's secretary of defense, Robert McNamara, played a key role in this decision. McNamara was interested in instituting a number of cost-accounting reforms in his department. He knew, however, that their introduction would be controversial and spark intense opposition from the aerospace lobby. By supporting Project Apollo within NASA, the aerospace industry would have additional business and McNamara would have more freedom in pursuing his reforms within the Defense Department (McDougall 1985, 320–21).

16. Rosholt 1966, 192–93.

17. Logsdon 1970, 129.

18. Ibid.

19. Rosholt 1966, 282.

20. Ibid., 283.

21. Ibid., 282.

legislators tried to get the president to prioritize his agenda, hoping that it might erode support for the agency. Kennedy carefully resisted these attempts, reminded legislators of their previous support for the agency, and personally stood behind NASA's efforts during this turbulent period.[22]

On the other hand, NASA began receiving greater support from the aerospace industry lobby. The aerospace industry was one of the fastest-growing industries in the United States at the time, and its voice increased as appropriations for Apollo escalated.[23] To promote the political power of its clientele, NASA tried to distribute contracts and facilities across the country.[24] The economic impact of the Apollo project on a district was often enough to alleviate the concerns of efficiency-minded legislators.

Financial concerns at this time were not limited to the overall size of the agency's budget. Misgivings also arose over the division of funds between NASA projects. In particular, many scientists began to speak up against NASA. Their concern was that the manned lunar project was being funded at the expense of unmanned space science endeavors. The challenge of Apollo, they argued, was primarily oriented toward engineering, not science. Informal polls at the Carnegie Institution found that non-NASA scientists opposed Apollo, 110 to 3.[25] These scientists were not concerned that NASA would take the wrong action with Apollo, but that the agency was not doing the right thing by funding more space science projects.

NASA encouraged the development of both types of groups, Apollo supporters in industry and space scientists outside the project, by emphasizing the diversity of its mission. Webb stressed to Kennedy that "we pursue an adequate well-balanced space program in all areas, including those not directly related to the manned lunar landing."[26] To facilitate this goal, NASA established a number of space science satellite projects. The agency also distributed its research funding as broadly as possible to bring more universities (and members of Congress) on board with the agency's agenda.[27] This strategy not only increased the political support for NASA, but also provided a safeguard from excessive political damage to the agency if it lost the "moon race."

NASA's manned space programs had progressed for six successful years when tragedy finally struck. On January 27, 1967, a flash fire broke out in the *Apollo 1* spacecraft while it was on the launch pad. The three astronauts inside the capsule, Virgil Grissom, Edward White, and Roger Chaffee, were killed as the fire quickly spread through the nearly pure oxygen atmosphere.

---

22. McDougall 1985, 393.
23. Rosholt 1966, 284.
24. McDougall 1985, 373–76.
25. Ibid., 390.
26. Ibid., 380.
27. Bilstein 1989, 65.

At the time of the accident, Lyndon Johnson was the president and a strong supporter of NASA. Given his political history, Johnson could hardly be anything else. Both in the Senate and as vice president, Johnson pushed space exploration as a way of advancing his political career. Beyond the political expediency of the move, Johnson also believed strongly in American technology and its potential to do good in the world. NASA, in Johnson's eyes, was the perfect example of what government could achieve through the management of technology.[28]

A congressional investigation of the *Apollo 1* fire was unavoidable. The president made it clear, however, that he stood behind NASA's mission. Such support probably helped derail stronger congressional opposition to the agency's program. As a result of the tragedy, there was a renewed commitment by political leaders to NASA's goal of a lunar landing and less emphasis on the cost-effectiveness of agency policy. While many areas of NASA policy changed because of the accident, the agency was not hurt so badly by the incident that it could not quickly resume its activities.[29] On November 9, *Apollo 4* was successfully launched using the Saturn V booster for the first time.

NASA ultimately fulfilled its dominant objective on July 20, 1969, with the flight of *Apollo 11*. Astronauts Neil Armstrong and Edwin Aldrin became the first human beings to walk on the moon. The United States, through NASA, had met Kennedy's challenge of landing a man on the moon before the end of the decade. The Soviets tried to upstage the U.S. achievement by sending *Luna XV* to scoop up moon soil and return it to Earth before *Apollo 11*, but the probe crashed on the moon about the same time the astronauts landed.

In retrospect, the success of Project Apollo benefited from several political factors. Presidential support for the agency mission was a major element in this cause. Kennedy proposed the lunar landing project and held firm in his support for the agency when it faced more serious opposition in 1963. Johnson saw that NASA appropriations remained adequate in spite of the pressures that his Great Society programs and the war in Vietnam placed on the federal budget. The president maintained his support of the agency and its mission even when NASA was confronted with the tragic fire of 1967.

Not only did Kennedy and Johnson act as NASA's champions, but they also both expressed the preference that the agency pursue type I reliability. These leaders and their advisers were astute enough to recognize that a major type I failure would only exacerbate the Soviets' propaganda success in the space race. They had seen firsthand the Soviets scoring political points off previous U.S. space failures and sought to avoid such an outcome under their

---

28. McDougall 1985, 406.
29. Bilstein 1989, 88.

watch. Furthermore, budgetary concerns, while not absent, were a low priority compared to the cold war objective of beating the Soviets. It is clear that this type of presidential support could have enormous consequences for the direction of agency reliability.

All this is not to say that other concerns and political actors did not surface. Indeed, NASA did cater to other interests and did establish some measure of type II reliability by allocating resources to these interests. Still, presidential support for type I reliability combined with the visibility asymmetry and the agency bias that carried over from the Vanguard experience generally allowed the agency to be dominated by concerns for type I reliability.

By 1969, however, it was not clear that NASA could maintain such a position. The success of Apollo had fulfilled the political demand that the United States beat the Soviet Union in some area of space exploration. In 1961, many Americans worried that the future belonged to the Soviets. Now polls indicated that the public was confident that the United States was "without peer in power and influence."[30] NASA certainly gained some political clout because of its achievement, but at the same time it lost the sense of urgency that had propelled it throughout the decade.

Moreover, new problems confronted politicians on the domestic front, all of which seemed to demand a great deal of time and money. Activists complained louder that money should be spent on "Spaceship Earth" and not on moon rockets. Even at the launching of *Apollo 11*, several groups gathered to protest against federal spending for space exploration.[31] At the moment of its greatest engineering triumph, NASA's political influence was waning. The agency needed to find a new mission that would sustain it in the present political environment.

NASA in the Shuttle Era

The political environment for NASA had indeed changed by 1969. Congressional supporters were satisfied with the success of Apollo and looking toward new challenges. Furthermore, the new president was Richard Nixon. While Nixon took advantage of the publicity surrounding Project Apollo, he was not considered a major supporter of the agency. Nixon's attitude was shaped partly during his years as vice president, during which he defended Eisenhower's conservative space policy. Moreover, Nixon had no close political advisers who were advocates of the space program.[32] Consequently,

---

30. McDougall 1985, 413.
31. *Ibid.,* 412.
32. Hoff 1993.

Nixon pledged during the 1968 presidential campaign to curtail NASA operations until the economy could afford more funding.[33]

On the other hand, Nixon found he could not completely oppose the agency. One major factor in favor of supporting NASA was the needs of the lagging aerospace industry. James Fletcher, the newly appointed NASA administrator, told Nixon that one of the agency's new projects, the space shuttle, would boost employment by 8,800 workers in 1972 and 24,000 by 1973.[34] The president's home state of California would benefit greatly from the increased expenditures, and the spending boost would be well timed for the 1972 elections. These factors played a major role in Nixon's decision to support additional NASA programs.[35] In the end, Nixon agreed to back the shuttle concept on the following conditions:[36]

No major increase in NASA's budget levels

Any manned program that would be developed in the billions-of-dollars category would have to satisfy OMB's "cost-effectiveness criteria"

The shuttle would have to advance the state of the art in space vehicles, but use as much of the Apollo technology as possible

The program would have to be achievable in a reasonably short time, but not a "crash program" in the sense that Apollo was

Demonstrating cost-effectiveness of the shuttle was critical to selling the project to both Nixon and Congress. To obtain the low-cost access to space demanded by political superiors, however, NASA felt it was necessary to get additional support from the Department of Defense.[37] If the Defense Department were to guarantee exclusive use of the shuttle for launching military satellites, it would be easier to justify calculations that would demonstrate the program's cost-effectiveness. The Defense Department requirements for the shuttle dictated a number of major design and operating changes. Institutional survival, however, dictated that NASA now take a more compromising position with other political actors than it had been accustomed to in the past.

Although Nixon was not a major proponent, the space program was able to survive with the minimal support offered by the White House. Nixon's successor, Gerald Ford, was much more supportive of the agency. Before coming to the White House, Ford had served on the House Committee on Astronautics and Space Exploration and had taken an interest in many science

---

33. Schichtle 1983, 73.
34. Logsdon 1986, 1104.
35. Ibid.
36. Emme 1981, 105.
37. Logsdon 1986, 1100.

policy issues. Ford and his director of the Office of Management and the Budget (OMB) were both sympathetic toward NASA and were willing to increase funding for the agency above the level of inflation.[38] The president was particularly impressed with the space telescope project.[39] Unfortunately for NASA, the combination of Watergate (which had weakened the presidency in general) and stagflation in the economy limited Ford's ability to pursue more initiatives on behalf of the agency.

As president, Jimmy Carter was mildly supportive of NASA overall, but the agency's mission was not a priority to the new administration. Some have argued that Carter's unfamiliarity with much of the space program led to a slow start for the president in this area.[40] Carter expounded on his position toward space exploration in Presidential Directive 42 on Civil Space Policy (fall 1978) in which he stated:

> It is neither feasible nor necessary at this time to commit the United States to a high-challenge space engineering initiative comparable to Apollo. As the resources and manpower requirements for shuttle development phase down, we will have the flexibility to give greater attention to new space applications and exploration, continue programs at present levels or contract them.[41]

It seems that while Carter would not undo what his predecessors set into motion, his administration had hoped to scale down the space program.

The transition into the Reagan administration seemed to be both good and bad for NASA. Ronald Reagan was personally enthusiastic about the space program. Presidential adviser Ed Meese observed that "Ronald Reagan has always had an interest in space. That interest was constant throughout his presidency and from even before."[42] In Reagan's mind, the space program was an example of the proper type of program that government should be pursuing.

Reagan was also aware of the commercial fallout from the space program. As governor of California, which receives four times more money in NASA prime contracts than any other state, Reagan watched the aerospace industry suffer during the years Congress was cutting the NASA budget. Reagan once remarked at a Republican Party dinner that "the only time you can get a quorum in the Senate these days is when the Democrats fly back to

---

38. Smith 1989, 176–77.
39. Ibid., 177.
40. Emme 1981, 134.
41. Quoted in Schichtle 1983, 82.
42. McCurdy 1990, 179.

Washington to vote against an aerospace appropriation."[43] As a result, Reagan took office with a general desire to expand the space program.[44]

Reagan's advisers, on the other hand, were often opposed to the agency. For example, David Stockman, Reagan's OMB director, routinely and publicly opposed the agency's mission and referred to several NASA projects as "high-tech socialism."[45] Casper Weinberger, Reagan's secretary of defense, also was opposed to increasing NASA programs and instead wanted the funds diverted to new military space applications.[46] The presidential science adviser, William Graham, was also hostile to NASA's manned space missions. Graham stymied several attempts by the agency to solicit presidential support for new space initiatives.[47] Initially, administration officials reacted to NASA by cutting the agency's budget by $600 million below Carter's fiscal year 1982 funding.[48] James Beggs, the new NASA administrator, knew President Reagan's sentiments and appealed the decision. Reagan's consensus style of leadership demanded that he seek a compromise between these positions. The balance that later developed was that the administration would moderately support NASA but the agency would stress cost-effectiveness in planning its missions. To this end, Beggs issued a formal policy statement on January 6, 1982, which stressed to NASA employees the need for greater achievements, "especially in the areas of cost and schedule control."[49]

During this time Congress had also pushed NASA to emphasize the cost-effectiveness of its policies. That became particularly true in an era of astronomical budget deficits. During hearings to review and commemorate the National Aeronautics and Space Act of 1958 on its twenty-fifth anniversary, legislators were generally pleased with NASA as it reflected on the agency's achievements. However, the questions eventually focused on the unpleasant issue of when the shuttle operations would reach a cost-effective status.[50] The shuttle had been sold to Congress as a self-supporting mode of space transportation for the future, and Congress was eager for NASA to achieve that payback status as soon as possible.

The more time progressed after the shuttle became operational, the more legislators became impatient with the agency. Questions about meeting the schedule and becoming cost-effective occurred more often during hearings. This pressure spilled over into other NASA programs. During hearings in

43. Ibid., 177.
44. Ibid., 178.
45. Stockman 1986, 164–65.
46. McCurdy 1990, 165.
47. Fink 1987, 19.
48. Schichtle 1983, 83.
49. NASA Memo, Administrator's Policy Statement, January 6, 1982.
50. U.S. House 1983, 252–53.

1985 on cost overruns with an ancillary shuttle program, Representative Bill Nelson (D-FL) became upset when officials started quibbling over the exact size of the overrun. Nelson responded that:

> You see, I have to deal in the world of getting votes from people to support the NASA program. If they say to me, why did you have a $110 million cost overrun on [the Shuttle/Centaur project], am I going to be able to say to them, well, that may only be a $90 million overrun.[51]

The fact that the subcommittee would have to recess momentarily to vote on the budget resolution was not lost on either the legislators or the agency. Pressure to avoid overruns and to advance the shuttle schedule to a point where it would become cost-effective to operate continued to mount in Congress.

Another congressional issue was the demand for programs that produced visible results for constituents. Representative Jack Buechner (R-MO) summarized this pressure best when he told NASA officials,

> We as representatives of the American taxpayers are faced with the most dramatic problem, and that is I have yet to have one of my constituents say, "God, there are some great ultraviolet tests being taken out there." You can't show them on television. People can't see the bang for their buck.[52]

If NASA was not meeting its shuttle schedule, it could not be producing results for which legislators could claim some measure of credit. The same logic also suggested to the agency that there were more rewards for doing many projects in a shorter period of time than for taking the time to execute one large project very well.

NASA felt additional scheduling pressure from the Department of Defense. In the early 1970s, the space agency argued that the shuttle was cost-effective because the military had reached an agreement with NASA guaranteeing its use of the shuttle for satellite launches. One disadvantage to this arrangement was that if NASA could not maintain its flight schedule, its biggest customer, the Defense Department, would publicly complain that the space agency was unable to meet its demands and suggest the need for unmanned boosters under direct control of the military.

Another change for NASA was that it no longer enjoyed the information advantage it had in the early 1960s. The experience of Apollo sparked broader

---

51. U.S. House 1985, 68.
52. U.S. House 1990, 29.

interest in space flight and encouraged the development of outside expertise. Furthermore, the military now had a sufficient source of independent expertise to question NASA policy. Eisenhower and Kennedy had originally endowed NASA with the majority of space resources, but this advantage steadily shifted over time to the military. As illustrated in Table 3.1, NASA controlled over 70 percent of federal funds for space in 1965. Twenty years later, the Defense Department had about twice as much space resources as NASA. If

TABLE 3.1. **Shift in Budget Authority for Federal Space Program, by Agency (1965–91)**

	NASA		Defense		Other	
Year	Budget	Percent	Budget	Percent	Budget	Percent
1965	5.14	73.9	1.57	22.6	0.24	3.5
1966	5.07	72.7	1.69	24.2	0.22	3.1
1967	4.83	72.0	1.66	24.8	0.22	3.2
1968	4.43	67.9	1.92	29.4	0.18	2.7
1969	3.82	64.0	2.01	33.7	0.14	2.4
1970	3.55	66.4	1.68	31.4	0.12	2.2
1971	3.10	65.4	1.51	31.9	0.13	2.7
1972	3.07	67.1	1.41	30.8	0.10	2.1
1973	3.09	64.1	1.62	33.6	0.11	2.3
1974	2.76	59.4	1.77	38.1	0.12	2.5
1975	2.92	59.3	1.89	38.5	0.11	2.2
1976	4.08	61.2	2.44	36.7	0.14	2.1
1977	3.44	57.5	2.41	40.3	0.13	2.2
1978	3.62	55.6	3.74	42.0	0.16	2.4
1979	4.03	55.6	3.04	41.9	0.18	2.5
1980	4.68	53.9	3.85	44.3	0.16	1.8
1981	4.99	50.0	4.83	48.4	0.16	2.3
1982	5.53	44.4	6.68	53.7	0.23	1.9
1983	6.33	40.6	9.02	57.9	0.24	1.6
1984	6.65	38.8	10.20	59.5	0.29	1.7
1985	6.93	34.3	12.77	63.3	0.47	2.4
1986	7.17	33.1	14.13	65.2	0.37	1.7
1987[a]	9.81	37.9	15.72	60.7	0.35	1.4
1988	8.76	33.2	17.20	65.1	0.46	1.7
1989	10.10	35.5	17.91	63.0	0.44	1.5
1990	12.14	43.2	15.62	55.6	0.33	1.2
1991	13.04	47.2	14.18	51.4	0.38	1.4

Source: Statistical Abstract of the United States, 1989, U.S. Department of Commerce. Data provided from the Office of Management and Budget.

Note: Budget authority in terms of billions of dollars. Percent represents agency budget as percentage of total federal spending on space programs.

[a]Additional one-year funding was allocated to NASA for the construction of the *Challenger* replacement shuttle, *Endeavor.*

NASA was not launching as often as the air force thought possible, the space agency policy could be credibly challenged by a military impatient to get its satellites into space. Not wanting to risk any further transfers of budgetary resources to the Department of Defense, NASA officials felt they had little choice but to comply with Defense demands.

NASA and the *Challenger* Disaster

NASA was not unaware of the technical problem that led to the destruction of *Challenger*. The agency had known for quite some time about the problem of O-ring seal erosion in the solid rocket motors and its potential consequences. NASA engineers first suspected the problem in 1977—before any shuttle had ever launched.[53] Over the years, NASA had accumulated launch data that suggested that the *Challenger* launch in particular was vulnerable to O-ring failure. Why NASA did not act on this issue sooner is a matter of politics. This segment focuses on the specific political incentives that led to the *Challenger* accident.[54]

As mentioned earlier, NASA was under intense pressure to meet its ambitious schedule so as to demonstrate the cost-effectiveness of the shuttle. This pressure had been with the space agency since the beginning of the shuttle program. For example, NASA held to its commitment to launch the first shuttle mission by March 1981, despite a fire in July 1980 that damaged one of the shuttle's main engines. NASA Administrator Robert Frosch stated at the time that "the engine study would not be allowed to impede the central effort to hold to the agreed-upon launch schedule."[55] As noted earlier, the political demand to meet the announced schedule only intensified over time.

This schedule pressure was exacerbated in the case of *Challenger,* for several reasons. First, if the *Challenger* launch were delayed any further, it would endanger the agency's ability to launch on time the upcoming Astro mission to observe Halley's Comet. This mission was needed to placate space scientists who felt NASA was unresponsive to their needs as well as to upstage the efforts of other nations, particularly the Soviet Union, in studying this rare phenomenon.[56] Although NASA could have used a satellite and unmanned booster to study the comet, the agency opted for using the shuttle in order to further justify the program and to gain publicity and exposure as scientists on board made detailed observations of Halley's Comet. Failing to

---

53. Presidential Commission 1986, 233.

54. The focus of this section is exclusively on NASA's political environment at the time of the accident. The administrative behavior of the agency will be discussed later in chapter 5.

55. NASA News Release, July 31, 1980, No. 80-122.

56. McConnell 1987, 134–35.

launch the Astro mission would have opened up the agency to criticism for missing this rare opportunity. Thus, *Challenger* and its Teacher-in-Space mission needed to be launched in a timely fashion to clear the way for the Halley's Comet mission.

Second, the number of media present for the Teacher-in-Space mission was particularly large, and NASA did not wish to be portrayed in front of this sizable gathering as unable to manage its program. This fear was intensified by the negative media reactions that had occurred with recent launch delays. As NASA scholar Maureen Casamayou notes, "Furthermore, for about a month before the *Challenger* launch, the agency had been subjected to ridicule by the press and media over the innumerable launch delays. The *Columbia* launch, for example, suffered seven delays, which were portrayed by the media as a 'running soap opera.'"[57] To make matters worse, NASA had "scrubbed" a previous opportunity for launching *Challenger* based on weather factors that later proved to be incorrect. *CBS News* anchor Dan Rather reported this fact on January 27 by stating, "Yet another costly, red-faced-all-around space shuttle launch delay . . . Bruce Hall has the latest on today's high-tech low comedy."[58] Such negative press is particularly harmful to an agency that lacks a large natural constituency as does NASA. It is clear that the normal political pressures to launch—already quite high—were exacerbated by the conditions surrounding the *Challenger* mission.[59]

These pressures contributed to the decision by NASA managers to dismiss the potential problem of O-ring erosion in the *Challenger* launch. But if NASA had known that O-ring erosion was occurring, why had it not acted well before the *Challenger* launch? One reason NASA was so slow to react to the O-ring problem had to do with the controversial procurement of the solid rocket boosters. NASA's Source Evaluation Board reviewed proposed designs for the solid rocket motors and ranked Lockheed's proposal marginally ahead of Morton Thiokol's. As NASA administrator, James Fletcher had the final decision in the contract award and chose to give it to Thiokol.[60] Lockheed immediately protested the choice and asked for the Government Accounting Office (GAO) to investigate the decision. Although GAO questioned some of

---

57. Casamayou 1993, 74.

58. Ibid., 75.

59. There were a number of allegations that the agency was also under pressure to launch because of the president's upcoming State of the Union address. Rumor had it that the president's staff had worked with NASA to have a live hookup with Teacher-in-Space Christa McAuliffe during the speech. The Rogers commission investigated the claim but could not find any evidence to substantiate this position (Presidential Commission 1986).

60. Some claim that Fletcher is part of the "Mormon Mafia" whose purpose is to bring government business to Utah. Thus, they argue his decision to award the contract to Thiokol was not made on technical grounds, but for political and economic reasons (McConnell 1987, 55–60).

the assessments of the Thiokol proposal, it concluded that the decision itself was legitimate. To justify this decision, Fletcher specifically praised the Thiokol design for its safety and its redundant O-ring design.[61] For NASA to publicly delay the shuttle schedule while the joint was redesigned would add to a controversy that the agency did not need to reignite. Thus, NASA and Thiokol quietly worked on a redesign of the booster joint but would not stop any shuttle flights because of the problem.

Another important reason for the schedule pressure contributing to the *Challenger* launch decision had to do with the Marshall Space Flight Center—the field center responsible for the solid rocket motor. This center had been slated for shutdown following the completion of Project Apollo.[62] As Fletcher told his successor, "closing Marshall has been on [OMB's] agenda ever since I came to NASA in 1971."[63] To prevent the shutdown from occurring, NASA Headquarters sent several high-visibility projects, such as the space telescope and the solid rocket motors, to Marshall. Despite these efforts, Marshall was still threatened with large reductions in personnel and other resources following Apollo.[64]

This problem became even more intense as the shuttle neared operational status. In 1978, OMB had expressed to NASA that it wished to impose major cuts at Marshall. NASA suggested "new roles" for the center, but OMB officials made it clear they were not interested.[65] While NASA as an institution faced strong pressure to run its operations cost-effectively, Marshall felt this demand more intensely. Consequently, the center did not want to be responsible for any delay in launching the shuttle.[66] Acknowledging that the O-ring erosion represented a significant danger to the shuttle would have put the troubled space center in a negative light and would give more ammunition to opponents who wanted to shut it down.

Still another factor in NASA's desire not to delay shuttle flights on account of the O-rings had to do with the status of some of its previous shuttle

---

61. Interestingly, a McDonnell-Douglas proposal actually anticipated problems with the joint. It recommended that an abort system be established using a "burn through wire" at each joint, which would sense any O-ring leakage and then terminate booster thrust and separate the orbiter's personnel from the main unit via an escape rocket. The proposal, however, would have added several thousand pounds to the shuttle and was deemed too expensive (McConnell 1987, 49–50).

62. Smith 1989, 83.

63. Ibid., 84.

64. NASA Memo, Marshall Space Flight Center News Release, March 5, 1974, No. 74-31.

65. NASA Memo, September 7, 1978, To: Associate Administrator for Management Operations; From: Assistant Associate Administrator for Management Operations; Subject: Institutional Assessment Presentation to OMB.

66. McConnell 1987, 112.

passengers. In 1985, NASA had sent up Senator Jake Garn and Representative Bill Nelson on shuttle flights.[67] While some saw this move as a political ploy on the part of the agency to secure congressional support, others argue that the two members of Congress used their political influence to force NASA into acquiescing to their desire to fly on the shuttle. In either case, the agency could suffer severe political repercussions if it were known that they allowed these public figures to travel in a shuttle that had a known design flaw. This political aspect further increased the agency's desire to suppress information about the booster joint problem.

In summary, NASA faced political pressure in the 1980s to meet its flight schedule and make the shuttle cost-effective to operate. There were also a number of particular political reasons why the critical design flaw in *Challenger* could not be seen as justification for stopping the mission. Under these circumstances, it is not hard to imagine that NASA managers would fail to acknowledge the severity of the O-ring erosion on shuttle operations. It is also not hard to imagine that the space agency would eventually suffer a major failure. The tragedy is that in the absence of these political factors, the design modification would have been relatively easy to implement and could have saved seven lives.

Space Politics after *Challenger*

Like the Vanguard TV-3 rocket in 1957, the loss of *Challenger* was a major technical failure with great political ramifications. President Reagan responded to the *Challenger* disaster by appointing an independent commission headed by William Rogers to investigate the causes of the failure and make recommendations to correct the problems. This elite panel held two months of hearings and delved into both the technical problems with the shuttle and the managerial problems at NASA. The Rogers Commission produced nine major recommendations, including the redesign of the booster joint, the establishment of an independent safety office in NASA, and a comprehensive review of the shuttle schedule and other flight procedures.

Congress did not miss this opportunity to exercise oversight as well. A number of congressional committees held hearings in advance of the Rogers Commission's review in order to prepare Congress to receive the final report. Once the report was finished, Congress held more than ten days of hearings to review its findings. During that time, some legislators strongly chastised the

---

67. While not directly chastising the members of Congress for lobbying to get onto a shuttle mission, the Rogers commission report argued that the late additions of Garn and Nelson disrupted NASA's ability to operate the shuttle effectively and that the short-notice changes in the manifest contributed to increased pressure on the strained launch system (Presidential Commission 1986, 166–70).

agency for its behavior. Others lamented that Congress had been in awe of the agency's accomplishments and unwilling to "apply the same strong oversight to NASA as it does to any other Government agency."[68] In response to these inquiries, NASA later announced to both the president and Congress a series of management programs and design modifications that would implement all of the Rogers Commission's recommendations.

Although many legislators clearly used this opportunity to assail NASA for its behavior in light of *Challenger*, Congress was initially more accepting of NASA following the accident. Gone was the talk of making the shuttle cost-effective; *safety* became the operative word. When hydrogen leaks in 1990 grounded the shuttle, NASA was not rebuked, but praised for its actions. In a hearing on both the Hubble space telescope and the shuttle problems, Representative Robert Walker (R-PA) made it a point to tell NASA officials, "I think I speak for most of my colleagues, if not all of us, when we say that we think you've been unfairly maligned for [grounding the shuttle fleet] . . . You did right."[69] Representative James Sensenbrenner (R-WI) later followed up on Walker's statement by saying,

I think you really got a bum rap relative to the grounding of the shuttle fleet. Your job is to make sure that when the shuttle goes up it is as safe as it can humanly be, and to send up an unsafe shuttle would be a tremendous let down to the Congress and the American public, not the least of which the astronauts who are on board, and I hope that you don't get anymore cartoons for doing your job right.[70]

The same committees that had once pressured the space agency to meet its schedule and bring the shuttle to a cost-effective point had changed their expectations.

This change did not last long. In the 1990s, concern over the federal budget deficit has increased and politicians on both sides of the aisle have begun to look at NASA as an expendable agency. Many members of the Clinton administration have expressed a desire to cut deeply into NASA funding, and the agency has been targeted with budget cuts in excess of 30 percent. At the same time, House Speaker Newt Gingrinch during Clinton's first term urged that NASA programs be privatized and the agency's future agenda substantially limited.[71] NASA Administrator Daniel Goldin acknowledged the new political realities when he said that "the American public wants

---

68. U.S. House 1986a, 2.

69. U.S. House 1990, 16.

70. Ibid., 23.

71. Newt Gingrich, Remarks to National Space Society Seminar on "Space Policy for the 21st Century," March 3, 1995, Washington, D.C.

a leaner, more efficient NASA, and we're prepared to meet that challenge."[72] In response to the demand for cost-effectiveness, NASA has proposed major cuts in safety personnel and programs, and no political leader has yet objected to the trial balloon proposal.

Managers within NASA's Office of Safety and Mission Quality acknowledge that, if anything, the agency's technology has become somewhat riskier to operate since the early days of space flight and the advent of astronautics. Based on technological factors alone, then, we should expect the agency to maintain a considerable emphasis on type I reliability because of both the large risk of approving unsafe launches and the high cost of such failures. Political incentives from the 1970s to the 1990s, however, have been encouraging the space agency toward greater type II reliability. In the beginning of chapter 2, we noted that a purely economic cost-benefit analysis would easily discourage NASA from launching *Challenger* when it did. The decision to do so led to highly undesirable results, but considering the political incentives of the agency, it was not irrational for NASA to go ahead with the launch.

Political Incentives and the FDA

Like NASA, the FDA's regulation of new pharmaceuticals is fraught with risks and trade-offs. But when discussing political incentives, many officials at the Food and Drug Administration vehemently deny that agency decisions are influenced by political considerations. From their perspective, the agency's professional status allows it to evade most political matters. Furthermore, these officials believe that their area of expertise is one that is not often in the limelight. As one FDA official stated, "our day-in, day-out operations attract little interest [among politicians]. We're a boring agency."[73]

In this segment we will see that this perception is incorrect. The FDA is indeed swayed by a number of political factors that shape the agency's objectives. In turn, these political considerations affect the types of reliability the FDA chooses to pursue at any point in time. To demonstrate this political connection, we begin with a brief review of the political history of the FDA. Following that we will focus on the impact the AIDS crisis and its effect on the agency's political environment. By the close of this section, the FDA's motivation for the policy choices it made regarding reliability should be evident.

---

72. NASA Press Release 95-73, May 19, 1995.
73. Author interview, FDA Center for Drugs, March 13, 1991.

The Formation of the FDA

The FDA's birth was itself the result of political turmoil. Prior to the establishment of the FDA, there was no regulation of pharmaceuticals. Before the turn of the century, a great deal of medication was marketed directly to the public as "miracle cures." These drugs were often found to be ineffective and sometimes dangerous. In response, a number of interest groups during the Progressive era began lobbying Congress to limit this "quackery." Most prominent among these groups were the American Medical Association and the American Pharmaceutical Association. Both organizations recognized that legislative efforts to limit the fraudulent promotion of medical drugs would serve their interests by raising consumer confidence in their professions.[74]

Despite the lobbying activities of these groups, however, Congress was reluctant to pass corrective legislation. Momentum for such regulation continued to grow nonetheless because of the increased attention of the media. Magazines such as *Collier's* and *Ladies' Home Journal,* for example, published numerous articles revealing the corruption in the patent-medicine trade.[75] More dramatically, Upton Sinclair's book *The Jungle,* dealing with the horrors of the meat-packing industry, alarmed President Theodore Roosevelt and turned him into an advocate of food and drug reform.[76] Roosevelt's support for reform was the critical element in compelling legislators to accept the Pure Food and Drugs Act of 1906.

The 1906 act itself did not create the FDA. Rather, responsibility for implementing this new law was given to Dr. Harvey Wiley, a key proponent of reform and the chief of the Bureau of Chemistry within the Agriculture Department.[77] In 1927, a separate enforcement agency, the Food, Drug and Insecticide Agency, was formed. In 1931, this agency became known as the Food and Drug Administration, but it remained within the jurisdiction of the Department of Agriculture.[78]

The new law gave the Bureau of Chemistry (and later the FDA) the authority to take action against any drug found to be either adulterated or misbranded. According to the act, a drug was considered adulterated if its strength or purity were found to be less than the level claimed by its labeling.[79] Misbranded drugs were those that made false or misleading claims

---

74. Quirk 1980, 193.
75. Weimer 1982, 241.
76. Quirk 1980, 194.
77. Dodge 1979, 1.
78. Ibid., 6.
79. Drugs that did not explicitly make a claim of strength or purity were judged against the standards set in either the United States Pharmacopoeia or National Formulary (Weimer 1982, 242).

about the product. Any drug found in violation of these criteria could be seized by the agency while its manufacturer faced possible prosecution in federal court under libel statutes.

In response to Supreme Court rulings, Congress amended the law in 1912 so that a drug manufacturer could be prosecuted for misbranding only if the agency could prove that the manufacturer's claims were both false and fraudulent. This change meant the agency now had to demonstrate that the false labeling claim had been made with the intent to deceive,[80] and it reduced the agency's already limited power. Additionally, the law could not be applied to any other promotional activity except the label, which allowed deceptive advertising of unsafe and worthless drugs to continue unabated.[81] As the weakness of the new law became evident, proponents began to lobby for more comprehensive regulation.

These proponents saw the advent of the New Deal in 1933 as a window of opportunity for drug law reform. Many of the same interest groups came back together to lobby for the measure. As had occurred prior to the first drug law, a number of muckraking books and articles appeared, which exposed some of the dangers associated with pharmaceuticals.[82] President Franklin D. Roosevelt initially agreed to support a change in the law but later backed away because of a political dispute with Senator Royal Copeland, a vocal supporter of the bill.[83] The lack of political support from the president, combined with opposition from some segments of the food and drug industry, stalled the reform effort for a number of years.

The stalemate quickly ended after the Elixir Sulfanilamide disaster in 1937. Sulfanilamide was widely recognized at that time as an effective cure for gonorrhea and septicemia. In its haste to capitalize on this finding, the Massengill Company released a liquid form of sulfanilamide, using diethylene glycol as the solvent, without doing any toxicity analysis. The drug painfully killed 107 people before it was removed. The FDA was able to remove the drug from the market only on the grounds that its labeling as an "elixir" implied an alcoholic content that the drug did not have. This incident vividly demonstrated the weakness of the law. Congress and the president remedied the situation by quickly passing the Federal Food, Drug and Cosmetic Act of 1938.

As one commentator noted, the 1938 law was "probably the most important piece of legislation ever passed on the regulatory functions of the

---

80. Quirk 1980, 194.

81. Ibid.

82. The most notable of these books, *100,000,000 Guinea Pigs,* argued that "in the eyes of the law, we are all guinea pigs, and any scoundrel who takes it into his head to enter the drug or food business can experiment on us" (Quirk 1980, 196).

83. Weimer 1982, 243.

agency."[84] The new act superseded the previous law, including the Sherley amendment, which limited the FDA's authority to cases of false and fraudulent labeling. The agency's jurisdiction was also expanded to cover cosmetics and medical devices. More important, the new legislation required that pharmaceutical manufacturers prove the safety of their drug before the FDA cleared it for general marketing. Additional provisions allowed the agency to conduct factory inspections and gave the FDA court injunction power as a remedy of seizure and prosecution.[85]

This legislative change was followed with an order in 1940 that altered the FDA's position in the executive branch. The FDA was moved from the jurisdiction of the Department of Agriculture to the Federal Security Agency, a precursor of the Department of Health, Education, and Welfare (HEW). This transfer was significant inasmuch as the regulation of food and drug safety was no longer a subordinate function within a department established primarily to aid food producers. Furthermore, the FDA was now aligned with an agency that had a significant health component in its mission. Not surprisingly, farmers expressed the greatest concern over the transfer of the FDA and its impact on their activities.[86]

Despite the misgivings of some producers, the FDA enjoyed strong support and quiet times for nearly twenty years. In 1959, Senator Estes Kefauver began to hold hearings on the pricing activities within the pharmaceutical industry. Although skillful in handling the media covering the hearings, Kefauver was unable to generate support from the White House for his proposed amendments to the drug law. The major provision of the Kefauver amendment at this time was the mandatory licensing of drug patents to any manufacturer who was willing to pay up to 8 percent in royalties. Although his initial focus was on pricing regulation, the senator was able to later reignite interest in the hearings by publicizing the thalidomide disaster that had recently occurred in Europe.

Thalidomide was a sedative given to pregnant women in Europe. Postmarketing studies revealed that the children of these women had a significantly higher rate of birth defects. FDA officer Frances Kelsey had refused to give thalidomide market clearance in the United States on the grounds that the manufacturer's application had not met the safety standards necessary for approval.[87] The thalidomide tragedy renewed concern for drug safety in this country and led to the passage of the Kefauver-Harris amendments in 1962.

---

84. Dodge 1979, 6.

85. Ibid., 6.

86. Ibid., 1.

87. The manufacturer had, however, distributed the drug to twelve hundred doctors for clinical testing. It is generally believed that this testing resulted in ten to sixteen birth defects in the United States (Weimer 1982, 245).

The final law did much to strengthen the FDA's safety and efficacy regulations, but unfortunately for Kefauver, it did not contain the mandatory licensing requirements he had advocated and did nothing to address his initial concern for greater price competition in the pharmaceutical industry.

The 1962 amendments expanded the FDA authority in several ways. The new law gave the agency greater control over the clinical trials needed to verify the safety of new pharmaceuticals. The amendments also required that manufacturers demonstrate the efficacy, as well as the safety, of all new drugs.[88] The law defined substantial evidence of safety and efficacy to be

> consisting of adequate and well-controlled investigations, including clinical investigations, by experts qualified by scientific training and experience to evaluate the effectiveness of the drug involved, on the basis of which it could be fairly and responsibly concluded by such experts that the drug will have the effect it purports or is represented to have.[89]

Since this period, Congress has occasionally debated changes in the FDA's authority and structure. The Kefauver-Harris amendments, however, still form the basis for much of the agency's procedures today.

Reviewing the political history of the FDA reveals how highly visible failures provided political leaders with a strong motivation to expand the agency's regulatory influence. The initial Food and Drug Act was prompted by the publicized and egregious abuses within industry. Revisions to the law in the 1930s faltered until the Elixir Sulfanilamide failure made headlines and moved politicians into action. Kefauver's hearings stalled until the thalidomide disaster in Europe rekindled interest in the newspapers and in Congress. Type I failures such as these are often dramatic and highly visible to the public. The result is that government officials are often eager to make reliability changes during these crises so as to appear responsive to the situation at hand. Although the FDA initially had many incentives to guard against type I failure, has this emphasis continued in the 1980s and 1990s? To answer this question, we begin by looking at the agency's interactions with other members in the political arena.

Initial Changes in the Political Environment of the FDA

A review of the FDA's political history seems to indicate that presidents have generally played an inactive role in the life of the agency. During interviews

---

88. This requirement was retroactively applied to drugs approved since 1938. Drugs marketed before 1938 were considered safe and effective based on historical experience and were therefore "grandfathered," provided no evidence to the contrary developed.

89. Quoted in Weimer 1982, 246.

with agency officials, most stated that beyond shaping the agency with some political appointments, the president rarely takes an active interest in the FDA. As one official said:

> I don't really think there's much presidential influence here. This isn't really a political agency. There's more of a hands-off approach taken by the White House. In fact, I think our biggest problem is that we're usually ignored—up until the AIDS crisis, that is.[90]

Even with the advent of the AIDS epidemic, some FDA officials still believe that the president shows little concern about the agency.

While presidents may not express much interest in the FDA, the agency has not been able to escape the influence of their subordinates. Since deregulation in the late 1970s, the Office of Management and the Budget has been concerned with minimizing the FDA's influence over the marketplace and thereby reducing the probability of committing a type II error. OMB is a traditional villain because of its responsibility for initiating many of the agency's budget cuts. One official, talking about the agency's relationship with OMB, argued that "the FDA regulates twenty-five cents of the consumer's dollar, but we're asked to do it all on a shoestring budget. We're not getting much support from OMB."[91] Budgetary control is not the only tool OMB has to influence FDA decisions, however. Executive Order 12291 extended OMB's authority to review the cost-effectiveness of FDA regulations. OMB's ability to screen agency regulations has severely limited the FDA's actions. Between 1981 and 1991, the FDA has proposed about four hundred regulations that have never been issued—the direct result of "the determination of the Reagan White House to reduce the scope of FDA regulation."[92]

One example of OMB's success in limiting FDA actions is the color dye controversy. After more than two years of study, the FDA concluded that six color dyes used in drugs and cosmetics caused cancer and moved to ban these products. OMB stymied repeated FDA efforts to ban the dyes, arguing that the cost of the ban exceeded the potential benefits.[93] This controversy and similar incidences have led some scholars to conclude that the FDA commissioners serving under the Reagan administration experienced greater limitations in their authority than their predecessors had ever known.[94]

Political appointees at the Department of Health and Human Services (HHS), the parent organization of the FDA, have also exercised control over the

---

90. Author interview, FDA Center for Biologics, March 12, 1991.
91. Author interview, FDA Legislative Affairs, December 11, 1990.
92. Philip J. Hilts, "Head of FDA Orders Review of Big Backlog," *New York Times,* June 10, 1991.
93. Kosterlitz 1985, 1968–69.
94. Eads and Fix 1984, 146.

agency. Often, these appointees work with OMB on its efforts to restrict the FDA.[95] As a result, there has been some discussion in Congress of making the FDA an independent agency similar to the Environmental Protection Agency (EPA). The official line at the FDA is that such a move is unnecessary since HHS and FDA are in complete agreement on major health issues. However, lower-level officials at the FDA, speaking on background, argue that a move away from HHS's domain would be beneficial to the agency and give it the autonomy needed to effectively carry out its operations.

While presidential aides in the 1980s have sought to get more pharmaceuticals out onto the market, most legislators have remained concerned over the safety of new drugs. According to Charles Schultze, the chief maxim of the American political system is never be seen doing direct harm.[96] This principle has consistently prevailed through most of Congress's dealings with the FDA. As Christopher Foreman of the Brookings Institution stated:

> The primary message conveyed to the agency by its political overseers for years before the HIV epidemic . . . had been to "go slow." In hearing after hearing, year after year (and even today, for nearly everything except AIDS), Congress has told the agency mostly one thing: above all else, do not approve, or allow to remain accessible, products . . . that cause demonstrable harm to identifiable victims.[97]

Even proponents of greater type II reliability have found it necessary to preface their remarks with an assurance that they do not wish to jeopardize the FDA's ability to certify the safety of new pharmaceuticals.[98]

The national emphasis on deregulation in the late 1970s did give these congressional proponents of type II reliability a more prominent voice. Greater concern was expressed over the "drug lag," which denied consumers of important new therapies in the process of protecting them from harmful ones. As a general rule, however, tinkering with the FDA's drug approval process offers few electoral benefits for most politicians. While the harm caused by releasing unsafe drugs generates ample publicity to motivate congressional reform of the approval process, the existence of type II errors rarely sparks such public concern.[99] As a result, the most comprehensive attempt to reform the FDA's

---

95. Appointees at HHS helped OMB in its efforts to stop the color dye ban mentioned earlier.

96. Schultze 1977, 70.

97. Foreman 1991, 31.

98. See, for example, U.S. House 1981.

99. The Orphan Drug Act of 1983 was a notable exception. "Orphan" drugs are those used for the treatment of rare diseases. Because of the small patient population for these illnesses, such drugs may offer a manufacturer little or no profit. The Orphan Drug Act was established to

approval process since 1962, the Drug Regulatory Reform Act of 1978, stalled out after lengthy congressional hearings.[100] That the FDA may be committing type II errors concerns many legislators, but not to the same extent that they worry about type I failures.

One reason Congress is oriented toward type I reliability is the behavior of many prominent consumer-interest groups. As a matter of principle, most of these public-interest groups are anxious about the possibility of the FDA allowing harmful drugs onto the market. Most notable among these groups are the Public Citizens' Health Research Group, Consumer Action for Improved Food and Drugs, and the Center for Science in the Public Interest.[101] Although these organizations often have less funding than their industry counterparts, they have been very successful in finding sympathetic legislators to champion their causes. The relationship between these consumer groups and the FDA, on the other hand, has been an antagonistic one. Embracing the traditional notion of bureaucratic capture, these groups accuse the FDA of collaborating with industry and perceive the current regulation of drug manufacturers as lax. These consumer groups may be effective in Congress and in the courts, but their self-appointed role as guardians of the nation's health has made them few friends in the halls of the FDA.

In contrast, the pharmaceutical industry has developed a more cooperative relationship with the FDA. Drug manufacturers, not surprisingly, are more concerned about reducing the chances for a type II error; that is, get all good drugs out into the market as quickly as possible. That the FDA has established clear acceptance standards has helped mollify this group. As one official put it, "What industry wants from us is a firm set of guidelines, and that's what we've given them."[102] Uniform standards make the system appear more equitable, which is not a small consideration in the pharmaceutical field. The longer the agency holds up a drug in review, the more time competitors have to catch up. (Pharmaceutical manufacturers routinely monitor their competitors' activity at the FDA through the Freedom of Information Act. A longer period in the FDA's domain gives competitors the opportunity to develop similar drugs to compete with the new product.) Without established guidelines, companies could claim that the FDA was unfairly eroding their market advantage. Thus, standard operating procedures help the agency minimize these complaints about equity and have kept the number of industry complaints down.

---

promote these pharmaceuticals by allowing companies to take tax deductions for 75 percent of the cost of clinical studies and granting exclusive marketing rights for seven years following approval.

100. Eads and Fix 1984, 81.

101. These three groups share an additional bond—they are all offshoots of the Nader organization.

102. Author interview, FDA Center for Drugs, March 13, 1991.

Of course, this standardization has not ended all complaints against the FDA. Individual companies have occasionally made the opposite claim—that they never know what to expect from the agency. These complaints usually follow rejection or delay by the FDA. As one officer stated:

> Companies can't always recognize the "dry wells." After they've invested millions of dollars on R&D for a new drug, they don't want to hear that it's unsafe or ineffective. At those times we are definitely not their best buddies.[103]

Still, however much pharmaceutical companies want the agency to favor type II reliability, most recognize the importance of the FDA's mission to limit type I failures. Such protection boosts consumer confidence in pharmaceuticals, which is vital to a thriving marketplace. Consequently, many drug companies are currently supportive of the proposed FDA revitalization bill.

It should not be too surprising that the FDA has historically emphasized type I reliability. As we have noted, the political consequences of allowing harmful drugs onto the market usually outweigh those of keeping good pharmaceuticals off. Former FDA Commissioner Alexander Schmitt summarized this well when he said in the 1970s:

> For example, in all of FDA's history, I am unable to find a single instance where a Congressional committee investigated the *failure* of FDA to approve a new drug. But, the times when hearings have been held to criticize our approval of new drugs have been so frequent that we aren't able to count them . . . The message of FDA staff could not be clearer. Whenever a controversy over a new drug is resolved by its approval, the Agency and the individuals involved likely will be investigated. Whenever such a drug is disapproved, no inquiry will be made. The Congressional pressure for our *negative* action on new drug applications is, therefore, intense. And it seems to be increasing, as everyone is becoming a self-acclaimed expert on carcinogenesis and drug testing.[104]

This belief remains as true today as it was in Schmitt's time. One FDA official stated in an interview that "we tend to be conservative . . . No one congratulates us about all the good drugs we've approved, but our [derriere] will be in a sling if we are ever found to approve a bad one."[105] As a consequence, the

---

103. Author interview, FDA Center for Drugs, June 18, 1991.
104. Quoted in Grabowski 1976, 76. Emphasis in the original.
105. Author interview, FDA Center for Drugs, June 17, 1991.

FDA's bureaucratic culture heavily emphasizes the pursuit of type I reliability in order to minimize political interference.

Even if the FDA's political environment did not demand greater type I reliability, the agency would still maintain this bias because of the medical training of its personnel. The officials in the pharmaceuticals division of the FDA are predominantly medical professionals.[106] Their medical education teaches them to save individual lives but does not equip them to perform cost-benefit analyses for society as a whole. When asked about the educational influence of FDA personnel, a manager at the Center for Drugs replied that "doctors are taught to protect the lives of their patients at all costs. It's certainly reasonable to think that this has an effect on our medical officers— but a good one, I think."[107] If the FDA were dominated by economists, it might be more mindful of the cost trade-offs between type I and type II errors.

The FDA's behavior is also shaped by the existence of a major information asymmetry with regard to type I and type II failures. If the FDA approves a bad drug, a type I error, the consequences are usually visible to the public and widely reported by the media.[108] On the other hand, holding up a good drug in the regulatory process, a type II error, is a problem generally known to a much smaller body of people—the pharmaceutical companies, a small number of independent researchers, and the agency itself.[109] Thus, the greater visibility of type I errors increases the opportunity for negative publicity and more political interference, causing the agency to allocate more effort and resources to prevent that type of error.

The FDA has shown a willingness to shift its position in cases where individual type II errors become widely known. An example of this shift can be seen in the recent case of the FDA's review for a new wonder drug, TPA. TPA, short for tissue plasminogen activator, is administered to heart-attack victims and is designed to dissolve blood clots near the heart that cause cardiac arrest. Although TPA performed its task admirably in clinical trials, there were questions raised about possible cerebral hemorrhaging caused by the drug. To minimize the probability of a type I error, the FDA required additional tests before approving TPA. During this time, however, TPA had

---

106. Furthermore, all but one of the FDA commissioners have been medical doctors.

107. Author interview, FDA Center for Drugs, June 18, 1991.

108. The greater the cost of the error, in terms of either number of people affected or the severity of their affliction, the more likely that the failure will be visible.

109. One may wonder why pharmaceutical companies don't protest more often when they believe a type II error is occurring. As noted earlier, these companies do indeed complain about such errors from time to time, but the FDA's uniform procedures help reduce this problem. Furthermore, by not publicly challenging the FDA, as many consumer groups regularly do, industry is able to promote more goodwill between itself and the agency, which better serves its overall interests.

achieved approval on an experimental basis only at thirty-two hospitals across the country. It just so happened that one of the patients saved using TPA at an experimental facility was Larry King, a famous radio talk-show host. Following his experience, King spent considerable time publicly attacking the FDA for not granting the drug full approval. Thus, as evidence of the drug's effectiveness became known to both the medical community and the general public, the FDA was under increasing pressure to approve the drug for general use. Commissioner Frank Young finally stepped in to expedite the process and granted TPA full approval. The final licensing of TPA was due in part to the greater awareness of the type II error that was taking place.[110]

Dealing with the AIDS Crisis

The existence of type II errors, as in the case of TPA, has been discovered from time to time, but it is the exception rather than the rule. Perhaps the biggest change in the FDA's political environment following the onset of the AIDS crisis, however, has been the increased visibility of type II errors for a broader classification of pharmaceuticals.

One reason that type II errors generally tend to be less visible is that there is no constituency willing to monitor and act on this issue on a regular basis. It is essentially a collective action problem. Action first requires information, but as Mancur Olson stated, "Information and calculation about a collective good is often itself a collective good."[111] Unfortunately, the group that should be collecting this information—consumers—is too large a segment to avoid the negative effects of the free-rider problem. If we limited the focus to certain subsets of this group, such as asthma sufferers, the members of such a subgroup might choose to organize a monitoring system focusing on their illness under certain conditions. Even these smaller groups, however, are often large enough to have to contend with the free-rider problem and the difficulties of collective action. While consumer groups, such as Public Citizens' Health Research Group, are already organized and might be able to watch for type II errors, these groups tend to concentrate their efforts on monitoring for type I errors and allow the type II problem to often go unnoticed. Consequently, type II errors committed by the FDA are rarely visible in the political arena.

This situation has changed with the advent of the AIDS crisis. The population group most directly affected by the development of the AIDS epidemic is the gay community. Data reveal that 75 percent of all AIDS transmission cases are between homosexual males.[112] Unlike other groups of

---

110. Shapiro and Silberner 1987.
111. Olson 1982, 25.
112. The remaining transmission categories are divided among intravenous drug users (15

patients, this group is able to overcome the collective action problem for several reasons. First, homosexuals represent a relatively small segment of the population, which reduces the magnitude the free-rider problem. The difficulty of collective action is further curtailed by the fact that AIDS is a terminal disease that is spreading through the gay community rather quickly, which makes the costs of inaction to group members quite large and discourages free riding. Finally, homosexuals have been previously organized on other issues, such as civil rights, and thus do not need to overcome the inertia associated with forming a new organization.

As a result, a number of gay-interest groups have focused a considerable amount of their attention on AIDS issues. Most prominent among them are Lambda Legal Defense Fund, Project Inform, the Gay Men's Health Crisis, and the AIDS Coalition To Unleash Power (ACT-UP). Leaders from these organizations spend a great deal of time communicating with FDA officials and other members of the Public Health Service. Furthermore, these groups have shown that they are willing to protest vocally and visibly about FDA policies they disagree with.

AIDS activists are primarily concerned about the FDA's chances of committing a type II failure. Their affliction is already terminal, so if a licensed drug proves to be deadly, it is viewed as simply accelerating the inevitable end.[113] On the other hand, type II failures—withholding drugs that could prove beneficial—are seen as devastating because of the intense need for new therapies to treat AIDS patients. This need is especially true given the limited options available for treating AIDS patients and the questionable value of these procedures. As a result, these interest groups monitor type II failures much more closely and are quick to object to any perceived error on the part of the FDA.

These interests have been able to find some congressional support to force the FDA toward more type II reliability. This emphasis has continued to grow as AIDS has moved into the heterosexual population. The catalyst of the FDA's new political environment has clearly been the activities of the gay community and the increased visibility it brings to type II failures.

---

percent), blood and blood products (3 percent), and undetermined (7 percent). See U.S. House 1987, 134.

113. This perception is actually the subject of a large ethical debate in the medical community. Some medical professionals believe that activities that shorten the life of terminal patients are still wrong. These people generally regard any cost-benefit analysis as meaningless where human life is involved. Many actual AIDS patients disagree and believe that if they are willing to accept the risks, they should be allowed to do so. Although this controversy is interesting, this work nevertheless focuses on the positive, rather than the normative, aspects of AIDS policy. For our purposes, therefore, it is sufficient to note that many AIDS activists are willing to accept greater levels of type I failure in order to lower the chances of a type II error occurring.

Further Changes in FDA Politics

For most of its history, the FDA clearly had an incentive to minimize the possibility of approving bad drugs—a type I error. As an agency dominated by physicians, the FDA has professional norms that dictate greater concern for type I errors. This finding was augmented by the fact that type I failures were generally more visible than type II errors. Finally, political superiors in the legislative and executive branches used the old adage of "do no direct harm" (avoid type I failures) as the prevailing rule for overseeing the management of pharmaceuticals. This last factor began to change in the 1980s as presidential appointees began concentrating efforts at reducing type II failures.

In the 1990s, a bit of a role reversal occurred. Clinton administration officials were happy with traditional FDA policies and showed little concern that the FDA's regulatory stance hurt the marketing of new drugs. In part, the administration's focus was on its national health care plan, and it sought approval for this proposal from consumer-advocate groups. These groups have been alarmed over type I errors, not type II; to get their support, the Clinton administration focused its wrath on pharmaceutical manufacturers, not the policies of the FDA. Furthermore, as believers in government activism, the administration members had no philosophical reason to be opposed to increasing FDA regulation.

Recent FDA activities, however, have started to raise questions in Congress. The volumes of new regulations, the restrictions on information that can be provided by companies to physicians regarding prescription drugs, the efforts of the FDA to extend its authority into tobacco regulation, and armed raids on vitamin manufacturers have caused some concern in Congress.[114] Congressional opposition was magnified by the 1994 congressional elections, which turned over control of both chambers to the Republican party and empowered its conservative members. The roles have reversed since the 1980s; now the executive branch is supportive of efforts to reduce type I errors while the legislative branch pushes for more type II reliability.

Of course, this concern for reducing type II error is not simply the result of electoral changes. Why has there been renewed concern over the FDA? With all the other important issues on the agenda, why has the FDA drawn the concern that it has from legislators? In part, the fact that AIDS activists have drawn attention to the type II errors committed by the agency regarding the

---

114. One of the more publicized raids occurred on May 6, 1992, in Washington state when FDA inspectors and local police conducted a no-knock raid of the Tacoma Clinic, a vitamin and health supplement distributor. FDA agents held the staff at gunpoint (to prevent anyone from hiding the vitamins) and seized more than $100,000 worth of products and office supplies. Although the FDA claimed the clinic was engaged in dangerous health practices, no charges were filed nor materials returned for more than two years following the raid.

approval AIDS drugs has raised broader concerns. Political leaders and other interest groups have begun to show much more concern for other lifesaving drugs that may be held up unnecessarily. The attention on type II errors has also been enhanced by the rise of the Internet, which has reduced the cost of information about new drug therapies and made it somewhat easier for other patient groups to begin mobilizing. Combined with the general conservative shift in Congress, these factors have created a strong incentive for the FDA to institute reforms and show greater concern for type II errors.

Conclusions

In the last two chapters, we have seen that there are strong political currents that have the power to shape agency decisions and routines. In the theoretical discussion in chapter 2, we noted that responsiveness to the perceived desires of active political leaders, the involvement of organized interest groups, and the visibility of each type of failure are some of the factors that can influence agency behavior. In the case analysis in chapter 3, we have seen that each of these ingredients was present in the political environments of NASA and the FDA. In particular, it is interesting to note that each agency had fairly strong political incentives to move from type I to type II reliability between the mid-1970s and the mid-1990s.

Although it is theoretically plausible that these agencies would respond in this way, it is important to ask whether such a shift actually occurred. When discussing issues of politics, NASA and FDA officials tend to resist the idea that politics plays a major factor in basic agency decisions. NASA personnel acknowledge that politics influences the agency but are often disdainful of this fact. Many FDA officials deny outright that politics affects the daily decisions or routines of the agency. It is easy to understand why these agencies are reluctant to admit that politics affects policy. Both agencies are dominated by professionals who take pride in the expertise they are able to bring to these important decisions; to the extent that politics is an influence, it is often seen as undermining the importance of expertise.

If it is true that political incentives shape agency decisions, then based on the information presented in this chapter, we should see both agencies becoming more responsive to type II errors and more vulnerable to type I failure. If political incentives are not relevant to these technologically oriented agencies, the fact that the technology has remained unchanged or more susceptible to type I failures should mean that neither NASA nor the FDA would seek to maintain or even increase its type II reliability. To determine which is the case, we need to look at the administrative behavior of these two agencies. But a further question now arises: Is it reasonable to assume that these two agencies responded to these pressures in the same way? If not, then what might account for these differences? To answer these questions, we must first work through a theoretical discussion of organizational structure and staffing and what their impact is on the reliability of agency decisions. After discussing these issues in chapters 4 and 5, we will return to the cases of NASA and the FDA to see if in fact these agencies are driven by political factors.

CHAPTER 4

Organizational Structure and the Design of Reliable Systems

As I have shown in the last chapter, both NASA and the FDA in the 1980s had to contend with growing political pressure to reduce the likelihood of potential type II failures. In response to these demands, we might expect that each agency instituted some significant organizational changes. This expectation, however, raises a number of important questions. What exactly can an agency do to shift the reliability of its decision-making process? Did NASA and the FDA institute the same policies in response to the similar pressures they each felt? If not, what factors caused these agencies to pursue their objectives in a different manner?

These are important questions, but more theoretical development is needed before they can be properly answered. As a first step in this process, I begin in this chapter by focusing on organizational design and its impact on the reliability of agency decisions. In chapter 5, I discuss the factors that influence the behavior of individual members of an organization. Finally, in chapter 6, I draw these two perspectives together to develop some hypotheses about the organizational choices of agencies like NASA and the FDA.

Basic Concepts of Structure and Reliability

General Assumptions

Throughout the remainder of this book I will be contrasting *component* and *system* reliability. It is important to clarify in advance what is meant by these terms. A *system* is a collection of subunits, known as *components,* that are linked together in a particular structure. In administrative theory, identifying components is dependent on the system level in question. If one were concentrating on the behavior of an agency, then the agency as a whole would be the system and the offices within it would be the components. Alternatively, if one were looking at the executive branch as a whole, that would be the system and each agency a component within the system. In an organizational context, determining what the components are depends largely on the system with which you are concerned. Although the logic is applicable to any level of analysis, in both the case studies of NASA and the FDA as well as this theoretical section, the system of concern is the agency and each component represents an office or individuals inside the agency.

Three other assumptions must also be specified. First, I assume initially that the probability of failure for each component in the system has already been determined, either by testing or by past history. Making this assumption is not unreasonable. Measuring personnel productivity is a subject that has been discussed in industrial engineering and other areas of management science, and the research from these areas makes it possible to generate statistically sound estimates of component performance and reliability. Nonetheless, I will later relax this assumption, in part to demonstrate that the theoretical framework is valuable even when the exact probabilities of component failure are not known. Making this assumption at the onset, however, is useful for developing the theory; since the components are assumed to be known quantities, the remaining question is how to assemble these components into a reliable network.

Second, I assume that organizational reliability is static, not dynamic. In the engineering literature, reliability is often treated as time-dependent so as to simulate the breakdown of mechanical components; the probability of such failure naturally increases with age. For administrative systems, however, it is not clear how component reliability would change over time. One might argue that agents become more reliable over time because they have greater experience and expertise with the issues and are thus better able to address them. On the other hand, it could be posited that agents are less reliable over time because they are more secure in their positions and lose their incentive to perform well. Additionally, interest-group capture of some public agency may affect the reliability of its performance. While these ideas raise interesting questions, for our needs here, static models of administrative reliability will provide sufficient insight.

Third, I assume that the states of all components are statistically independent. In other words, the failure of one component or subsystem does not affect the probability of failure of other components. Those who study public administration may question the validity of this assumption. Later in this chapter, I will discuss some features of organizations that may call this premise into question, and I will formally relax the assumption. Using concepts from probability theory, I will show later that the possibility of component interaction does not negate the general results of reliability theory. Therefore, making the assumption of component independence at this point is a useful simplifying assumption that does not undercut the generalizability of the results.

With these assumptions in hand, we can now focus our attention on the possible structural configurations that are commonly found in organizations.

Types of Organizational Structures

Several basic organizational forms are employed in the development of administrative systems. The first is a serial structure, a form that is often found in organizations. In a traditional serial structure, pictured in figure 4.1a, the first component must correctly process a policy initiative before sending it on to the next component. To be effective, policy must successfully pass through each of these components. The result is that, in order for the system as a whole to fail, it is only necessary for one of the components in series to fail. If any one component were to fail to pass the policy to the next unit, then all the components that followed it would be unable to act and the policy could not get through the system.

Another possible organizational form is the establishment of parallel linkages between components. In a parallel structure, such as the one illustrated in figure 4.1b, a policy may pass through any one of the components in order to get to the implementation stage. It is different from the serial structure inasmuch as that even if one or more units fail to pass the policy along, it may still be able to make it through the system. The end result is that for a policy to fail to get through this type of system, all components must fail.

One variation of this structural form is the k-out-of-m unit network. In certain cases, we require that a certain number k of the m units in an active parallel redundant system must work for the system to be successful. One example of this type of system might be the requirement that at least two of the space shuttle's four major computers be on-line for launch. An organizational application of this system may be an agency director's decision rule not to implement any policy that a majority of his or her staff cannot agree upon ($k = (m/2) + 1$).

There are two special cases of the k-out-of-m unit network that merit attention. The first is where $k = 1$, in which case we are back to a simple parallel system. The second case is where $k = m$, which effectively reduces the structure to a serial system. (See appendix at the end of this chapter for proof.) In the latter case, although the network is configured as an active parallel system, in terms of reliability it is behaving as a serial structure. To differentiate between this type of system and a traditional serial network, we will classify this type of structure as a *serially independent system*. This name signifies that while the system is essentially a serial one, its components operate completely independently from each other.

In an organizational context, an important distinction between a serially independent system and the traditional serial structure is the difference in processing time. In a traditional serial system, the first component must process the information, and then pass it on to the next component for processing,

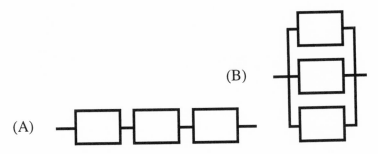

(B)

(A)

Fig. 4.1. Redundant systems in series and in parallel. *A*, serial configuration; *B*, parallel configuration.

and this procedure continues until all the components have processed the information. The total processing time of the system is the sum of processing times for each component plus some factor to account for transmission delay between units. In contrast, the serially independent system allows all components to operate simultaneously. The time needed for the serially independent system to complete its task is simply the time it takes the slowest component to finish its operations. So while both structures yield the same level of reliability, serially independent systems require less processing time.

Larger organizations often utilize combinations of serial and parallel structural forms. Two examples of this utilization can be seen in figure 4.2. The first case is that of a series-parallel system. In this structure, there are several parallel subsystems linked together in a serial fashion. Figure 4.2b illustrates the case of a parallel-series configuration. It is the result of several serial substructures combined into a larger parallel network. As these two examples illustrate, most large and complex structures can be decomposed into smaller units for easier analysis.

The Advantage of Parallel Systems
in a Two-State World

Components aligned in a series configuration are perhaps the easiest systems to analyze as well as the most commonly encountered. As we noted earlier, in order for the system as a whole to fail, it is only necessary for one of the components in series to fail. Defining the probability of failure for component i as f_i, a mathematical statement of the reliability of a serial system with m components would be:

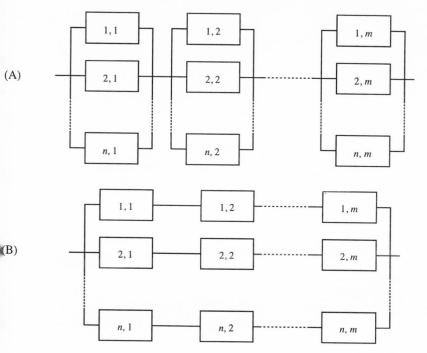

Fig. 4.2. Combinations of structures with *m* units in series and *n* units in parallel. *A*, series-parallel configuration; *B*, parallel-series configuration.

$$R_{sys} = \prod_{i=1}^{m} (1 - f_i) \tag{4.1}$$

As we can see, there are two factors that determine the reliability of a series system: component reliability and the number of components in the system. To increase the reliability of this type of system, we must either increase the reliability of the components or decrease the total number of components employed. As illustrated in figure 4.3, marginal gains in system reliability from increasing component performance decrease as component reliability increases. When the costs of increasing component reliability rise exponentially, it is more effective to simply reduce the total number of serial components in order to reach reliability goals.

Perhaps the most common means of increasing reliability in a two-state world is to add parallel components to a system. It is assumed that all branches

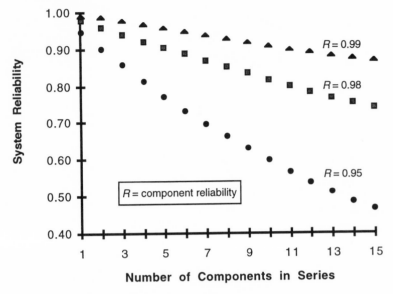

Fig. 4.3. Declining reliability with serial systems

are active and that a signal needs to pass through only one branch to be successfully transmitted. Since it is assumed that all branches must fail in order for the system to fail, the reliability function for a parallel system with n components is simply:

$$R_{sys} = 1 - \prod_{i=1}^{n} f_i \qquad (4.2)$$

Figure 4.4 illustrates the relationship between component reliability, the number of parallel elements, and overall system reliability. In this case, we see that the marginal gains from adding parallel channels decrease as the number of parallel components increases.

In comparing figures 4.3 and 4.4, the attractiveness of parallel systems in a two-state world is clear. Holding component reliability constant, the addition of redundancy in a parallel fashion will raise the reliability of the overall system, while creating serial redundancies decreases total system reliability. It is not surprising, therefore, that many scholars in this area have spurned serial systems and focused instead on parallel linkages when discussing this issue. Pressman and Wildavsky (1973) have criticized the existence of "multiple clearance points"—a serial system—for an implementive decision because it

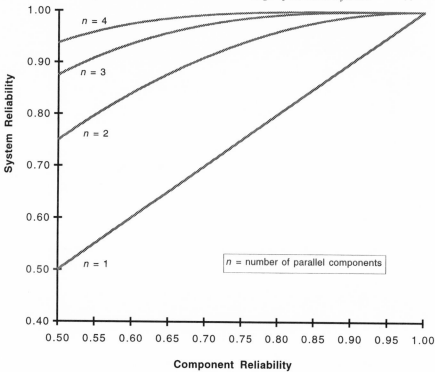

Fig. 4.4.   Increasing reliability with parallel systems

reduces the likelihood that any policy can ever be executed. Landau (1969) directs the same logic against "streamlined" serial structures, claiming that such systems are more susceptible to failure than those with parallel redundancies. As a result, the major policy prescription of Landau's work (1969, 1973, 1991) and others (Bendor 1985; Lerner 1986) has been to emphasize the use of parallel linkages to create more reliable organizations.

However, if it is true that serial systems are generally less reliable, then why are such structures ever adopted by organizations? To fully answer this question, we must go beyond the two-state world to allow for multiple forms of error.

Type I and Type II Errors in an Administrative Setting

As we have seen in the two-state world, serial structures are less reliable than others of comparable size. Nonetheless, it is clear that this structural form has been employed repeatedly in the development of bureaucracies. The reason this type of organizational structure has survived, I will suggest, is that it is valuable when we must design systems to accommodate multiple types of error. In the last section, it was assumed that there existed only two states for every component: good (operating) and failed (not operating). In this section, I discuss how organizational reliability changes when we account for both type I and type II errors.

In general, a series structure is better suited to stop type I errors from occurring. Since the null hypothesis is that the agency should not take any new action, if any component chooses to pass the proposed policy through its part of the system, then it is rejecting the null hypothesis. For any policy decision to successfully pass through a serial system, all units must agree to pass it along. If rejecting the null hypothesis was actually the incorrect decision (a type I error), then all units must commit such an error for the serial system as a whole to fail. To see an example of this, consider NASA's launch decision process. A serial decision structure is more effective in preventing unsafe launches (type I errors). To approve an unsafe launch in a serial system, every unit must err. The more hurdles established, via increasing numbers of serial components, the harder it is for an unsafe launch proposal to pass through the system unopposed.

With regard to type II errors, however, series structures are less effective. In a serial system, if even one unit accepts the null hypothesis of no new action, then the policy cannot be passed through the rest of the serial system. If accepting the null hypothesis was actually incorrect (a type II error), then the whole system would have failed. Thus, for a type II error to occur at the system level, only one component in series must fail in this manner for the overall system to fail. Returning to the launch decision example, if only one unit in the serial launch decision structure falsely believes the launch should be aborted, then a safe launch will be aborted even though the rest of the units had or would have correctly identified the launch as safe. As the number of serial components increases, the probability that at least one component will commit a type II error—leading to system failure—rises as well.

Likewise, parallel systems have both advantages and disadvantages in a three-state world. Serial systems work to limit type I errors while parallel structures reduce the likelihood that a type II error occurs. That is because it is necessary for all components to fail in this manner for the parallel system to commit a type II error. To see this process, let us assume that the FDA chooses to establish a parallel structure for processing New Drug Applications (NDAs). Such a parallel system would reduce the likelihood that a good drug is denied or delayed approval (a type II error). The reason is that it would only take one unit to correctly identify an NDA as beneficial before it was granted approval; even if other units mistakenly thought the drug was bad, approval would be correctly granted. As the number of parallel linkages increases, the likelihood that one of them will correctly reject the null hypothesis also rises.

While the likelihood of type II failures declines in parallel systems, these structures often lead to higher levels of type I errors. In a parallel system, if one unit errs and incorrectly rejects the null hypothesis, the policy moves forward and a type I error occurs; it is only necessary for the incorrect action to pass through one channel in order to be implemented by the system. In the previous FDA example, the parallel structure made it more likely that good drugs got into the market, where they could help people in need. But the same structure that made it more likely for good drugs to be approved also makes it more likely that bad drugs will be approved. The reason is that if just one unit incorrectly believes the drug is safe and effective, the drug will be approved by the agency. If it only takes one unit in a parallel system to move a policy decision forward, then it only takes one error to lead to organizational failure. Consequently, the more independent parallel branches that are attached to a structure, the more likely it is that a type I error will occur but the less likely that a type II error will be committed by the system.

In hypothesis testing, the probability of type I and type II errors can be simultaneously reduced by increasing the sample size. Similarly, we can lower the probability of both types of error occurring in reliability theory by adding additional components to the system, both in series and in parallel. Administrative networks that contain both parallel and series subsystems can be analyzed by applying the same guiding principles mentioned earlier in a technique known as the decomposition or system reduction method. To use this technique effectively, however, will require that we formalize these ideas as mathematical expressions. That will be done in the following modeling exercise.[1]

Modeling the Impact of Structure
on Organizational Reliability

Differences between Technological Performance
and Administrative Decisions

In developing mathematical expressions of organizational performance, I will be drawing primarily on materials developed originally in the field of engineering reliability theory (Barlow and Proschan 1965; Aggarwal, Misra, and Gupta 1975; Dhillon 1983). To transfer these concepts to an administrative setting, however, it is necessary to include additional factors not normally

---

1. Readers who are not interested in the technical presentation may skip over the modeling exercise and the mathematical example that follows it without loss of continuity.

considered in engineering. Engineers are concerned primarily with the likelihood of technological failure. Administrators overseeing the management of risky technologies are concerned with more than the prospect of technological failure; they must also consider how likely it is that a potential error will be recognized by organizational members who will then take appropriate action to mitigate the problem. Thus, these models must include both the probability of technological failure and the likelihood of an appropriate response by organizational members.

We can also look at this issue from a probability perspective. What we are focusing on in this book is the probability of type I and type II errors. In a strict interpretation of hypothesis testing, type I and type II errors are the following conditional probabilities:

$$P[\text{type I error}] = P[H_0 \text{ is rejected} \mid H_0 \text{ is actually true}]$$

$$P[\text{type II error}] = P[H_0 \text{ is maintained} \mid H_0 \text{ is actually false}]$$

where the null hypothesis is represented by the term H_0. To calculate the probability of an actual failure, we need to multiply each of these conditional probabilities by the probability of the conditions. For example, a type I failure occurs when H_0 is rejected *and* H_0 is actually true. Because two events must occur to achieve this outcome, the probability of a type I error is a joint probability that can be found with the following expression:

$$P[H_0 \text{ is rejected } and \text{ } H_0 \text{ is true}] = P[H_0 \text{ is rejected} \mid H_0 \text{ is true}] \times$$

$$P[H_0 \text{ is true}]$$

The right-hand side of this expression contains both the likelihood of an appropriate response by organizational members ($P[H_0$ is rejected $\mid H_0$ is true]) and the probability of technological failure ($P[H_0$ is true]). By inference, the same principle is true for calculating type II failures.

To solidify this notion, consider two organizational subunits, each of which rejects H_0 when it is actually true in 10 percent of all cases ($P[H_0$ is rejected $\mid H_0$ is true] = 0.10). In one case, the organizational subunit works with a technology that is fairly reliable—H_0 is true in only 10 percent of all cases. The chance that this subunit commits a type I failure is only 1 percent. The other subunit works with a far less reliable technology for which H_0 is true in 80 percent of all cases. The likelihood of a type I failure from this subunit is 8 percent—eight times higher than in the first case. Even though the subunits themselves are equally reliable, the differences in technological performance lead to significant differences in the probability of failure.

While technological differences are important, variations in organizational performance can also be significant. Consider again two subunits working with the same technology. This technology is fairly reliable—H_0 is true in 20 percent of all cases. The first subunit fails to recognize that the null hypothesis is true in only 10 percent of cases where H_0 is true. Thus, the first subunit commits a type I failure in only 2 percent of all cases. In contrast, the second subunit is far less reliable, having a 25 percent chance of rejecting H_0 when it is fact true. The result is that the second subunit fails 2.5 times more often using the same technology as the first unit. These examples clearly show that it is important to factor into our models both the probability of technological failure and the likelihood of an appropriate response by organizational members in order to get an accurate view of agency reliability.

Mathematical Formulation of Serial System Performance

In order to express organizational reliability in mathematical terms, we must first define some notation. The probability that the null hypothesis is true is (q) while the probability that it is false is $(1 - q)$. In other words, the probability that the technology in question cannot be safely and effectively employed will be represented as (q).[2] The likelihood that an organizational component commits a type I error ($P[H_0$ is rejected $\mid H_0$ is true]) will be represented by the term α_i. Likewise, the probability that the ith organizational component commits a type II error will be represented by the term β_i. The chances of the ith component being responsible for a type I or type II failure—which is a function of both administrative error and technological failure—will be signified by the terms $f_{I,i}$ and $f_{II,i}$ respectively. The prospect of an administrative system committing a type I or type II failure will be denoted by F_I, F_{II} respectively.

As noted earlier, for any policy to successfully pass through a serial system, all units must agree to pass it along. If rejecting the null hypothesis was actually the incorrect decision (leading to a type I error), then every component in the administrative structure must commit such an error for the serial system as a whole to fail. Thus, mathematically we can identify both the probability of a type I failure occurring in a serial system with m components and the reliability of the system against this error (R_I) as[3]

---

2. This could be respecified so that q equals the probability that the null hypothesis is false—the technology is safe and effective. Such a change would alter the equations that follow but does not affect the results substantially.

3. My training as an engineer has taught me to think of such problems in terms of the likelihood of failure. Over time, however, I have come to recognize that many people find it easier to think of this subject in terms of the probability of reliable performance. The two perspectives

$$F_I = \prod_{i=1}^{m} f_{I,i} = \prod_{i=1}^{m} \alpha_i q \tag{4.3}$$

$$R_I = 1 - \prod_{i=1}^{m} f_{I,i} = 1 - \prod_{i=1}^{m} \alpha_i q. \tag{4.4}$$

Serial structures are less effective when it comes to preventing type II failures. If even one component accepts the null hypothesis of no new action, then the policy does not pass through the serial system. If accepting the null hypothesis was actually incorrect (a type II error), then the whole system would have failed. Since only one component in series must commit a type II failure for the system to fail, the probability that will fail in this manner is

$$F_{II} = 1 - \prod_{i=1}^{m} (1 - f_{II,i}) = 1 - \prod_{i=1}^{m} (1 - \beta_i(1 - q)) \tag{4.5}$$

$$R_{II} = \prod_{i=1}^{m} (1 - f_{II,i}) = \prod_{i=1}^{m} (1 - \beta_i(1 - q)). \tag{4.6}$$

We may also be interested in the overall reliability of the system—the likelihood that an agency would commit either a type I or a type II error. To find this, we assume that, for a given event at a given time, it is not possible for an administrative system to commit both a type I and a type II error simultaneously. This assumption is not unreasonable. A type I error requires that the agency act while a type II error demands that the agency postpone any action. An organization cannot both act and not act at the same time. Consider NASA's decision to launch the shuttle. The space agency can either decide to launch the shuttle now (possibly resulting in a type I error) or abort the launch until another time (possibly resulting in a type II error.) It cannot decide to both launch and abort at the same time.

Given this argument, we can conclude that type I and type II errors are, at any point in time, mutually exclusive events. Therefore, the probability of either a type I or a type II error in a serial system can be found as

$$P(F_I \cup F_{II}) = P(F_I) + P(F_{II}) = \prod_{i=1}^{m} \alpha_i q + \left(1 - \prod_{i=1}^{m} (1 - \beta_i(1 - q)) \right).$$

are complimentary, but I will present both formats in this section in order to appeal to a broad range of readers.

The overall reliability of the serial system is then found to be

$$R_{sys} = 1 - P(F_I \cup F_{II}) = 1 - \left(\prod_{i=1}^{m} \alpha_i q + \left(1 - \prod_{i=1}^{m} (1 - \beta_i(1 - q)) \right) \right)$$

$$R_{sys} = \prod_{i=1}^{m} (1 - \beta_i(1 - q)) - \prod_{i=1}^{m} \alpha_i q. \tag{4.7}$$

If we concern ourselves only with the system's overall performance, we can find the number of elements in series that, for a given level of component reliability, will result in the optimal level of reliability. The system reliability of a series network consisting of m identical and independent components is

$$R_{sys} = [1 - \beta(1 - q)]^m - [\alpha q]^m. \tag{4.8}$$

Differentiating this equation with respect to m and setting the result equal to zero will give us the optimal number of components to be linked in series in order to maximize the system's reliability. This result, which is derived in the appendix at the end of this chapter, is

$$m^* = \frac{\ln \left(\frac{\ln(\alpha q)}{\ln(1 - \beta(1 - q))} \right)}{\ln \frac{(1 - \beta(1 - q))}{(\alpha q)}}. \tag{4.9}$$

Mathematical Formulation of Parallel System Performance

As the reader will have realized by now, there is an inverse relationship between the reliabilities of series and parallel systems. For instance, although series structures are ineffective against type II errors, parallel systems are able to reduce the probability of such errors occurring because it is necessary for all components to fail in this manner for the overall system to commit a type II error. Likewise, type I errors are increased in such a network because it is only necessary for the incorrect action to pass through one channel in order to be implemented by the system. Therefore, the more independent parallel branches that are attached to a structure, the more likely it is that a type I error will occur but the less likely that a type II error will be committed by the system.

The mathematical formulation of the reliability of a parallel system with n components is

$$F_I = 1 - \prod_{i=1}^{m} (1 - f_{I,i}) = 1 - \prod_{i=1}^{m} (1 - \alpha_i q) \qquad (4.10)$$

$$R_I = \prod_{i=1}^{m} (1 - f_{I,i}) = \prod_{i=1}^{m} (1 - \alpha_i q) \qquad (4.11)$$

$$F_{II} = \prod_{i=1}^{m} f_{II,i} = \prod_{i=1}^{m} \beta_i (1 - q) \qquad (4.12)$$

$$R_{II} = 1 - \prod_{i=1}^{m} f_{II,i} = 1 - \prod_{i=1}^{m} \beta_i (1 - q) \qquad (4.13)$$

$$R_{sys} = \prod_{i=1}^{m} (1 - \alpha_i q) - \prod_{i=1}^{m} \beta_i (1 - q). \qquad (4.14)$$

Just as we were able to do earlier for the series structure, we can calculate the optimal number of identical and independent components linked in parallel. The system reliability of a parallel network consisting of n identical and independent components is

$$R_{sys} = [1 - \alpha q]^n - [\beta (1 - q)]^n \qquad (4.15)$$

Differentiating this equation with respect to n and setting the result equal to zero will give us the optimal number of components to be linked in parallel in order to maximize the system's reliability. This result, derived in the appendix at the end of this chapter, is as follows:

$$n^* = \frac{\ln \left(\dfrac{\ln(\beta(1 - q))}{\ln(1 - \alpha q)} \right)}{\ln \dfrac{(1 - \alpha q)}{(\beta(1 - q))}}. \qquad (4.16)$$

Combinations of Serial and Parallel Systems

In hypothesis testing, the probability of type I and type II errors can be simultaneously reduced by increasing the sample size. Similarly, we can lower the probability of both types of error occurring in reliability theory by adding additional components to the system, both in series and in parallel.

With regard to multiple errors, we may employ the expressions derived earlier to analyze the reliability of networks that contain both parallel and series subsystems. To do so, we must first reduce the overall structure into a set of serial and/or parallel subsystems. The various subsystems are evaluated to find the probability of type I and type II failure at this level. Each subsystem is then treated as a single component in a larger model of the overall structure. Using this system reduction method, we are able to find the reliability of more complex administrative networks.

Finding the optimal number of components in a mixed structure is more difficult than it was for simple series or parallel systems. Consider a combined system having m components in series and n components in parallel. We can raise the overall reliability level of the system to a point arbitrarily close to 1 by simply increasing the number of components in both series and parallel without bound (Barlow and Proschan 1965, 187). However, given a fixed number of components in either series or parallel, we can find the optimal number of components needed in the other dimension, as discussed here for both series-parallel systems and parallel-series systems.

First, let us consider a series-parallel system having m components in series and n components in parallel, as seen earlier in figure 4.2a. All components are assumed to be identical and independent. Regarding the system only as a series, we find that its overall reliability is

$$R_{\text{sys-sp}} = (1 - F_{\text{II}})^m - (F_{\text{I}})^m$$

Next, we must find the probability of type I and type II errors in each parallel subsystem.

$$F_{\text{I}} = 1 - (1 - \alpha_i q)^n \qquad F_{\text{II}} = (\beta_i(1 - q))^n$$

Combining these equations, we find that the overall system reliability of the $n \times m$ series-parallel network is

$$R_{\text{sys-sp}} = [1 - (\beta_i(1 - q))^n]^m - [1 - (1 - \alpha_i q)^n]^m \qquad (4.17)$$

Once we have the equation for the overall reliability of the system and have decided whether to fix the level of m or n, we can find the optimal number of components in the other dimension by differentiating $R_{\text{sys-sp}}$ with respect to the variable we seek to optimize and setting the result equal to zero. There are a number of computer routines available that are also capable of solving this type of problem.

This approach also works for parallel-series systems. Figure 4.2b shows a parallel-series network of $n \times m$ independent and identical components. Using the same method as shown earlier, we find the overall system reliability of a parallel-series system to be

$$R_{\text{sys-ps}} = [1 - (\alpha_i q)^m]^n - [1 - (1 - \beta_i(1 - q))^m]^n. \qquad (4.18)$$

Again, once we have the equation for the overall reliability of the system and have decided whether to fixed the level of m or n, we can find the optimal number of components in the other dimension by differentiating $R_{\text{sys-ps}}$ with respect to the variable we seek to optimize and setting the result equal to zero.

An Example of the Impact of Organizational Structure

Before demonstrating how all this may be applied in organizational analysis of NASA and the FDA, I first work through the necessary calculations using the example of a hypothetical agency. This hypothetical agency is headed by a director or political superior who has four subordinates (a, b, c, d) reporting directly to her.[4] In this example, we assume that each subordinate has a probability of committing a type I error of $\alpha_i = 0.150$, but commits type II errors with a probability of $\beta_i = 0.225$. In this case, the technology the agency works with is somewhat risky and fails one-third of the time; hence, the probability that the null hypothesis is true is $q = 0.333$. Factoring in the likelihood of administrative error and technological failure, we find the chance that any one subordinate would be responsible for a type I failure is only 5 percent ($f_{I,i} = 0.050$). The chance is 15 percent for a type II failure ($f_{II,i} = 0.150$).

The director begins by establishing a basic parallel network as shown in figure 4.5. The likelihood that this organizational design will be able to avoid error can be characterized as

$$R_{\text{I}} = \prod_{i=1}^{4} (1 - \alpha_i q) = (0.950)^4 = 0.815$$

$$R_{\text{II}} = 1 - \prod_{i=1}^{4} \beta_i(1 - q) = 1 - (0.150)^4 = 0.999.$$

While the basic parallel structure does an outstanding job guarding against type II errors, it is not as effective in preventing type I errors. To rectify this problem, the director decides to reorganize her subordinates into a basic serial structure. This new system—illustrated in figure 4.6—is far more reliable against type I failures but is now vulnerable to type II failures in almost half of all cases.

---

4. To more clearly differentiate between the director and the subordinates, I will assume in this chapter that the director is female while all the subordinates are male.

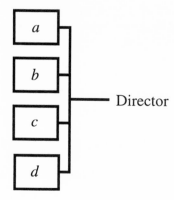

Fig. 4.5.   Initial organizational structure of hypothetical agency

$$R_{\mathrm{I}} = 1 - \prod_{i=1}^{4} \alpha_i q = 1 - (0.050)^4 \cong 1.000$$

$$R_{\mathrm{II}} = \prod_{i=1}^{4} (1 - \beta_i(1 - q)) = (0.850)^4 = 0.522.$$

Hoping to find a middle ground between these outcomes, the director begins experimenting with a number of alternative structures. She begins by retaining the original parallel structure but now moves one of the subordinates into a supervisory position over his other three colleagues. The resulting system is diagrammed in figure 4.7a.

To find the reliability of this structure, we need to recognize that the fundamental structure in this case is a series system. The three subordinates operating in parallel can effectively be reduced to a single unit as illustrated in figure 4.7b. The likelihood of the parallel subsystem committing either a type I or a type II failure would be

$$f_{\mathrm{I},3p} = 1 - \prod_{i=1}^{3} (1 - \alpha_i q) = 1 - (0.950)^3 = 0.143$$

$$f_{\mathrm{II},3p} = \prod_{i=1}^{3} \beta_i(1 - q) = (0.150)^3 = 0.003.$$

Fig. 4.6. Alternative serial organizational structure

The reliability of the overall serial system could then be found as

$$R_{\mathrm{I}} = 1 - \prod_{i=1}^{2} f_{\mathrm{I},i} = 1 - (0.143)(0.050) = 0.993$$

$$R_{\mathrm{II}} = \prod_{i=1}^{2} (1 - f_{\mathrm{II},i}) = (0.997)(0.850) = 0.847.$$

As an alternative, the director may choose to create two separate teams with her four subordinates. Each two-person team would have to agree on a recommendation or policy decision before passing it up to the director. In this regard, the teams would act as serially independent subsystems. However, the director has set these two teams up in a parallel structure so that if either team approves a certain policy decision, it will be acted upon. The resulting parallel-series structure can be seen in figure 4.8a.

This new structure can be reduced to a simple parallel network with two components, as demonstrated in figure 4.8b. The probability of failure for each team is

$$f_{\mathrm{I,team}} = \prod_{i=1}^{2} \alpha_i q = (0.050)^2 = 0.003$$

$$f_{\mathrm{II,team}} = 1 - \prod_{i=1}^{2} (1 - \beta_i(1 - q)) = 1 - (0.850)^2 = 0.278.$$

The reliability of the basic parallel network can be characterized as

$$R_{\mathrm{I}} = \prod_{i=1}^{2} (1 - f_{\mathrm{I},i}) = (0.998)^2 = 0.995$$

$$R_{\mathrm{II}} = 1 - \prod_{i=1}^{2} f_{\mathrm{II},i} = 1 - (0.278)^2 = 0.923.$$

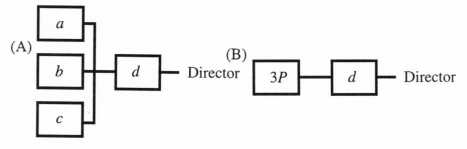

Fig. 4.7.   First mixed organizational structure. *A,* organizational structure; *B,* reduced agency structure with (*a, b, c*) reduced to unit 3*P*.

As the third alternative, the director considers establishing two divisions that operate in a serial fashion—that is to say that both divisions must approve the decision to employ the technology before that policy can be acted upon. Within the divisions, however, the subordinates are structured in parallel subsystems; if either subordinate approves the decision, it will be moved forward for action. This series-parallel network is illustrated in figure 4.9.

Once again, figure 4.9 demonstrates how the parallel subsystems can be reduced to single units within a serial structure. The probability for failure for each subsystem would be

$$f_{I,div} = 1 - \prod_{i=1}^{2} (1 - \alpha_i q) = 1 - (0.950)^2 = 0.098$$

$$f_{II,div} = \prod_{i=1}^{2} \beta_i (1 - q) = (0.150)^2 = 0.023.$$

The overall performance of the serial system can be characterized as

$$R_I = 1 - \prod_{i=1}^{2} f_{I,i} = 1 - (0.098)^2 = 0.990$$

$$R_{II} = \prod_{i=1}^{2} (1 - f_{II,i}) = (0.998)^2 = 0.956.$$

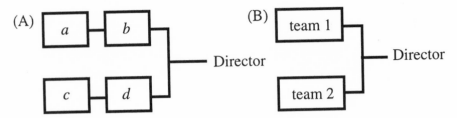

Fig. 4.8. Second mixed organizational structure. *A,* parallel-series structure; *B,* agency structure reduced to two parallel teams.

Looking at this example, several conclusions can be drawn at this point. First, as I have previously argued, organizational structure can have an important impact on administrative reliability. Second, the choice of structure provides insights into an agency's priorities. Which of these five structures should the director utilize? If the director was only concerned about type I failure, then the basic serial structure would undoubtedly be the best choice for the organization. If type II failure was the only factor, then the director's initial parallel network was best. Combinations of series and parallel subsystems yield results that strike a balance between type I and type II reliability. Since different structures are more susceptible to these two forms of errors at differential rates, looking at structural changes within an agency can provide some insight into its true preferences and priorities with regard to different types of reliability.

The Question of Subordinate Independence in Organizations

The principles of organizational structure and reliability established in this chapter rest on the validity of certain assumptions. These assumptions were clearly elucidated, and most of these points would be considered noncontroversial to public administration scholars. As noted earlier, however, one premise does raise concern and generate dissent: the assumption that each component in the administrative network operates independently of the others. If we were talking about machines—the original subject of reliability studies—then this assumption is less controversial simply because machines are not sentient and are unaware of their environment. But people in organizations realize that they are part of a larger group, and that knowledge may cause them to act differently than they might if they were lone decision makers. Normal-accident theorists would argue that because people are not the same as machines, reliability theory cannot be effectively applied to organizations. In this final section, I want to

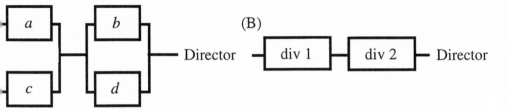

Fig. 4.9.   Third mixed organizational structure. *A,* **series-parallel structure;** *B,* **agency structure reduced to two serial divisions.**

consider at greater length the issue of organizational reliability and the assumption of independent subordinate judgments.

It seems almost trivial to say that people are not simply machines; few
people would be willing to argue otherwise. But in applying the results of
reliability theory in an organizational context, it is important to remember that
people, unlike machines, are social animals. As such, individuals seek acceptance among groups of people they deem important. Being risk averse, most
people wish to avoid any actions that may cause them to look bad or hurt their
standing in the group. In making decisions, people consider both the relevant
facts as well as how the choice will be perceived by their friends and colleagues
(Miller 1992). Since this social behavior can affect the performance and
reliability of an organization, let us spend a few moments considering each of
these problems.

In seeking acceptance from the larger group, people often take cues from
others in determining what would be appropriate behavior. This principle was
illustrated well in some classic experiments by Asch (1952). In these experiments, three subjects were placed in a room with an investigator, who would
draw three lines of unequal length on the blackboard and ask the three to state
which line was longest. In actuality, two of the three subjects were colleagues of
Asch who were instructed to follow a certain pattern in their answers: initially
they reported correctly and then after a short time they falsely stated which line
was longest. The actual subject always struggled before answering whenever
the colleagues falsely reported. A substantial portion of the subjects in the study
actually waited until the others answered and then made the same false report as
the colleagues.

In a similar vein, the experiments by Milgram (1974) demonstrated the
degree to which people were willing to comply with commands from an
authority figure. Dressed as a scientist, the authority figure would order the
subject to administer electrical shocks to the supposed subject in the next room
(who pretended to receive the jolts, but never actually felt any shocks). Al-

though the supposed subject acted as if in great pain, the real subject would often continue to administer jolts of electricity on the orders of the authority figure even as the doses reached nearly lethal levels. In some cases Milgram used two shock givers, with one being a colleague who was instructed to go along with administering the initial shocks and resist as the dosages increased. As the colleague began to resist, the true subject was also more likely to resist the orders of the authority figure.

What these experiments clearly show is that, in a group setting, people are influenced by the behavior of others. Individuals take cues about what is considered appropriate behavior from others who are like them. In the context of the discussion about organizational reliability, it seems clear that such social pressures may influence the behavior of components in the system. When faced with others who agree on a particular policy choice, it may be hard for an individual to oppose the group decision, even if he or she does not agree with the choice.

Another potential threat to independence in an organizational setting is the problem of subordinate shirking. There are times when members of an organization find it to their advantage to evade their work responsibilities and trust that the efforts of others are sufficient for the agency to meet its goal. Shirking occurs because it offers two advantages to the shirker. First, by free riding on the efforts of others, the shirking subordinate may reap the same reward without making the commensurate effort. Second, shirking allows a risk-averse agent to pass or spread blame for failure to other organizational members. Of course, these advantages are not universally available, but to the extent that this is possible, it is reasonable to expect that some subordinates will choose to shirk.

What would be the impact of shirking on organizational reliability? In a serial system, the shirker may simply pass along the response of the previous subordinate without providing any independent check on the content of the message. In a parallel system, a shirker can learn the position of another colleague and make the same report to his superior. In either case, what we have is effectively a lesser number of components in the administrative system. This doesn't really change previous results—it simply means that the formal structure is not the same as the effective structure.

The Impact of Cue Taking and Shirking

Normal-accident theorists have been quick to claim that these human behaviors represent a serious threat to the application of reliability theory to organizational science. Surprisingly, little effort has been made to formally analyze the impact of cue taking and shirking on organizational reliability. The only effort in this area has been some work by Sagan (1994) in which he calculates the probability of failure for a parallel system assuming independence and then assuming that dependence reduces component performance by some fixed amount. While an examination of Sagan's modeling attempt reveals a number of problems (it considers only parallel systems, operates in a limited two-state world, and could lead to negative probabilities of success), a critique of the functional form of his model misses the most important point. Sagan assumes that we know each unit is acting in a dependent manner. If we know that this is a problem, organizational theorists have a number of solutions that can be used to counteract these effects, including—but not limited to—firing the shirkers and replacing them with new subordinates. The real problem in applying these principles of organizational reliability is that an agency director is uncertain whether subordinates are acting independently.

How does the possibility of subordinate cue taking or shirking affect the director's assessment of the organization's reliability? To answer this question, let us begin by examining the performance of two subordinates: 1, who may be a cue taker or shirker, and 2, who may be a cue giver or leader with regard to a particular form of error. Furthermore, let us assume that each is equally competent so that if they were acting separately, their likelihood of failure would be the same. In the modeling exercise at the end of this section, it will be shown that if we could be assured that subordinate 2, the cue giver or leader, was always acting independently, then the probability of failure for subordinate 1 is the same as it would be if the director knew there was no shirking. That is to say, even if we thought that subordinate 1 might fail to be independent, the director's assessment of subordinate 1 would not change if subordinate 2 was known to be independent. Why is that the case? The reason is straightforward: even if engaged in cue taking or shirking, subordinate 1 is as likely to pass up a correct message received by his fellow agent as he would if he were acting independently.

This conclusion rests on two assumptions. First, if both subordinates are acting independently, the probability of failure is the same for each subordinate; we will relax this assumption momentarily. Second, the director is sure that subordinate 2 is definitely not shirking or otherwise violating the assumption of independence. This second assumption is not unreasonable when dealing with serial systems. Consider a serially structured organization engaged in bottom-up processing. The field unit who makes the initial report has no one else to cue off of, and his shirking behavior would be too obvious to escape notice. Subsequent subordinates in the serial system may engage in this behavior, but we can be reasonably confident that the lead unit is acting independently. Likewise, in a top-down command structure, the first unit who gives the command has no one to take a cue from, thus we can be confident of this unit's independence even if the other subordinates are questionable. But the assessment of the other subordinates, so long as there is some doubt about whether they are shirking or cue taking, does not change in the eyes of the director, and all our previous results about organizational reliability and structure remain intact.

What, then, about parallel systems? Arguing that subordinate 2 always acts independently in a parallel system is a bit of a stretch; in the absence of structural sequencing, it is quite possible that both units can choose to either shirk or cue-take simultaneously, creating the possibility of a common mode failure. The term *common mode failure* has taken on a number of definitions in the course of the high-reliability–normal-accident debate. In an organizational context, I define a common mode failure simply as the failure that occurs when two or more units interact in a dependent manner, with the resulting probability of failure being greater than if either had acted independently. For example, in the case of shirking, common mode failures occur when each unit counts on others to pick up the slack in his own performance, with the end result being that little overall effort is made to prevent a failure. The result in this case is that the likelihood of a system failure is greater than would be expected if one or more units acted independently.[5]

In a parallel system, therefore, we must consider three factors that could influence organizational reliability. First, there is the possibility of a common mode failure. Second, in a parallel system there is no guarantee that subordinate 2 is acting independently. Third, we cannot be sure if the cue taker is as reliable as, more reliable than, or less reliable than the cue giver. How would our results change if we were to relax the previous assumption that each subordinate was equally competent?

To answer this question, we begin with the case that if independent, subordinate 1 is more reliable than subordinate 2 with regard to a particular error. Of course, if both are shirking, then the probability of common mode failure is greater than if either acted independently. In this case, we would find that the probability of failure by subordinate 1 is greater if there is a possibility that his actions are dependent on those of subordinate 2. Understanding why that may be is not difficult. If he is acting independently, subordinate 1 is the more reliable of the two units. By either shirking or cue taking, subordinate 1 is following the lead of a less-reliable colleague, thereby increasing his chance of failure.

What would happen if the situation were reversed and subordinate 2 was the more reliable of the two units? That is to say that if independent, subordinate 2 is more reliable than subordinate 1 with regard to a particular error. In this case, it is possible that the reliability of subordinate 1 increases and the likelihood of failure decreases. To the extent that the cue giver is the more

5. If it is not clear to the reader now, it should be clear by the end of the next chapter that simply because two units act dependently does not guarantee that they will commit an error, but it does increase the chances.

reliable unit, it can actually help increase the reliability of the cue taker. Under such circumstances, subordinate 1—the cue taker—can decrease his probability of failure by following the lead of a more expert colleague. Of course, this gain is tempered by the possibility that subordinate 2 in this case is also shirking, and the net result is a possible common mode failure. But contrary to the claims of normal accident theorists, there are certain circumstances in which organizational reliability may actually be improved by the interdependence of organizational members.

The foil in this result, however, is that the director has no guarantee that the more reliable subordinate is the cue giver and the less reliable is the cue taker. Given this uncertainty, are there any policy implications that follow from this analysis? We can recall from chapter 1 that a number of high reliability theorists argued that the development a "culture of reliability" within an organization would be a key element in its success. Insofar as this culture promotes the norms of professionalism, it may help minimize the problem of cue taking and shirking in the first place. Further, to the extent that this culture of reliability emphasizes the importance of expertise, it raises the chance that more reliable subordinates are viewed within the organization as leaders and cue givers. Thus, the culture of reliability that high-reliability theorists discuss in their work may be one means by which we can prevent the problem of subordinate dependence from interfering with our efforts to improve the reliability of the organization as a whole.

These conclusions can be verified through the use of formal modeling.[6] Again we are focusing on the performance of two subordinates: 1, who may be a cue taker or shirker, and 2, who may be a cue giver or leader with regard to a particular form of error.[7] We will use Φ_i to represent the state of subordinate i acting in an independent fashion (i.e., no cue taking or shirking). Finally, let us make three further assumptions. First, if both subordinates are acting independently, the probability of failure is the same for each subordinate: $P[f_1 \mid \Phi_1] = P[f_2 \mid \Phi_2]$. Second, if both subordinates are acting dependently (state Ψ), then the probability of failure is greater than if one were independent: $P[f_i \mid \Psi] > P[f_i \mid \Phi_i]$. Third, if subordinate 1 is cuing off of 2, then the probability of failure for subordinate 1 would be: $P[f_1 \mid \bar{\Phi}_1] = P[f_2]$.

In our formulation, since the director is uncertain whether the subordinate is acting independently, the subordinate's probability of failure is determined from the definition of marginal probability. As a result, subordinate 1's probability of a particular type of failure is

---

6. Readers who are not interested in the technical presentation may choose to skip over this modeling exercise without loss of continuity.

7. We should recognize that a subordinate may take cues with regard to one type of error but not the other. For that reason I generalize the model for any particular type of error f. Thus, f_i could represent either α_i or β_i.

$$P[f_1] = P[f_1 \mid \Phi_1]P[\Phi_1] + P[f_1 \mid \bar{\Phi}_1]P[\bar{\Phi}_1]. \tag{4.19}$$

Substituting into this equation the assumptions made earlier and simplifying, we get

$$P[f_1] = P[f_1 \mid \Phi_1]P[\Phi_1] + (P[f_2 \mid \bar{\Phi}_2]P[\Phi_2]$$

$$+ P[f_2 \mid \Psi]P[\bar{\Phi}_2])P[\bar{\Phi}f_1]$$

$$P[f_1] = P[f_1 \mid \Phi_1](P[\Phi_1] + P[\Phi_2]P[\bar{\Phi}_1])$$

$$+ P[f_2 \mid \Psi]P[\bar{\Phi}_2]P[\bar{\Phi}_1]. \tag{4.20}$$

Let us take a moment to consider this result. If we could be assured that subordinate 2, the cue giver or leader, was always acting independently, then this expression would reduce further to $P[f_1] = P[f_1 \mid \Phi_1]$. That is to say, even if we thought that subordinate 1 might fail to be independent, the director's assessment of subordinate 1 would not change if subordinate 2 was known to be independent. This result occurs because even if he is engaged in cue taking or shirking, subordinate 1 is just as likely to pass up a correct message received by his fellow agent as he would if he were acting independently.

We should also be careful to note that if the director knew for a fact that subordinate 1 was cue taking, then her estimate of the subordinate's reliability would be lower, reducing to: $P[f_1] = P[f_2 \mid \Phi_2]P[\Phi_2] + P[f_2 \mid \Psi]P[\bar{\Phi}_2]$. Of course, as noted earlier, if the director had such information, then there are a number of alternatives available to her to address the problem.

How would our results change if we were to relax the previous assumption that $P[f_1 \mid \Phi_1] = P[f_2 \mid \bar{\Phi}_2]$? In other words, how might the director's assessment change if she were uncertain whether the potential cue taker was as reliable as, more reliable than, or less reliable than the cue giver? To answer this question, we begin with the case that if independent, subordinate 1 is more reliable than subordinate 2 with regard to a particular error. Of course, if both are shirking, then the probability of common mode failure is greater than if either acted independently. Stated mathematically, we are assuming that $P[f_i \mid \Psi] > P[f_2 \mid \Phi_2] > P[f_1 \mid \Phi_1]$. This latter assumption can be rewritten as

$$P[f_2 \mid \Phi_2] = P[f_1 \mid \Phi_1] + \varepsilon$$

$$P[f_2 \mid \Psi] = P[f_1 \mid \Phi_1] + \varepsilon + \omega,$$

where ε and ω are some incremental increases in the likelihood of failure when compared to the probability of failure for subordinate 1. Again, subordinate 1's probability of committing a particular type of failure is

$$P[f_1] = P[f_1 \mid \Phi_1]P[\Phi_1] + P[f_1 \mid \bar{\Phi}_1]P[\bar{\Phi}_1]$$

$$P[f_1] = P[f_1 \mid \Phi_1]P[\Phi_1] + (P[f_2 \mid \Phi_2]P[\Phi_2]$$

$$+ P[f_2 \mid \Psi]P[\bar{\Phi}_2])P[\bar{\Phi}_1].$$

Substituting our new assumption and simplifying, we find

$$P[f_1] = P[f_1 \mid \Phi_1]P[\Phi_1] + ([P[f_1 \mid \Phi_1] + \varepsilon]P[\Phi_2]$$

$$+ [P[f_1 \mid \Phi_1] + \varepsilon + v]P[\bar{\Phi}_2])P[\bar{\Phi}_1]$$

$$P[f_1] = P[f_1 \mid \Phi_1][P[\Phi_1] + P[\Phi_2]P[\bar{\Phi}_1] + P[\bar{\Phi}_2]P[\bar{\Phi}_1]]$$

$$+ P[\bar{\Phi}_1][P[\Phi_2] \, (\varepsilon) + P[\bar{\Phi}_2] \, (\varepsilon + \omega)]$$

$$P[f_1] = P[f_1 \mid \Phi_1] + P[\bar{\Phi}_1][\varepsilon + \omega \, P[\bar{\Phi}_2]]. \tag{4.21}$$

In this case, we see for any $0 < \varepsilon, \omega < 1$ that the probability of failure by subordinate 1 is greater if there is a possibility that his actions are dependent on those of subordinate 2. Understanding why that may be is not difficult. If he is independent, subordinate 1 is the more reliable of the two units. By either shirking or cue taking, subordinate 1 is following the lead of a less-reliable colleague, thereby increasing his chance of failure.

What would happen if situation were reversed and subordinate 2 was the more reliable of the two units? We will assume now that $P[f_i \mid \Psi] > P[f_1 \mid \Phi_1] > P[f_2 \mid \Phi_2]$. That is to say that if independent, subordinate 2 is more reliable than subordinate 1 with regard to a particular error. This assumption can be rewritten as

$$P[f_2 \mid \Phi_2] = P[f_1 \mid \Phi_1] - \varepsilon$$

$$P[f_2 \mid \Psi] = P[f_1 \mid \Phi_1] - \varepsilon + \omega,$$

where ε and ω are some incremental changes in the likelihood of failure when compared to the probability of failure for subordinate 1. Calculating subordinate 1's probability of committing a particular type of failure, we find

$$P[f_1] = P[f_1 \mid \Phi_1]P[\Phi_1] + P[f_1 \mid \bar{\Phi}_1]P[\bar{\Phi}_1]$$

$$P[f_1] = P[f_1 \mid \Phi_1]P[\Phi_1] + (P[f_2 \mid \Phi_2]P[\Phi_2]$$

$$+ P[f_2 \mid \Psi]P[\bar{\Phi}_2])P[\bar{\Phi}_1]$$

$$P[f_1] = P[f_1 \mid \Phi_1]P[\Phi_1] + ([P[f_1 \mid \Phi_1] - \varepsilon]P[\Phi_2] + [P[f_1 \mid \Phi_1]$$

$$- \varepsilon + \omega]P[\bar{\Phi}_2])P[\bar{\Phi}_1]$$

$$P[f_1] = P[f_1 \mid \Phi_1][P[\Phi_1] + P[\Phi_2]P[\bar{\Phi}_1] + P[\bar{\Phi}_2]P[\bar{\Phi}_1]]$$

$$+ P[\bar{\Phi}_1][P[\Phi_2] (-\varepsilon) + P[\bar{\Phi}_2] (-\varepsilon + \omega)]$$

$$P[f_1] = P[f_1 \mid \Phi_1] + P[\bar{\Phi}_1][-\varepsilon + \omega P[\bar{\Phi}_2]]. \tag{4.22}$$

In this case, it is possible that the reliability of subordinate 1 increases, since for any $[\varepsilon > \omega P\bar{\Phi}_2]$, the likelihood of failure decreases. If the cue giver is the more reliable unit, the reliability of the cue taker is enhanced as well. Under such circumstances, subordinate 1—the cue taker—can decrease his probability of failure by following the lead of a more expert colleague. Of course, this gain is tempered by the possibility that the leader—subordinate 2 in this case—is also shirking, leading to a possible common mode failure. What this analysis clearly demonstrates is that the interdependence of organizational members can sometimes improve, rather than hinder, the overall reliability of organizational performance.

Overall, the material presented in this chapter provides us with important insights regarding the impact of organizational structure and performance. Some critics might contend that it is difficult to know the exact value of component reliability in administrative systems, making it hard to apply these findings very broadly. It should be noted, however, that it is possible to perform such an analysis even if we do not know the exact values of component reliability for both types of error. In many cases we are still able to apply these principles by making some reasonable assumptions about the reliability of the components. More generally, when circumstances dictate greater effort toward one form of reliability, we can use these principles to develop a set of structures that are relatively better at minimizing the error of concern. The theory can also be used to recognize potential weak points in more complex organizations and allow us to reinforce them with regard to the particular error of concern. Whether we choose to reinforce these organizational weaknesses with redundant units or more expert subordinates is a question we will take up in the next chapter.

APPENDIX: PROOFS FOR CHAPTER 4

Proof that a *k*-out-of-*m* Unit Network Reduces to Serial System where *k* = *m*

Since the success or failure of each of the *m* units can be modeled as a Bernoulli process, we can use the binomial distribution to describe the system reliability for a *k*-out-of-*m* unit network. Letting f represent the probability of failure for each independent unit, the overall reliability of a *k*-out-of-*m* unit network may be represented mathematically as

$$R_{k/m} = \sum_{i=k}^{m} \binom{m}{i} (1 - f)^i f^{k-i}.$$

When *k* = *m*, this expression reduces to

$$R_{k/m} = \binom{m}{m} (1 - f)^m f^{m-m}.$$

This expression further reduces to

$$R = (1 - f_i)^m$$

Note that this expression is equivalent to equation 4.1, which represents the reliability of a serial system in a two-state world.

Series Systems Optimization

The system reliability of a series network consisting of *m* identical and independent components is

$$R_{sys} = [1 - \beta(1 - q)]^m - [\alpha q]^m.$$

Differentiating this equation with respect to *m* and setting the result equal to zero will give us the optimal number of components to be linked in series in order to maximize the system's reliability:

$$\frac{\partial R}{\partial m} = [(1 - \beta(1 - q))^m \ln(1 - \beta(1 - q))] - [(\alpha q)^m \ln(\alpha q)] = 0$$

$$(1 - \beta(1 - q))^m \ln(1 - \beta(1 - q)) = (\alpha q)^m \ln(\alpha q).$$

Taking the natural log of each side and grouping like terms,

$$m\left(\ln \frac{(1 - \beta(1 - q))}{(\alpha\, q)} \right) = \ln\left(\frac{\ln(\alpha\, q)}{\ln(1 - \beta(1 - q))} \right)$$

$$m^* = \frac{\ln\left(\dfrac{\ln(\alpha\, q)}{\ln(1 - \beta(1 - q))} \right)}{\ln \dfrac{(1 - \beta(1 - q))}{(\alpha\, q)}}.$$

Parallel System Optimization

The system reliability of a parallel network consisting of n identical and independent components is as follows:

$$R_{\text{sys}} = [1 - \alpha\, q]^n - [\beta(1 - q)]^n.$$

Differentiating this equation with respect to n and setting the result equal to zero will give us the optimal number of components to linked be in parallel in order to maximize the system's reliability:

$$\frac{\partial R}{\partial n} = [(1 - \alpha\, q)^n \ln(1 - \alpha\, q)] - [(\beta(1 - q))^n \ln(\beta(1 - q))] = 0$$

$$(1 - \alpha\, q)^n \ln(1 - \alpha\, q) = (\beta(1 - q))^n \ln(\beta(1 - q)).$$

Taking the natural log of each side and grouping like terms,

$$n\left(\ln \frac{(1 - \alpha\, q)}{(\beta(1 - q))} \right) = \ln\left(\frac{\ln(\beta(1 - q))}{\ln(1 - \alpha\, q)} \right)$$

$$n^* = \frac{\ln\left(\dfrac{\ln(\beta(1 - q))}{\ln(1 - \alpha\, q)} \right)}{\ln \dfrac{(1 - \alpha\, q)}{(\beta(1 - q))}}.$$

CHAPTER 5

Subordinate Expertise and Reliable Organizations

It was established in the previous chapter that reorganization can affect the reliability of agency decisions. That is important when we consider that one of the more popular activities of politicians involved in administrative affairs is to reorganize the bureaucracy. Of course, there are a number of reasons why this practice is so prevalent. In some cases, as in the Nixon administration, reorganization is done to achieve greater control over a bureaucracy perceived to be hostile to the political aims of the president (Aberbach and Rockman 1976). In other cases, reorganizations are undertaken to purposely undermine agency performance. For example, political appointees in the Reagan administration constantly reorganized the EPA's enforcement division in order to keep it off balance and prevent it from carrying out any actions against polluting industries (Lester 1989). But far and away, the most commonly cited reason for bureaucratic reorganization is the desire to achieve greater efficiency.

This concern for bureaucratic efficiency is the result of two related phenomena in American politics. The first of these is the enormous growth of bureaucracy at all levels of government. At the turn of the century, there were fewer than half a million federal employees; after the New Deal forty years later, there were about two million federal bureaucrats. Today the number of federal employees has grown to approximately three million. Similar growth in the bureaucracy has occurred at state and local levels during the same period. But while the public may desire more government programs, it does not necessarily want more government bureaucrats. When people express anger over the amount of "red tape" in bureaucracy, they are showing displeasure not only with the amount of paperwork the government requires, but also with the army of bureaucrats who slowly process the work through an unnecessarily complex administrative network. Indeed, polls routinely show that two-thirds of Americans believe that the government employs more people than are needed (Goodsell 1985). It is often thought that if bureaucracies could be streamlined, then government would be able to accomplish as much, or more, with only a fraction of the costs.

This desire to reorganize the bureaucracy and make it a more efficient operation has also been fueled by growing concern over the deficit. Public anxiety over the federal budget deficit has risen as this deficit has increased by several orders of magnitude (Wildavsky 1984, Schick 1983). At the same time, the American public has also made it clear that spending cuts are generally preferred to tax increases as a means of reducing the budget deficit (Sears and Citrin 1982; Peterson 1985). Although there is strong public support to lower overall government spending, when asked about cutting into a specific program, many people favor either continuing services at the same level or even increasing program support (Ladd 1979; Citrin 1979; Welch 1985). Even at the state and local level, voters have strongly supported a number of tax revolt initiatives, such as Proposition 13 in California, but have complained whenever public services are scaled back accordingly (Kuttner 1980; Sears and Citrin 1982; DeHaven-Smith 1985). It seems as if the voting public is sending contradictory messages to its elected officials: reduce spending without necessarily decreasing government services. Politicians often find that the easiest way to satisfy these conflicting demands is to pledge to roll back government spending through the creation of a leaner and more efficient bureaucracy.

It comes as little surprise, then, that twelve of the sixteen presidents elected in this century have either introduced plans to reorganize the executive branch or established task forces to study bureaucratic reorganization with the express purpose of increasing governmental efficiency (Arnold 1986). With the onset of stagflation in the early 1970s and the meteoric rise of budget deficits in the 1980s, presidents have faced additional pressure to streamline the operations of a growing federal bureaucracy. Consequently, Nixon made various attempts to streamline the government from 1971 to the end of his administration in 1974. Nixon's efforts were motivated both by the desire to increase his political control over the bureaucracy and by the need to increase the efficiency of government operations (Nixon 1970, 1972; Aberbach and Rockman 1976). Carter stated quite clearly that "[M]y administration is determined to reorganize and streamline the executive branch of government . . . to improve the efficiency and the sensitivity of the federal government bureaucracy" (Meier 1980). In 1982, Reagan appointed the Grace commission to identify opportunities for increased efficiency and reduced costs in federal operations. Among the major recommendations the Grace commission put forth was a reduction in the number of federal employees (Grace 1984; U.S. Congressional Budget Office and General Accounting Office 1984). Most recently, the Clinton-Gore initiative to "reinvent government" seeks to reduce the cost of federal operations in part by streamlining the massive federal bureaucracy and eliminating more than a quarter million government jobs.

Research in public administration has made it clear, however, that changes in an organization's structure can have a significant impact on the reliability of administrative decision making. In earlier work, Landau (1969), Bendor (1985), and Lerner (1986) have all stated that streamlining the bureaucracy may increase the number of failures it experiences. Indeed, we have noted in the previous chapter that, depending on how an organization's structure is altered, an agency may be increasingly vulnerable to different types of errors. In sum, it is quite clear that changes in an agency's administrative structure can affect the likelihood of failure and that any reorganization or streamlining should not be done without considering these consequences.

Is the public generally willing to accept the potential consequences that would follow from streamlining the federal bureaucracy? The evidence presented earlier does not suggest that it would. The result is that political leaders seem to be caught in a no-win situation: bureaucratic efficiency comes at the expense of government effectiveness and the public demands both. Proponents of bureaucratic reduction have argued, however, that under the right circumstances this trade-off need not occur. An organization's effectiveness can be maintained through the process of streamlining if the agency simultaneously seeks to hire more qualified people or raises the performance criteria to which bureaucrats are held. For example, in discussing changes in the structure of Defense Department and other government laboratories, John Deutch has argued that hiring fewer, but more prominent, scientists would both save the government money and increase the productivity of these labs (Deutch 1991). Likewise, "reinventing government" spokespeople suggest that downsizing and flattening organizations gives subordinates a bigger stake in agency outputs, thus improving their performance (Osborne and Gaebler 1992).

Indeed, in considering the issue of reliability and structure, we must concede that there are actually two fundamental strategies an organization may use in altering the reliability in its overall system performance. The first of these I refer to as a *systems strategy*. A systems strategy involves modifying the number of components within the system or changing their location within it, or both. For example, if an agency was concerned about decreasing the possibility of a type II error, it could achieve this result using the systems strategy in one of three ways. First, it could eliminate some of the serial elements in the system. Second, the agency could reorganize its components into a parallel structure. Third, it could increase the number of components in order to create additional parallel linkages within the system. For the most part, chapter 4 focused on the impact of the systems strategy within organizations.

As an alternative, however, an agency could employ a *component strategy* to increase its organizational reliability. An agency engaging in this type of strategy would require greater performance from some or all of the components that make up the system while keeping the basic administrative structure intact. Of course, it should be clear that these are not necessarily mutually exclusive strategies. Consider the example of an agency that is trying to reduce its staff due to budget cuts. By reducing the number of serial components within its organization, the agency is engaging in a systems strategy that makes itself more vulnerable to committing a type I error. To compensate for this vulnerability, the agency may also adopt a component strategy in order to reduce the probability of a type I error being committed by any of the remaining components. While these strategies may be implemented concurrently, we will see later in this chapter that they are not compatible under all circumstances.

Given that there are two strategies for altering organizational reliability, why might an agency choose to employ one strategy rather than the other? To answer this question, we must consider the costs involved in the design and execution of an organizational structure.[1] The cost of creating an administrative system is a function of both the number of components used and the quality of each of these components. If the costs needed to raise the reliability of each component outweigh the costs of either reconfiguring or utilizing new components, then we would expect to see the agency rely on a systems strategy. Conversely, if it is less expensive to change component performance than it is to institute a systems overhaul, then a component strategy would be preferred.

How expensive are more reliable components to an agency? Surprisingly, we have no answer to this question in the current literature. Indeed, while we must concede that it may be possible to maintain or increase organizational performance through higher personnel standards, we lack the analytical tools needed to objectively and accurately assess the claims of Deutch and other advocates of reduced bureaucracy. How would organizational reliability change when an agency is allowed to vary both its structural and component parameters? In terms of the preceding discussion, we would like to know how bureaucratic performance might change if an agency not only streamlined its administrative structure, but also sought to adjust its personnel standards. Succinctly stated, the question addressed in this chapter is: When is it better for an agency to employ fewer, more expert subordinates (i.e., follow a component strategy) rather than a larger number of policy generalists (i.e., engage in a systems strategy)? To answer this question, we must first discuss what is meant by subordinate expertise and the different types of tasks agencies engage in.

---

1. The focus here will be on the costs of building an administrative system, not on the costs of failure. The cost of failure is important for an agency to consider, but as noted in chapter 2, it primarily influences the political decision of what type of reliability the agency needs to focus on. It is assumed here that an agency knows how much type I and type II reliability it needs to achieve—the relevant question is how the agency will go about meeting these goals.

Expertise and Different Types of Tasks

If greater expertise is supposed to enhance the reliable performance of organizational components, then it makes sense to ask this question: What exactly is meant by *expertise* and how is it acquired? Expertise is knowledge that can be applied in an effort to resolve uncertainty over policy decisions. Such knowledge comes from a variety of sources. Education and training certainly provide opportunities for individuals to increase their expertise in a particular field. Likewise, prior experience can furnish individuals and organizations with knowledge of what has worked in the past and what is likely to work well in the future. Expertise may also be enhanced through the use of tests and experiments. Such tests and experiments may offer greater insights on the state of the world, which consequently can affect policy decisions.

Is it always beneficial to acquire greater expertise? In specifying how expertise is gained, one thing is clear: expertise is costly. Education and training can take quite a bit of time and money. Not only does learning from past experience involve opportunity costs, but such learning often comes from dissecting past failures (the school of hard knocks), which can be costly in their own right. Tests and experiments—where possible—can also be monetarily expensive and time intensive. If expertise were costless, more expertise would always be preferred to less. Given that there are real costs to gaining expertise, how much subordinate expertise should an agency seek to acquire?

Whether it is beneficial to seek greater subordinate expertise is dependent upon the types of tasks in which an agency is engaged. For some types of tasks, expertise can be rather hard to come by; in other cases, it may be easier to obtain the information that enhances a subordinate's expertise level. Herbert Simon (1965) has argued that an agency's tasks can be classified by the extent to which they require either programmed or nonprogrammed decisions. Programmed decisions are those that occur routinely or repetitively. Although Simon was careful to note that programmed tasks are not necessarily simpleminded ones, the key to programmed decisions is that, because of their repetitive nature, they can be structured into specific procedural instructions and easily delegated. In contrast, nonprogrammed decisions are usually required in unique and complex circumstances. Because of the novel circumstances associated with nonprogrammed decisions, they usually do not lend themselves to a well-defined treatment. Rather, these tasks require a large amount of good judgment and creativity in order to be handled effectively. Each of these forms of decision making places different demands on agency performance and the ability of subordinates to gain further expertise. Consequently, it is reasonable to expect that a director's decision of how many subordinates to employ and at what level of expertise will depend in part on whether the task in question is programmable or not.

How does this distinction between programmed and nonprogrammed tasks affect the desirability of expertise? The first difference that should be considered is the availability of an appropriate context for experts to operate within. To have value, knowledge must be placed within a context that makes it useful for policy decisions. For example, an expert may be able to determine with a high degree of accuracy that a particular policy option has an 85 percent chance of success. Is that high enough to justify a decision to implement this option? How might this decision change if the likelihood of success were higher or lower? Knowledge alone does not guarantee reliable performance; context is needed to make this knowledge applicable.

There are important differences in this regard between programmed and nonprogrammed tasks. Because programmed tasks are repetitive, past experience not only enhances expertise, but it also provides a context in which new information can be analyzed. In the previous example, there was uncertainty over the appropriate decision given an 85 percent chance of success. If the agency had been down this or similar roads before, that experience could provide a context for the information that would essentially reveal whether such a policy should be implemented. In contrast, nonprogrammed tasks are novel and unique; past agency experience provides little information that can be used to establish a context for expertise to operate within. Without an appropriate context, it may well be that the performance of experts is not much better than that of policy generalists.

Context is necessary, but the cost of greater expertise is even more critical in deciding whether to utilize a component or systems strategy. How does the cost of expertise change as we increase subordinate expertise? One might think that greater expertise becomes increasingly costly to acquire. The first observations and information obtained are the easiest to come by; we get that information first because there is a low cost in obtaining it. After that, each successive bit of data becomes increasingly more difficult to obtain and hence more costly. This, in fact, seems to be the case for nonprogrammed tasks. For these tasks education, training, and past experience provide some limited information to guide decision making. To get better estimates, however, will require that some testing, experiments, and simulations be done. The simplest, least costly tests are usually done first. More information beyond that requires even more complex and costly tests. On the whole, the marginal cost of expertise seems to rise rapidly for nonprogrammed tasks.

But we might also surmise that in some cases the marginal costs of expertise are decreasing. There are some initial costs in gaining education and training, and there are start-up costs to setting up a new program. Once the groundwork is established, however, new information that comes in from experience is easily integrated and expertise is enhanced. Such is often the case for programmed tasks. The repetitive nature of programmed decision making means that additional data are more easily gained because of the reservoir of past experience and the repeated nature of the task. In such cases, additional information may cost more, but its unit price is unlikely to be higher than the price of previously obtained data. Indeed, it may well be that because of economies of scale, obtaining additional data may cost less than the initial sampling. In contrast with nonprogrammed tasks, the marginal cost of expertise in a programmed decision-making setting may actually be declining rather than rising.

What consequences do these cost differences have in determining whether it is better for an agency to pursue a systems strategy or a component strategy? In the case of programmed decisions, the marginal costs of expertise are decreasing, and thus the marginal value of expertise rises. In such cases, it makes sense for an agency to engage in a component strategy that relies on fewer, but more expert, subordinates; it is both possible and cost-effective to pursue such an option. In cases of nonprogrammed tasks, however, the marginal cost of expertise rises, thus decreasing the value of greater expertise. Organizations primarily involved with nonprogrammed tasks generally find that there are limits to the amount of additional expertise that can be acquired given the existence of resource constraints. Even if such expertise could be acquired, there is no guarantee that the agency will have the proper context needed to utilize such knowledge. In such cases, an agency director may be better off relying on structure and a systems strategy to achieve the desired ends rather than putting trust in subordinate expertise.

Although the logic applies to a variety of organizations, it should be noted that the resource constraints that limit the usefulness of a component strategy in a nonprogrammed task setting are more restraining for public agencies than for private organizations. As noted in the introduction to this chapter, the demand to cut budgets and place greater limitations on the resources available to public agencies has been increasing over time. Likewise, there has been some difficulty attracting quality personnel into public administration, especially in areas requiring advanced technical knowledge. There are a number of reasons for that. Some scholars have pointed to the decline in prestige associated with public service or to legal changes that limit the "revolving door" phenomena as reasons for this difficulty (C. Levine 1990). Making this situation worse is the fact that even with recent reforms, federal pay trails the private sector for comparable jobs; this disparity increases at higher skill levels. With greater budgetary pressure at most levels of government, it is not likely that this disparity will be erased in the near future. The fiscal stress experienced throughout government also limits the opportunities an agency has to provide additional training for its personnel. Overall, it is much more difficult for public-sector organizations engaged in nonprogrammed decision making to alter the reliability of component performance.

Although every organization faces a mixture of both programmed and nonprogrammed decision-making opportunities, the nature of an agency's mission often dictates that one form of decision making will become predominant. Agencies that are primarily engaged in programmed decision making should be inclined to use a component strategy in their efforts to alter organizational reliability. While altering program parameters is not a costless exercise, it is often less expensive than either adding new components or instituting a reorganization, as would be required by a systems strategy. In contrast, we should expect that agencies relying heavily on nonprogrammed decision making would utilize a systems strategy in their efforts to alter organizational reliability. The constraints placed on these public organizations make it quite difficult to adopt a component strategy; a systems strategy is these agencies' choice because they have few alternatives.

Agency Performance and the Director's Dilemma

These hypotheses can be corroborated through the use of a mathematical model.[2] To evaluate the impact of streamlining the bureaucracy, we must first construct a model of the operations of a typical agency. In this case, we return to our previous example of a hypothetical agency that is headed by a director or political superior.[3] This director has the final word regarding all policy decisions of the bureau. To gain the best achievable policy outcome, the director seeks to organize or adjust the components within the administrative structure of the agency so as to receive the most accurate information possible.

Of course, what the director must ultimately decide is whether the agency should pursue a certain policy initiative. Decision theorists have made it clear that the director's final choice is dependent on her evaluation of the state of the world (Raiffa 1968; Stokey and Zeckhauser 1978; Mullen and Roth 1991). This evaluation focuses primarily on two factors: the value of each possible outcome and the likelihood of obtaining that outcome. To determine the best course of action, the director calculates the expected value of each option by multiplying the value of the outcome by the probability of obtaining it and then chooses the option that yields the largest expected value.

To see how the director's evaluation affects her final decision, consider a simple case of two choices: implement policy A or remain with the status quo. The status quo leads to an outcome valued at some level (x). Policy A, if successful, would increase the value of the outcome to ($x + y$). If unsuccessful, policy A reduces the value of the outcome to ($x - z$). The likelihood of success with policy A is denoted as π. The expected value of policy A would be $EV(A) = \pi(x + y) + (1 - \pi)(x - z)$. For the status quo (SQ), we are

---

2. Readers who are not interested in the technical presentation may skip over the modeling exercise and move to the section entitled "Bureaucratic Reform Revisited" without loss of continuity.

3. Again, in order to more clearly differentiate between the director and the subordinates, I will assume in this chapter that the director is female while all the subordinates are male.

certain of getting outcome x, so its expected value would simply be $EV(SQ) = x$. Only if $EV(A) > EV(SQ)$ would the director choose to implement policy A over the status quo. Using a little algebra, therefore, we find that it would be best for the director to choose policy A whenever the likelihood of success is greater than $\pi^* = z/(y + z)$. For situations when the likelihood of success is less than or equal to π^*, the director would be better off staying with the status quo.[4]

As a general rule, the decision to pursue a particular policy would be considered rational if the probability of a successful outcome is greater than some critical value. Formally, if π represents the likelihood of a successful outcome and the critical value is π^*, then the director should enact the policy if $\pi > \pi^*$. If $\pi \le \pi^*$, the director should reject this policy and consider alternatives. It should be noted that this simple decision rule is general enough to be applied to more complex decisions. For example, it may be that the director must choose between three or more different policy options. Using principles of decision theory, the director first calculates the outcome value of each option and then determines whether the value of π_1 is sufficiently great so as to make its expected value the most preferred outcome. If not, she proceeds to the next best option and determines whether π_2 is large enough to make its expected value the most preferred outcome. The process continues until the the best expected outcome is determined. Of course, it is clear that the more complex decision is simply an iterative process of the basic decision rule used here.

Unfortunately for the director, she does not know the probability of success. In order to determine this value, the director seeks the input of her subordinates, who are closer to the situation and have greater knowledge about the circumstances. Although subordinates also lack perfect information about π, they are able to generate estimates of π based on their prior experience and current observations. Presuming that subordinates operate along the lines of classic Weberian bureaucrats, we can assume that the estimate P reported by a subordinate is, on average, equal to the true value π.

The director aggregates the estimates of the subordinates and compares the result to the critical value, π^*. The value of π^* is a function of the value of different policy outcomes. As discussed at length in chapter 2, an agency's evaluation of a particular policy outcome is dependent on both political and technical factors. For this reason, responsibility for calculating the critical value π^* is left to the director. Just as the true value of π is often unknown,

---

4. In cases where the probability of success was exactly equal to π^*, the director should technically be indifferent between Policy A and the status quo. However, since Policy A involves greater risk than the status quo, most individuals would give presumption to the status quo. Hence, the likelihood of success must exceed this critical value before Policy A is adopted.

however, the exact value of π^* is also generally unknown and must be estimated. The agency's formal decision rule, then, is

$P > P^*$ enact policy
$P \leq P^*$ abort policy

where P^* is the director's estimate of π^*. Of course, as stated earlier, the policy is only justified when $\pi > \pi^*$. If $\pi \leq \pi^*$ but the agency estimates $P > P^*$, then the agency will decide to act when it should not—a type I error. If $\pi > \pi^*$ and the agency concludes that $P \leq P^*$, then the agency will fail to act when it should—a type II error. The agency's choices and consequences are summarized in figure 5.1.

Of course, the director's responsibility is not limited to deciding what policies should or should not be enacted; she must also create an organizational structure that will help her do so. Assuming that the director has some preference for the balance between type I and type II reliability, she has two general options regarding staffing and structure available to her. One option would be to hire a large number of "generalists" who are knowledgeable in many policy areas but do not have much expertise in any particular field. Although the estimate of any one subordinate would not be highly accurate, through proper structuring of the subordinates the director could ensure that the agency still achieved the desired balance between type I and type II reliability. Another possible option would be for the director to hire a smaller number of more "expert" subordinates. Instead of depending on structural features to ensure reliability, she would be counting more on the greater knowledge and expertise of her subordinates to avoid errors.

What is the optimal choice for the director when considering both the number of subordinates and their degree of expertise? Given that the agency must work within certain budgetary constraints, the director's preference for multiple generalists versus fewer experts depends in part on how much expertise costs. There are two primary ways in which we can introduce cost factors into our analysis. First, we can assume that bureaucrats have fixed budgets and they attempt to achieve the maximum level of reliability possible while spending their entire budget. This approach is in line with Wildavsky's notion that administrators must spend their entire allocation or face losing it in the future (1984, 31). Such a strategy can be expressed through the following formulation:

Maximize $R_s = \mathrm{f}(y_1, y_2, y_3, \ldots y_m)$

such that $\displaystyle\sum_{i=1}^{m} a_i c_i(y_i) \leq B,$

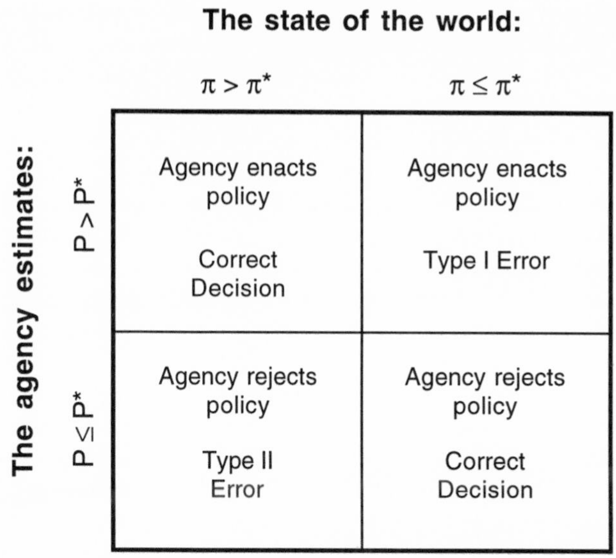

The state of the world:

	$\pi > \pi^*$	$\pi \leq \pi^*$
$P > P^*$	Agency enacts policy Correct Decision	Agency enacts policy Type I Error
$P \leq P^*$	Agency rejects policy Type II Error	Agency rejects policy Correct Decision

The agency estimates:

Fig. 5.1. Summary of agency choices and possible errors

where R_s is the overall system reliability, y_i is the expertise of component i, c_i is the cost of a component having expertise y_i, B is the total amount of funds budgeted for the system, and a_i is a weight associated with the cost of linking components into the system.

James March and Herbert Simon have argued, however, that in most instances, organizations do not seek optimal solutions, but rather settle for satisfactory alternatives. (1958, 140) Additionally, William Niskanen (1975) has argued that public agencies often seek to maximize their discretionary budget—the difference between the allocated budget and the minimum budget necessary to produce the output. Applying these concepts within our framework, we would assume that bureaucrats do not attempt to maximize the reliability of their agency, but rather set acceptable levels of failure and then build the least expensive system necessary to obtain the chosen level of reliability. We can model the agency's behavior under such circumstances as follows:

$$\text{Minimize } C_R = \sum_{i=1}^{m} a_i c_i(y_i)$$

such that $R_s = f(y_1, y_2, y_3, \ldots y_m) \geq R_q$,

where C_R is the costs of creating a minimal performance system and R_q is the minimum level of reliability required by the agency.[5]

Each of these strategies may be observed under different sets of circumstances. For example, if the agency is competing with another agency and the criterion for success is performance effectiveness, not cost considerations, we would expect to see the first strategy employed. If the agency is trying to expand its influence, it may adopt the second method in order to save money, which could be diverted to new areas. There are numerous situations under which these different strategies will be used. What we should recognize is that given that bureaucrats act in a somewhat rational manner, we will see them try to either minimize their costs or maximize their agency's reliability.

Both of these cost formulations may be solved within certain bounds using techniques in linear and dynamic programming. This approach requires, however, that we hold the reliability per component, and thus the cost per unit, constant. Doing so allows us to focus on the optimal number of units within each type of structure possible. Utilizing mathematical programming techniques, we can find the optimal number of components for each type of possible organization and then choose the structure that yields the greatest benefits under the given constraints. Finding solutions to the unconstrained problem of variable component reliability and variable system structure is far more complex. The general formulation is a mixed integer nonlinear programming problem and thus difficult to solve using normal system optimization techniques. While limited comparisons are certainly possible, the large number of possible permutations makes it difficult to even develop a heuristic search device to find an optimal solution.

Given the impossibility of calculating an optimal solution, what should the director do? In deciding how many subordinates to hire and at what level of expertise, are there any principles the director could employ to help make this choice? Fortunately, it is possible to answer the more general question of whether it is better to employ multiple generalists or smaller numbers of experts; the answer depends on two factors. First, we must define more precisely what we mean by *experts* and *generalists*. Second, we must consider the type of task in which the agency is primarily engaged.

---

5. At first glance, it may appear as if these two approaches are mathematical duals that share the same optimal solution. It should be remembered, however, that in the case of mathematical duals, the resource constraints (or RHS) of the primal serve as the technological coefficients of the dual. In this case, the resource constraint of the maximization problem is not the technological coefficient of the minimization problem; rather, it is the variable we seek to minimize. Furthermore, the minimization problem contains a new variable, R_q, which does not appear in the maximization problem but should if these two were actually mathematical duals. Readers seeking more information on mathematical duals should see Winston 1995.

Defining Subordinate Expertise

To determine how "expert" a subordinate is, we need to model the process by which he determines P, his estimate of the probability of success. As noted earlier, the estimate P is assumed to be, on average, equal to the parameter π. Of course, any particular estimate that a subordinate generates may vary from π due to human indeterminacy and other stochastic factors. Since it is essentially a random variable, the subordinate's estimate P is best represented by a probability distribution. The most appropriate probability distribution in this case is the beta distribution. Because it is a continuous distribution bound in the range between 0 and 1, the beta distribution is typically used to model the estimates of a population proportion (Hey 1983; Robinson 1985; Cyert and DeGroot 1987). Furthermore, the beta distribution has been applied in past organizational research as a means of estimating proportion parameters (Heckman and Willis 1977; Brehm and Gates 1993). Thus, we can describe a subordinate's estimate of P using the beta distribution as follows:

$$f_P(x;\, r,\, n) = \begin{cases} \dfrac{\Gamma(n)}{\Gamma(r)\Gamma(n-r)}\, x^{r-1}\, (1-x)^{n-r-1} & 0 \leq x \leq 1;\, r,\, n > 0 \\ 0 & \text{otherwise} \end{cases}$$

where $(n,\, r)$ are additional parameters.

One advantage to modeling the subordinate's estimate in this manner is that we can determine the probability of committing either a type I or a type II error. The probability of failure is represented graphically in figure 5.2. For instances where $\pi \leq \pi^*$, the probability of a type I error is the area under the beta distribution from π^* to 1. When $\pi > \pi^*$, the probability of a type II error is the area under the curve from 0 to π^*. Methods for determining the numerical values for these probabilities are discussed in the appendix to this chapter.

Critical in determining the value of these beta-distributed probabilities are the parameters r and n. These parameters determine the mean, variance, and overall shape of the distribution. Figure 5.3 demonstrates how the beta distribution varies with changes in r and n. The mean of the beta distribution is simply r/n, which is equivalent to the sample proportion. For all $r/n > 0.500$, the underlying probability distribution is negatively skewed; likewise, for all $r/n < 0.500$, the distribution is positively skewed. When $r/n = 0.500$, the distribution is perfectly symmetrical.

In addition to their technical function, these parameters have an important substantive interpretation in this model. It can be said that a distribution $B(r,\, n)$ is the result of having observed a sample of size n in which r observations have the characteristic in question and $n - r$ observations do not (Hey

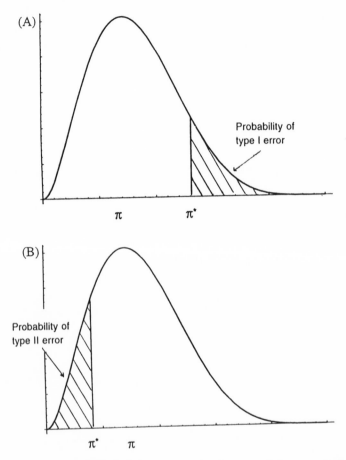

Fig. 5.2.   The probabilities of type I and type II errors. A, for $\pi \leq \pi^*$; B, for $\pi > \pi^*$.

1983, 120). Using this interpretation to compare the expertise of two subordinates, we would say the more expert subordinate is the one who is able to effectively sample a greater number of n units. To make this point clearer, consider two different subordinates. Subordinate 1 makes ten observations and finds that success occurs in four cases and failure in six cases. Subordinate 2 makes twenty observations and finds that success occurs in eight cases and failure in twelve cases. Assuming there are no differences in sampling technique, we would be inclined to say that subordinate 2 is more reliable because he has more data on which to base his estimate and thus is less likely to be swayed by anomalous observations.

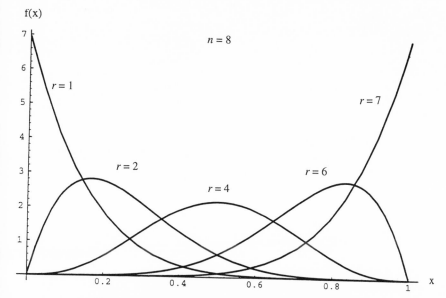

Fig. 5.3. Various realizations of the beta distribution

Moreover, we would say that subordinate 2 is more reliable because there is less variance in the distribution of his estimates. The variance of the beta distribution is given as

$$\sigma_P^2 = \frac{r(n - r)}{n^2 (n + 1)}.$$

It is evident that the variance of this distribution declines as the parameter n increases. In other words, the relative efficiency of the estimator increases as n increases. Of course, in statistics we strive for efficient estimators since using them increases the likelihood that our estimate is close or equal to the true parameter. In this case, a decreasing variance reduces the probability of making either a type I or a type II error. Consider ten subordinates illustrated in figure 5.4 who make ten observations each. On average, the expected value of their estimate $E(P) = \pi$, but due to stochastic factors, their actual estimates could vary quite widely. Contrast this with ten subordinates who each make twenty observations. On average, the expected value of their estimate is also $E(P) = \pi$, but there is less variance in the range of their estimates. For some $\pi^* < \pi$, it is clear that the probability of a type II failure is less for the subordinates who sample more.

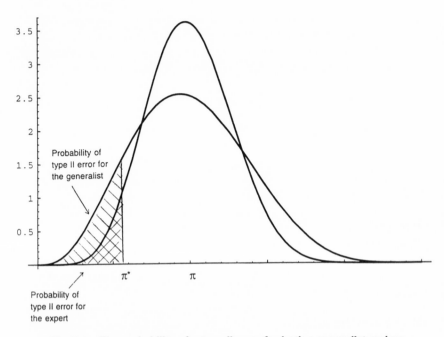

Fig. 5.4.   The probability of a type II error for both a generalist and an expert

There are, of course, other dimensions to expertise, such as education and prior experience, which are also relevant to this discussion. After being asked by the director to estimate π, the subordinate actually has three choices: (1) he may simply report his estimate P based on his prior experience and education, (2) he may choose to obtain new data and base his estimate on those results alone, or (3) he may conduct the tests and use the new information to update his beliefs about the value of π. We could use Bayesian updating to capture this process. In this model, a subordinate's prior experience and education can be summarized by a similar set of parameters (q, m) that can be interpreted as before.[6] The parameters (r, n) represent the additional data the subordinate may have chosen to acquire. Then assuming random sampling and using

---

6. Two small technical points must be made at this juncture. First, it should be noted that using (q, m) to capture past experience represents no change from our previous interpretation of r and n. Expressing education in terms of beta parameters, however, is a bit more difficult since there is no magic formula that translates years of education into levels of r and n. Nonetheless, it is plausible to think that under some circumstances we might choose to add some adjustment to the beta parameters to account for relevant educational experience.

Second, in the case where the component has no experience with which to formulate priors, one could use $B(0,0)$ as the initial prior. While there is some problem with this approach (the resulting function has an infinite area underneath it, making it an improper density function), it

Bayes' Theorem, it can be shown that the subordinate's new posterior distribution of P would still be beta-distributed but with a smaller variance for any $(q, m) > 0$ (Cyert and DeGroot 1987). It would be from this distribution that a subordinate's estimate P is finally drawn and reported to the director.

Expertise in Programmed and Nonprogrammed Tasks

In some cases, expertise is rather hard to come by; in other cases, it may be much easier to make the observations that enhance a subordinate's expertise level. Thus, a second factor that must be considered is the type of task in which the agency is primarily engaged. As noted earlier, an agency's tasks can be classified by the extent to which they require either programmed or nonprogrammed decisions. Each of these forms of decision making places different demands on agency performance and the ability of subordinates to gain further expertise. Consequently, it is reasonable to expect that a director's decision of how many subordinates to employ and at what level of expertise will depend in part on whether the task in question is programmable or not.

The first way in which these differences manifest themselves is in regard to how accurately π^* can be determined. This is important because π^* provides a context for the decision and helps determine whether it is wise to enact a given policy. Because of the repetition involved in programmed tasks, past experience can be very useful in the agency's attempts to define the critical value above which enacting a policy is justified. It is quite reasonable to expect that with programmed tasks there is little uncertainty over the true value of π^*. In contrast, nonprogrammed tasks entail greater levels of uncertainty and thus make it more difficult to accurately determine π^*.

How does uncertainty over π^* affect the probability that an expert or a generalist will commit some type of error? Unfortunately, evaluating the beta distribution from either 0 to π^* or between π^* to 1 does not yield a closed-form expression.[7] As a result, it is not possible to develop theorems using the traditional method of proof. Nonetheless, it is possible to use numerical methods to calculate values of the distribution for various levels of π and π^* and from this infer several properties about the value of increasing subordinate expertise.[8]

---

nonetheless works in the sense that the posterior distribution is perfectly proper, and it works well in that it satisfies our intuition. For sufficiently large samples, the prior could be set at $B(1,1)$ since the effects of such a low prior would be washed out by the larger sample in the posterior analysis.

7. This issue is discussed at greater length and in more mathematical detail in the appendix to this chapter.

8. The probabilities shown in figures 5.5 through 5.8 were calculated using numerical approximation algorithms found in *Mathematica*, version 2.2.2. The values generated by these algorithms are accurate to nineteen decimal places.

Figures 5.5 and 5.6 consider the problem of uncertainty over π^* for two asymmetric realizations of the beta distribution. In figure 5.5, the likelihood of the policy success is 3 out of 4, or $\pi = 0.750$, with π^* being either 0.850 (allowing the possibility of a type I error) or 0.667 (leading to a possible type II error). In figure 5.6, the true probability of policy success is $\pi = 0.333$ (a 1 in 3 chance of success), with π^* being either 0.450 (possible type I error) or 0.200 (possible type II error). The agency in these examples does not know π^* exactly, but estimates $P^* = \pi^* \pm \epsilon$. Assuming that the agency is as likely to overestimate π^* as it is to underestimate it, we can calculate the expected increase in the probability of a either a type I or a type II error given this uncertainty.[9]

What is quite clear from these figures is that as uncertainty over π^* rises, increasing a subordinate's expertise level makes less of a difference in his likelihood of committing a particular type of error. In other words, the marginal gain in error reduction declines with increasing expertise, and this decline occurs more rapidly with greater uncertainty over the critical value. Indeed, we see that as the uncertainty level increases, greater subordinate expertise makes little difference in probability of failure and may even increase the likelihood of committing an error. The clear lesson here is that greater expertise about the state of the world is of less value when we do not have the proper context for analyzing the data.

How does this apply to our discussion of programmed and non-programmed tasks? As we noted earlier, the repetitiveness of programmed tasks makes it possible for an agency to determine π^* more easily and accurately than in cases where the nonprogrammed tasks are the norm. Thus, when the agency is engaged in programmed tasks, it is possible to reduce the likelihood of failure by increasing subordinate expertise. As uncertainty over π^* increases—as is the case for nonprogrammed tasks—the overall performance of experts is often not much better than that of policy generalists. In such cases, the director may be better off relying on structure to achieve the desired ends rather than putting her trust in subordinate expertise.

Programmed and nonprogrammed tasks also differ in regard to the costs associated with gaining greater expertise. When dealing with nonprogrammed tasks, where the problems are novel and complex, each additional bit of information becomes increasingly harder to obtain. After all, previous training

---

9. This assumption allows us to use a uniform distribution for the value of ϵ in the numerical analysis. Although it is a very reasonable assumption, one might argue that depending on the policy being considered, the agency may choose to discount uncertainty in one direction so as to decrease the possibility of committing a certain type of error, the result being a skewed distribution of ϵ. Doing so would inevitably lead, however, to an increase in the probability of the other type of failure. As noted earlier, agencies need to strike a balance between these two forms of error; purposely distorting its assessment of π^* will not help the agency achieve the balance it desires.

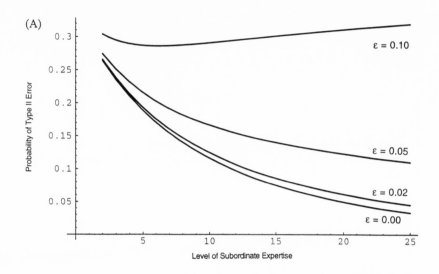

(A)

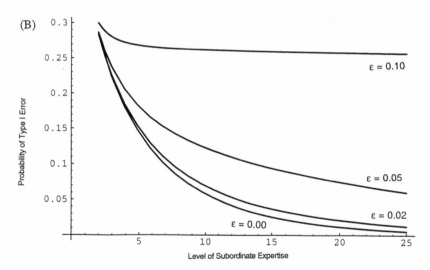

(B)

Fig. 5.5. The probability of error for increasing uncertainty; $\pi = 0.750$.
A, probability of type II error declines with increasing uncertainty, $\pi^* = 0.667$; *B*, probability of type I error declines with increasing uncertainty, $\pi^* = 0.850$.

(A)

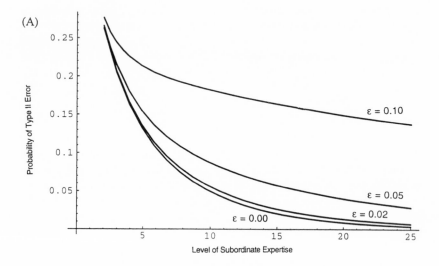

ε = 0.10

ε = 0.05

ε = 0.02

ε = 0.00

Probability of Type II Error

Level of Subordinate Expertise

(B)

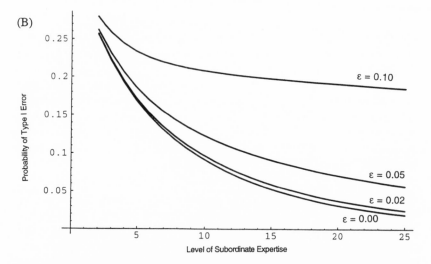

ε = 0.10

ε = 0.05

ε = 0.02

ε = 0.00

Probability of Type I Error

Level of Subordinate Expertise

Fig. 5.6.   The probability of error for increasing uncertainty; $\pi = 0.333$.
A, probability of type II error declines with increasing uncertainty, $\pi^* = 0.200$; *B,* probability of type I error declines with increasing uncertainty, $\pi^* = 0.450$.

and experience have less relevance in unique circumstances, and the complexity of the decision environment makes accurate and compelling data more difficult to acquire. It is quite reasonable to assume that the cost of additional sampling increases exponentially for nonprogrammed tasks. In contrast, the repetitive nature of programmed decision making means that additional data are more easily gained because of the reservoir of past experience and the repeated nature of the task. In such cases, additional information may cost more, but its unit price is unlikely to be higher than the price of previously obtained data. Economies of scale may exist with programmed tasks so that additional data may be obtained at a cost less than the initial sampling. In contrast with nonprogrammed tasks, the marginal cost of expertise in a programmed decision-making setting may actually be declining exponentially.

To determine the impact of these differences, costs need to be put in perspective with performance. To do so, I compare the the marginal reduction in error with the cost necessary for achieving that reduction. This comparison is akin to determining the marginal "value" of expertise.[10] Figures 5.7 and 5.8 illustrate changes in the marginal value of expertise for the case where the chances of success are 3 out of 4 ($\pi = 0.750$), but that the decision would be justified so long as the success rate was greater than 2 out of 3 ($\pi^* = 0.667$). The primary difference between these figures is that one assumes that marginal costs are increasing while the other assumes that marginal costs are declining.

To find the marginal cost of expertise, we must keep in mind that expertise is enhanced by raising the effective sample size a subordinate may draw from. To operationalize without loss of generality, marginal costs (m_i) are defined as $m_i = \alpha k^i$, where $\alpha = 1$ and $k \geq 1$ in the case of figure 5.7. In this figure, the marginal cost of expertise increases exponentially so that each observation becomes increasingly costly to make. To understand it better, consider the case where $\alpha = 1$ and $k = 1.10$. That means that the first observation costs only $1.10 to make, the second costs $1.21, the tenth observation costs $2.59, and the twentieth observation costs $6.73. As in the case of nonprogrammed tasks, each new bit of data becomes increasingly expensive to gather. Unfortunately, the gain in error reduction becomes smaller with greater expertise. The result, seen in figure 5.7, is that the marginal value of expertise declines rather rapidly as the costs of sampling increase exponentially.

In contrast, figure 5.8 demonstrates the change in the marginal value of expertise as marginal costs decrease. Considering cases where $k \leq 1$, we see that as unit cost of additional observations declines, the marginal value of expertise can level out or may actually increase. In these cases—which occur

---

10. The marginal value of expertise is calculated in these examples by dividing the marginal reduction in error by the cost necessary for achieving that reduction, with the units of the marginal value being error reduction per dollar.

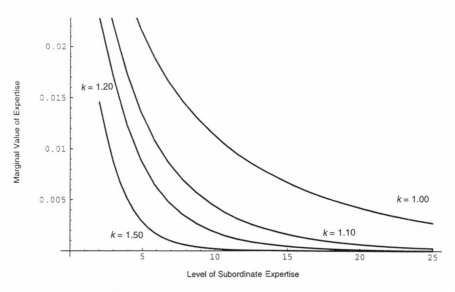

Fig. 5.7.   The marginal value of expertise declines as cost of expertise
increases exponentially

more often with programmed tasks—it is to the director's advantage to employ more expert subordinates and to rely on their greater knowledge and ability to avoid possible errors.

Simon's distinction between programmed and nonprogrammed tasks is a useful taxonomy when applied to particular instances of decision making. The subordinates of most agencies, however, will face over time a mixture of programmed and nonprogrammed tasks. As a result, the notion of an optimal balance between increasing subordinate expertise and increasing structural redundancy becomes even more difficult to achieve since it is dependent on the type of task an agency is engaged in at any particular time. For the director trying to determine the appropriate staffing and structure of her agency, it follows that the decision over how many subordinates to hire and at what level of expertise should be shaped by the degree to which the agency, due to its mission and technology, can be broadly classified as either a programmed or a nonprogrammed decision-making body.

The more an agency is involved in nonprogrammed tasks, the less appeal streamlining an agency has. If the director is motivated to minimize the costs of organization, then she would shy away from relying too heavily on subordinate expertise, because the rising marginal cost causes sharp declines in the marginal value of expertise. If the goal was to maximize overall agency reliability for a fixed budget, the director might choose to utilize a redundant structure of less-expert subordinates in the hope that the system as a whole

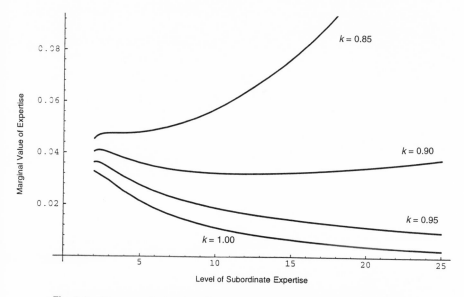

Fig. 5.8. The marginal value of expertise rises as cost of expertise decreases exponentially

could compensate for the uncertainty that exists over the critical value π^*. Regardless of whether a director seeks to minimize costs or maximize performance, the advantages of a streamlined organization decline as the number of nonprogrammed tasks confronting the agency rises.

In the same manner, an agency dealing predominantly with programmed tasks may find streamlining an attractive option. In such a setting, the value of increasing expertise is unhindered by ambiguity over the critical point where policy action is justified. Likewise, because of the repetitive nature of its tasks, the marginal cost of expertise generally declines, thus making increasing expertise a more affordable option. As the percentage of programmed tasks rises, the director may well find that the agency is able to withstand personnel cuts while maintaining organizational performance by altering the performance standards required of its subordinates.

Bureaucratic Reform Revisited

At the beginning of this chapter, we noted that concern over the growing federal debt is fueling current demands to downsize and streamline government operations. Although political economists have repeatedly shown that the phenomenal growth of entitlement spending is the major factor in our budget deficit problem (Peterson and Howe 1988; Kettl 1992), the political difficulty associated with curtailing benefits in any significant way lead politicians to pledge instead to get rid of the deficit by cutting "bureaucratic waste." Since personnel expenses often amount to a sizable portion of agency costs, reducing the total number of people employed in the public sector becomes the quickest way of identifying and eliminating this problem.

By pushing for bureaucratic downsizing, political leaders hope to maintain desired government services for constituents but provide them at a lower delivery cost in order to satisfy the deficit hawks. While reducing the number of employees in an agency is possible, it has become clear in this chapter that there are bounds on the effectiveness of this strategy. When an agency is involved in programmed tasks, it may be possible to offset some of the effects of personnel losses by raising a subordinate's performance standards. This option becomes severely limited in cases of nonprogrammed tasks. The uniqueness and complexity of nonprogrammed tasks makes it both cost-ineffective and infeasible for an agency to maintain a standard of reliable performance by increasing subordinate expertise alone. In the long run, such agencies will find that they are better off utilizing greater numbers of less-expert subordinates and organizing them into an administrative system that is able to achieve the desired ends.

Some bureaucratic reformers believe that the solution to this political dilemma lies in increased privatization of government services. Privatization advocates often argue that the private sector is able to the do the same job as public agencies with fewer human resources and lower costs. The superior efficiency of the private sector, while questioned by some public administration scholars (Downs and Larkey 1986), is generally accepted as true by many political leaders and the population at large. It is important to recognize, however, that the limitations of downsizing discussed here apply to both public and private organizations. Although it is true that many public agencies face more binding resource constraints than private sector firms, no assumption in the modeling section of this chapter strictly limits these conclusions to public administration. The result is that even private-sector organizations engaged in nonprogrammed tasks face constraints in their ability to maintain performance while trimming personnel. Not surprisingly, successful companies like 3M and Hewlett Packard do not choose to downsize their research and development functions or other areas involving nonprogrammed tasks (Peters and Waterman 1982). Thus, to the extent that a privatized program would remain a nonprogrammed task, simply shifting the burden to the private sector will not allow for substantial personnel reductions without affecting overall performance.

Closely related to the issue of bureaucratic downsizing, many people have advocated that government adopt many of the private sector's management techniques in order to further increase efficiency. Methods such as Total Quality Management and Just-In-Time processing are generally hailed as new management tools that could improve performance and help eliminate unnecessary expenses. At their core, these techniques seek to improve the performance of individual components within the organization. It should be clear from the results generated here that such efficiency-enhancing methods may not always be appropriate. These techniques may be valuable where the process—such as manufacturing—is well understood and can be programmed; agencies engaged in this type of task may find these practices useful as well. Those agencies engaged primarily in nonprogrammed decisions, however, will find such methods to be of considerably less value.

To this point, the discussion has focused on how these reforms will affect the decision-making abilities of public agencies. While it is clear that these reforms will have an important and direct impact on policy decisions, it is also true that there may be indirect effects as well. As noted in the last section, many agencies are involved in a mix of both programmed and nonprogrammed tasks, with some agencies oriented toward more nonprogrammed tasks and others engaged in more programmed decisions. Of course, it is often possible for an agency to shift its efforts away from one set of tasks and toward another. Given that agencies view failure as undesirable and something to be avoided, this analysis suggests that such agencies may choose to emphasize programmatic tasks and reduce responsiveness through innovation and adaptive learning if these reforms are implemented. If we want a particular agency to maintain its emphasis on nonprogrammed tasks, then we ought to be cautious in our efforts to reform that agency.

It is clear that some reform proponents would find a shift toward more programmed tasks to be an undesirable policy consequence. In particular, advocates of "reinventing government" not only press for leaner organizations, but they also stress the need for public bureaucracies to become more responsive to the varied demands of its constituents (Osborne and Gaebler 1992). In discussing bureaucratic responsiveness, Wilson (1967) has noted that concerns over equity and responsiveness place conflicting demands on bureaucratic performance; equity drives an agency to develop larger "rule books" and rigidly adhere to those rules while responsiveness dictates that the agency throw out the rule book and make decisions based on more individual needs. The same tension between equity and responsiveness arises in the context of bureaucratic streamlining. Agencies that place less emphasis on responsiveness and show more concern for equity typically rely more on programmed decision making—the large rule books—which makes streamlining a more feasible option. Increasing bureaucratic responsiveness requires that an agency have a greater capacity for nonprogrammed decision making, but that in turn makes it more difficult to save money by streamlining the organization. By developing a proper theoretical framework for discussing bureaucratic reform, we are able to see that some of the goals promoted by champions of reform are not fully compatible and could lead to undesirable outcomes.

Of course, there may be other factors that prohibit an agency from relying on greater subordinate expertise to make up for cuts in overall personnel levels. For example, in this model I have assumed that subordinates are essentially unbiased estimators of the state of the world. Under the right incentives, however, a subordinate may choose to strategically deceive the director by passing up biased information. Presidential historians have argued that FDR's concern over potentially biased advice was one reason that he employed a substantial amount of redundancy in the executive branch (Schlesinger 1958; Wilensky 1969). Further analysis of this problem may well demonstrate that the existence of strategic behavior serves to limit the opportunities available to trim agency staffs and force directors to rely more on structural redundancy for achieving organizational reliability.

Of course, we should recognize that the limitations of bureaucratic downsizing only apply if we want government to maintain or enhance the quality of its performance. Some political leaders today advocate downsizing precisely because they want to reduce agency output. But as noted earlier, most people don't necessarily want less government services—just less spending. This demand can be met and the impact of bureaucratic downsizing can be counteracted by employing a component strategy in some cases, but certainly not all. Political leaders who advocate various bureaucratic reforms and reorganizations should be mindful of the limitations of these methods.

Implications for Agencies Managing High-Risk Technologies

It is particularly important to consider the consequences of bureaucratic reform when dealing with agencies that manage or regulate risky technologies. It is unfortunate that so many of the political leaders attempting to rein in government spending through bureaucratic downsizing or other reforms see their methods as a "one-size-fits-all" strategy that can be applied across the board. But as we have noted here, cutting staffs and reorganizing agencies without regard to the types of tasks an agency is involved in can easily lead to lower performance and greater rates of failure. For agencies involved in hazardous technologies, such consideration is critical because increasing incidence of failure will ultimately lead to catastrophic consequences.

It is interesting to note that the general public often views engineering systems as well-defined, precise, and objective applications of technical knowledge. Whenever technical failure occurs, however, investigators find just the opposite is true; they uncover a system "characterized by ambiguity, disagreement, deviation from design specifications and operating standards, and ad hoc rule making" (Vaughan 1996, 200). This characterization applies to quite a number of technologies. Brian Wynne (1988) has argued that many technologies are "unruly" in the sense that there is limited information available to guide sound engineering decisions. According to Wynne, "Beneath a public image of rule-following behavior and the associated belief that accidents are due to deviation from those clear rules, experts are operating with far greater levels of ambiguity, needing to make uncertain judgements in less than clearly structured situations" (1988, 153).

The result is that many agencies responsible for managing risky technologies are engaged in tasks that require nonprogrammed decision making. That is especially true at the beginning of an agency's existence, for two reasons. The first reason is that a new agency usually has little past experience to draw upon when facing new policy decisions. The second reason is that new agencies are often dealing with new or developing technologies; by definition, most of the tasks this new agency will handle are nonprogrammed ones. For similar reasons, agencies responsible for technologies that are undergoing rapid changes will be facing novel and unique circumstances that dictate a nonprogrammed approach to decision making. Thus, in many cases, bureaucratic downsizing could have disastrous consequences for agencies dealing with risky technologies.

This is not to say that all reform efforts are inappropriate for all agencies involved with risky technologies. There are some cases where technological agencies are engaged in a greater degree of programmable tasks than some of their counterparts. It can be true of some regulatory agencies that are dealing with technologies that change at a more moderate pace. Regulatory agencies have a fair degree of repetitiveness in their tasks, and if technological change is more modest, then there are opportunities to develop routines and standards that can help guide agency decision making. While the reforms mentioned earlier may be more successful in these cases, it is not clear whether such examples represent the rule or the exceptions for agencies responsible for risky technologies.

Having spent the past two chapters developing theories to explain how agencies can alter the reliability of their decision-making processes, it is time to put these hypotheses to the test. In particular, do agencies involved in nonprogrammed tasks rely more on systems strategies while organizations engaged in programmed tasks utilize component strategies? To see if these hypotheses are true, we will move from theory to case study in the next chapter by resuming our discussion of NASA and the FDA.

APPENDIX — CHAPTER 5

In this chapter, it was noted that the probability of subordinates committing either a type I or a type II error could be found using the beta distribution.

Mathematically, we can define the probability of a subordinate committing either a type I or a type II error as:

$$Pr[\text{Type I error}] = \frac{\Gamma(n)}{\Gamma(r)\Gamma(n-r)} \int_{\pi^*}^{1} x^{r-1}(1-x)^{n-r-1}\, dx \quad \text{if } \pi^* > \pi$$

$$Pr[\text{Type II error}] = \frac{\Gamma(n)}{\Gamma(r)\Gamma(n-r)} \int_{0}^{\pi^*} x^{r-1}(1-x)^{n-r-1}\, dx \quad \text{if } \pi^* \leq \pi.$$

Integrating the beta function from 0 to 1 yields two possible solutions, as demonstrated in the following:

$$I_{\pi^*}(r, n) = \frac{\Gamma(n)}{\Gamma(r)\Gamma(n-r)} \int_{0}^{\pi^*} x^{r-1}(1-x)^{n-r-1}\, dx =$$

$$\frac{\Gamma(n)}{\Gamma(r)\Gamma(n-r)} \left[\frac{\pi^{*r}(1-\pi^*)^{n-r-1}}{n-1} + \frac{n-r-1}{n-1} \int_{0}^{\pi^*} x^{r-1}(1-x)^{n-r-2}\, dx \right]$$

$$= \frac{\Gamma(n)}{\Gamma(r)\Gamma(n-r)} \frac{1}{n-r} \left[-\pi^{*r}(1-\pi^*)^{n-r} + n \int_{0}^{\pi^*} x^{r-1}(1-x)^{n-r}\, dx \right].$$

Unfortunately, each of these solutions to the incomplete beta function contains yet another integral. The new integral can be solved in a manner similar to the first step, yielding yet another integral. While it is possible to repeatedly integrate by parts, this method will not yield a final solution without making a number of restrictive assumptions. As a result, it is not possible to obtain a closed-form solution that would allow us to develop any mathematical proofs using the beta distribution. Nonetheless, it is possible to use numerical methods to determine these values with a high degree of accuracy. In chapter 5, *Mathematica* (ver. 2.2.2) was used to approximate these values and create figures 5.5 through 5.8.

CHAPTER 6

Systems versus Components:
Seeking Greater Reliability at NASA
and the FDA

Wernher von Braun, the father of modern rocketry, once said, "We can lick gravity, but sometimes the paperwork is overwhelming."[1] The success of the space program, however, has as much to do with organizational management as it does with technological advancement. Without large-scale cooperation within NASA and between other agencies, reaching our objectives in space would require a much longer time frame to achieve. To understand the successes and failures of U.S. space policy, therefore, it is necessary is look at the administrative behavior of NASA.

In this chapter, we return to our study of policy-making at the National Aeronautics and Space Administration and at the Food and Drug Administration. We noted in chapter 3 that NASA and the FDA both had political incentives early in their history to reduce the likelihood of type I failures. Through the 1970s and 1980s, the political environment of each agency shifted so that both NASA and the FDA were encouraged to lessen the probability of type II errors even though there was no technological reason for the change. In this chapter, we seek to determine whether the two agencies maintained their commitment to minimizing type I errors or whether they were moved by the political incentives that were encouraging a shift toward more type II reliability.

To make this determination, however, we need to be mindful of the different ways in which organizations may seek to alter their performance. One possibility is that the agency relies on a systems strategy to avoid certain types of error, that is, modifying the number of components within the system or changing their location within it. It may also be that an agency chooses to increase organizational performance by requiring greater performance from some or all of the components that make up the system while keeping the basic administrative structure intact. As we hypothesized in the previous chapter, the decision to pursue one strategy over the other is depen-

---

1. Quoted in A. Levine 1982, v.

dent on the degree to which the organization engages in programmed decision making.

Comparing the behavior of NASA and the FDA also gives us an opportunity to test this hypothesis. While these two agencies have many similarities, they have one clear difference. The FDA is able to engage more often in programmed decision making during its review of new pharmaceuticals while NASA utilizes much more nonprogrammed decision making as it carries out its mission to explore outer space. To substantiate this point, consider first the FDA's drug approval process. As a regulatory agency, the FDA primarily engages in repetitive tasks while reviewing and approving pharmaceuticals. In the five-year period from 1988 through 1992, the agency received an average of

1,500 submissions for Investigational New Drug (IND) exemptions to permit clinical testing of new pharmaceuticals

130 New Drug Applications (NDA), representing completed testing of new chemical entities

900 to 1,000 Abbreviated New Drug Applications (ANDA), which are used to process generic drug applications[2]

While each new chemical entity represents special challenges for the FDA staff, the amount of repetition makes it nonetheless possible for the agency to establish general acceptance criteria within each pharmaceutical classification. Consequently, these criteria have been translated into specific procedural instructions to guide medical officers in their review of new pharmaceuticals.

NASA, on the other hand, is an agency engaged predominantly in nonprogrammed decision making. NASA's job is essentially to develop new and complex technologies for space exploration. The fruits of the agency's research and development efforts must later operate in the highly uncertain environment of outer space. Inasmuch as the technologies and applications being developed are novel, NASA tasks generally involve little repetition, which makes it difficult to codify many of the agency's operating procedures. This is not to say that NASA is devoid of standard operating procedures (SOPs). Most of the agency's SOPs, however, deal with administrative issues such as compensation and personnel, and not with questions of engineering judgment or scientific merit. NASA is compelled to rely on nonprogrammed decision making because the nature of its task is such that it has no other choice.

If the hypothesis—that the form of decision making an agency utilizes influences the organization's strategy toward the achievement of its reliability goals—is false, then we would expect to see that, given the similarities in

---

2. Figures were provided by officials at the FDA's Center for Drugs, May 20, 1993.

their political incentives, NASA and the FDA would follow similar paths in their effort to shift from type I to type II reliability. If the hypothesis is true, then we would expect to see NASA relying on a systems strategy while the FDA achieves its goals through the use of a component strategy.

Pursuing Organizational Reliability at NASA

To verify this hypothesis, let us first discuss the problems NASA faces in altering component reliability. Given the nonprogrammed nature of many NASA decisions, if the agency were to use a component strategy, it would have to do one of two things. It could choose to remove ineffective components and replace them with higher-quality personnel, or it could provide for additional training for each component in order to stimulate better judgment and creativity. Unfortunately for NASA, budgetary and civil service constraints inhibits the agency's ability to make either of these component adjustments.

While the space agency has been able to recruit reasonably good engineers and scientists based on the glamour of its mission, there are a number of factors that limit NASA from securing higher-caliber personnel. The greatest constraint facing the agency is the difference in salary between what NASA, as a government agency, can offer an employee and what the private sector can provide. Although this problem is to some degree governmentwide, it is particularly acute for NASA, which must recruit technically skilled people.[3] Under civil service regulations, NASA can rarely offer its employees a salary comparable to what they could command in the private sector. This problem will likely worsen as the pool of available talent in science and engineering is expected to decline by 25 percent over the next decade.[4] The result will be more intense competition for employees even within the private sector, making NASA recruitment efforts more difficult.

To demonstrate this pay difference, NASA commissioned a study in December 1987 that surveyed eight major aerospace companies and compared salary levels in the public and private sectors. This survey revealed that the salary of "freshout" recruits at NASA lagged 33 percent behind the private market.[5] The pay disparity became worse at higher levels. The study found that a NASA center director, who received $77,500 per year, would be paid more than $155,000 in salary and bonuses for comparable work in the private

---

3. For example, 55.6 percent of NASA employees were scientists and engineers and another 10.4 percent were part of the technical support staff in fiscal year 1990. (These figures were provided by the Office of Human Resources at NASA.)

4. NASA Technical Memorandum 1990, 44.

5. NASA defines *freshouts* as hires with a bachelor's degree at federal pay grades 5 or 7, master's degree at pay grades 9 or 11, and doctorate at pay grade 12.

sector. *USA Today* on September 27, 1988, published its own comparison of the pay differential problem at NASA. The paper found that NASA Administrator James Fletcher earned $89,500 in salary for managing an agency budget of $10 billion. The chair of General Dynamics, on the other hand, reportedly earned $1 million a year and controlled a company with $9.3 billion in net sales, $5.7 billion of which were in aerospace. Such pay discrepancies make it hard for NASA to attract quality workers and even more difficult to retain them later.[6]

New ethics laws have been established to shut down this "revolving door" between industry and government. These policies have also had an adverse effect on NASA's ability to recruit and retain employees. Immediately after the new regulations were announced in 1989, two of the highest-ranking civil servants at NASA, Noel Hinners and James Odom, decided to depart for industry while they still could.[7] By May 1989, twenty-five NASA managers had left the agency because of the new regulations.[8] William Lenoir filled one of these vacancies by accepting the post of space station director, but not without reservations. He told reporters, "The conflict-of-interest laws scare the hell out of me . . . I'm taking a personal risk, but there are some things that are just too damn important."[9] Lenoir's status as a former astronaut helped the agency's recruitment in this case, but this example may be more the exception than the rule. According to the Office of Human Resources at NASA, in 1991 five people from the private sector were approached regarding the position of associate administrator for aeronautics and space technology. All five declined the offer, citing both inadequate compensation and postemployment restrictions as the two major factors influencing their decision.

NASA is most successful in its efforts to attract young engineers. One factor in this success is the agency's participation in cooperative education programs. According to figures provided by the Office of Human Resources, 69.3 percent of NASA's freshout hires in 1990 were individuals who had done some co-op work with NASA before graduation. However, as time progresses and these individuals advance on the career ladder, they often find that private-sector service is far more lucrative. Figure 6.1 illustrates hire-loss differences for scientists and engineers at NASA by grade. As the figure clearly demonstrates, many of these people make the transition into the private sector

---

6. This problem is particularly acute in certain high-cost areas of the country. Combined with NASA's inability to directly reimburse for relocation expenses, this discrepancy has also made it hard to move employees to different parts of the agency.

7. Dr. Noel Hinners held the third-ranking position at NASA when he decided to leave the agency on May 14, 1989. James Odom was the director of NASA's space station project at the time of his departure.

8. "25 Departing NASA Managers Cite Ethics Rules," *Aerospace Daily,* May 18, 1989.

9. Kathy Sawyer, "NASA Space Station Chief Named," *Washington Post,* May 19, 1989.

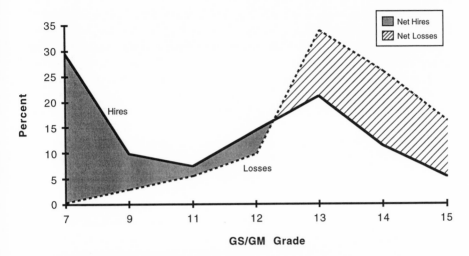

Fig. 6.1. NASA scientists and engineers hire and loss rates by GS/GM grade, 1990 (as percent of total in occupation). (Data from *The Civil Workforce, FY1990*, Office of Human Resources, National Aeronautics and Space Administration, p. 41.)

later in their career. Without the financial resources needed to recruit quality managers from industry for upper-level positions, NASA must look more to its own internal pool of candidates to fill these slots.

This internal pool has some limitations. The Augustine committee *Report on the Future of the U.S. Space Program* expressed concern over the bimodal age distribution of NASA employees. NASA has a large number of employees who have been with the agency since the early days of Project Apollo and has had some success at recruiting young engineers, but it has a noticeable gap in the 35-to-49 age bracket. As the report noted, since this is precisely the group from which future senior managers are usually drawn, NASA faces more intense staffing troubles ahead.[10] Overall, the shrinking pool of upper level candidates further complicates any attempt by NASA to rely on a component strategy.

In addition to the need to hire and maintain quality employees, NASA must also be able to remove ineffectual personnel if it wishes to employ a component strategy. The Augustine committee stressed in its review of the U.S. space program that NASA needs to increase not only its hiring potential, but its firing ability as well. Removing any civil servant, however, is a difficult process and is an option that is not often pursued. As one official in NASA's

---

10. NASA Technical Memorandum 1990, 45.

Human Resources Division stated, "We usually get calls from managers who want to fire an employee, but after we explain what they have to do to get rid of this person, most don't find it's worth the effort."[11] This handicap, combined with the other limitations mentioned earlier, inhibits the agency's ability to pursue changes in organizational reliability through a component strategy.

There is a second option NASA has in raising component reliability— provide for additional training for each component in order to stimulate better judgment and creativity. Of course, just to maintain component reliability, NASA faces a number of formidable challenges. Scientists and engineers must be made aware of continuing advancements in the fast-paced area of science and technology. A memo from the NASA management office expresses this concern well:

> As scientific and technical knowledge continues to grow exponentially, our S&E's face increasing obsolescence of their current skills and expertise. The half-life of undergraduate education is declining most quickly in those disciplines upon which NASA is most dependent (e.g., computer science, electronics, physics, etc.). Although involvement in research maintains some degree of currency, few of our technical staff can keep up with the state of the art through [on-the-job training] alone.[12]

NASA tries to overcome this problem in a number of ways. One means is the agency's funding of postgraduate education. NASA uses this option not only to keep its staff sharp, but also as a means of encouraging young recruits to join the agency. Postgraduate education could also be an avenue through which the agency might increase component quality. Unfortunately, the money required to enact such a measure is so great that the scope would necessarily be limited. Indeed, as the memo later points out, increasing budget limitations hamper NASA's ability to carry out this objective on as large a scale as some agency officials would like.

As the previous quotation also suggests, another way for NASA employees to maintain their expertise is through research. Certain field centers, such as the Ames Research Center, have little trouble providing such on-the-job opportunities. Others, such as the Marshall Space Flight Center, have a more difficult time due to the continuing pressure to cut budgets. In a December 1972 memo to headquarters, MSFC Director Eberhard Rees stressed the center's need for an in-house research and development (R&D) capacity to

---

11. Author interview, NASA Human Resources Division, March 14, 1991.

12. NASA Memo, September 28, 1989; To: Assistant Deputy Administrator; From: Deputy Associate Administrator for Management; Subject: Personnel and Pay Policy Impediments Analysis.

keep the staff fresh on technological developments and to provide an adequate check on contractors. To this end, Rees strongly urged headquarters to resist further reductions at the center in terms of both human and financial resources.[13] Unfortunately for Marshall, it was announced fifteen months later that the center would indeed be reorganized to accommodate a reduction in its workforce and that it would lose much of its capacity for in-house R&D work in the process. This loss of in-house R&D opportunities has not been limited to Marshall, but rather has occurred throughout NASA (McCurdy 1993). Such losses no doubt hurt the agency's ability to keep its staff abreast of new technological developments and to utilize a component strategy in its efforts to alter organizational reliability.

If NASA found it difficult to pursue changes in organizational reliability via component modification, how can the agency go about achieving its goals? To compensate for those limitations, NASA has historically relied on a systems strategy to achieve its desired reliability goals. To demonstrate this strategy, let us begin with a broad overview of the NASA organizational structure and some of the changes that have been implemented there. After that, we examine changes within two specific areas of NASA's structure, which the Rogers commission mentioned in its report on the *Challenger* accident in 1986. The first area of concern involves the organization of NASA's reliability and quality assurance (R&QA) functions.[14] The second area involves changes that took place in the agency's launch decision structure.

An Organizational Overview of NASA

Studying NASA's organizational structure is not an easy task. Writing about NASA history in the Apollo era, Arnold Levine said that "[t]he internal administrative history of NASA is much more difficult to write about than its external affairs."[15] One complication is that the agency's decentralized structure has historically led to tensions between the field centers and NASA headquarters. Further, not all administrative changes have had the desired effect. For example, the NASA reorganization in 1961 experienced difficulties because "neither center directors nor headquarters program directors were

---

13. NASA Memo, December 2, 1972; To: HQ/Deputy Administrator George Low; From: MSFC Director Eberhard Rees; Subject: In-House Capability.

14. The reliability and quality assurance (R&QA) function at NASA refers to those offices and individuals that are specifically charged with agency oversight on matters of reliability and safety. As I will demonstrate in the following passage, this function is not limited to a single office and has undergone a number of changes over time.

15. A. Levine 1982, 27.

quite certain of their function and responsibilities."[16] We will therefore discuss the overall NASA organization only briefly before focusing on more specific changes within the agency's reliability and quality assurance function and the launch decision process.

In studying the organizational history of NASA, one is struck by the fluidity of the agency's structural form. Since the beginning of Project Apollo in 1961, NASA has instituted thirteen major changes in its organizational structure as well as a number of minor adjustments.[17] Such behavior seems consistent with the hypothesis that NASA should pursue changes in reliability through its system linkages. Of course, not all organizational changes at NASA have been instituted because of reliability concerns. New administrators often choose to revise the administrative structure to suit their managerial preferences. For example, administrator Robert Frosch reorganized the agency in 1977 following his appointment by President Carter. As noted earlier in chapter 3, no real change in the political environment of NASA occurred at that time. As the new administrator, however, Frosch had his own preferences regarding organizational structure, which he later imposed upon the agency. There are many notable examples, however, of changes occurring at NASA in order to modify organizational reliability. One such instance is discussed here.

As also noted in chapter 3, the agency received some pressure to moderate its emphasis on type I reliability starting in 1963. To this end, NASA administrator James Webb instituted a number of changes that would "reduce the layering of authority so that fewer officials and fewer documents would be needed to authorize projects."[18] After the political fallout from the Apollo fire in 1967, however, Webb reversed his policy. He established the Office of Organization and Management on March 15, 1967, and by giving it broad supervisory powers, he effectively placed the office as a new serial component in the administrative system. As Webb himself noted,

We gave this Office of Organization and Management police authorities over the system. . . . I am giving them real teeth. I am saying to Harry [Finger], "If these fellows don't satisfy you with respect to the components to the system, cut off the water. Don't give them any money." He's

16. Ibid., 38.

17. A major organizational change is considered one in which changes occurred in either program or project management or in the lines of authority for field center operations. A minor change was one that dealt primarily with administrative support offices, such as personnel and general counsel. Information on the details of organizational changes was provided by the NASA History Office.

18. A. Levine 1982, 47. In effect, Webb was trying to reduce the number of serial components in the system and thus increase Type II reliability.

got the authority to allocate the money, he's got the authority to issue in his own right a modification of a project approval document.[19]

This additional serial component was intended to make NASA more reliable with regard to type I failures.[20]

The Office of Organization and Management and its role in the NASA system changed over time. In 1972, the office lost approximately half its staff, effectively reducing its scope of influence. By October 1978, the office was dissolved and its functions split up among the remaining offices. Chapter 3 documents the increased political pressure on NASA to pursue type II reliability. By eliminating this serial component from the system, the agency was able to reduce the probability that a type II error would occur (but increased the odds of a type I failure taking place). NASA not only had the motive to make such changes, but through reorganization had the means to achieve its policy objectives with regard to agency reliability.

Changes Within NASA's Reliability and Quality Assessment Function

Prior to 1961, NASA had no explicit reliability and quality assessment function within the agency. In trying to match the Soviet space achievements, NASA devoted little of its effort toward preventing bad launches (type I error) and used almost all its resources trying to launch as often as possible (avoiding type II error). As a result, the agency's mission success rate from 1958 to 1961 was dismal.[21]

At that point, the Soviet Union seemed to be winning the space race inasmuch as it was able to draw attention to its many successes while the United States had experienced a number of visible failures.[22] It became clear that the only hope of beating the Soviets was for the United States to play down the numbers of launches and emphasize mission quality. This fact underscored the need for an agencywide effort to increase type I reliability.

---

19. Quoted in A. Levine 1982, 55.

20. The Office of Organization and Management actually consisted of a main office and four suboffices. The effective result is the addition of up to five serial components in the administrative system.

21. Weiss 1971, 1.

22. The Soviets' control over the media allowed them to limit their coverage to the successful flights. Vanguard TV-3, on the other hand, was a highly publicized failure for the United States. The United States learned from this experience and tried to minimize press coverage in later launch activities. Such news cannot be kept a complete secret in our society, however, and the continued contrast between Soviet success and American failure made a political impact at home and abroad.

Consequently, NASA Administrator Webb established the first R&QA function within the space agency in 1961.

The R&QA function was initially formed on three levels: within headquarters, at the field centers, and in the contractors' plants. As such, it represents a classic example of serial redundancy. For a mistake to be made by NASA, the error would have to pass through all three checkpoints undetected. As we have noted earlier, system reliability with regard to type I error increases with each additional serial component. Constructing such an organizational structure is wholly consistent with the agency's increased concern over type I reliability at that time.

Following the success of the Apollo program in the 1970s, NASA faced less demand for type I reliability and more for type II reliability. In the Apollo era, NASA's primary concern was for successful achievement. The agency had a specific mandate that it knew had to be fulfilled at any cost. Having secured victory in the race to the moon, NASA faced increasingly tighter budget constraints. At the same time, the demand from politicians for services continued unabated, which meant that NASA now had to do more with fewer resources available. As a result of the changing political and economic landscape, the agency focus in the shuttle era had shifted to the efficiency and cost-effectiveness of its policies.

By demanding that NASA develop more cost-effective policies, politicians put the agency under greater pressure to pursue type II reliability. As noted earlier, type II failure costs are generally associated with wasted resources and inefficient behavior. From a short-term perspective, then, a concern for type II reliability appeared to be more sensible than type I reliability. The greater pressure for efficient space policy, therefore, led NASA to allocate more of its resources to type II reliability.

The results of this shift are visible in the changes in the R&QA structure since 1970. At the headquarters level, there was a consolidation of the R&QA Office with the Safety Office to take advantage of economies of scale.[23] Later in 1973, the R&QA Office was combined with other staff and placed under the associate administrator for organization and management.[24] Some of the R&QA work was integrated with the Office of Procurement at that time.[25]

---

23. While these two offices had overlapping responsibility, the Reliability and Quality Assurance Office was primarily concerned with hardware and technological issues while the Safety Office focused on human factors and included responsibility for worker safety procedures.

24. NASA Memo, Special Announcement, February 6, 1973; Subject: Establishment of Office of Safety and Reliability and Quality Assurance.

25. The Office of Procurement was another unit within the Office of Organization and Management. The first new major project assigned to the R&QA Office was to work on maintaining reliability while lowering parts acquisition costs (NASA Memo, March 9, 1973; From: Director, Office of Safety and Reliability and Quality Assurance; Re: Parts Acquisition and Reliability).

Further consolidations occurred in 1977, and all safety and reliability-oriented functions were transferred to the Office of the Chief Engineer.

Placement of the R&QA function within the Office of the Chief Engineer did not promote type I reliability. NASA documentation makes it clear that while safety and reliability were considered important, they were a secondary function of the chief engineer's office.[26] The efforts of R&QA were also hampered by the continual loss of personnel. From 1970 to 1985, NASA experienced a 31 percent decline in total personnel, but within the total R&QA function, this decline was more than 62 percent. As a result, the NASA staff allocated to R&QA was just over 5.1 percent in 1970; in 1985 it was less than 2.8 percent.[27]

By the end of 1985, the R&QA staff at NASA Headquarters totaled only seventeen people. As Chief Engineer Silveira stated in an interview, "We were trying to use the field center organizations rather than having that function here."[28] NASA had all but eliminated one of the serial components in its safety, reliability, and quality assurance function. This action reduced the probability of NASA committing a type II error but increased the chances of experiencing a type I failure.

The R&QA function was not immune to changes at the field centers. This level experienced reductions in staff as well.[29] From 1970 to 1985, the three major centers for manned space flight—the Johnson Space Center, the Kennedy Space Center, and the Marshall Space Flight Center—cut R&QA personnel by 38, 54, and 84 percent, respectively.[30] The heavy cuts at Marshall in particular were understandable given the pressure the center was under to be cost-effective. Again, cutting R&QA personnel can be seen as reducing the serial linkages at this level, which can serve to prevent type I errors.

In addition to the personnel reduction, the field centers' ability to supervise the activities of contractors was limited in this period. NASA normally seeks to "penetrate" its contractors to provide an adequate check on their work. Aerospace contractors, however, generally conduct business with the Department of Defense as well as NASA. The Defense Department in the 1970s became concerned that too many NASA inspectors at the contractors' plants could jeopardize national security and wanted to place a cap on the

26. NASA Internal Report, *The NASA Organization,* September 1983.

27. These figures were calculated from numbers provided to Congress by the chief engineer. See U.S. House 1986b, 59.

28. Mark Tapscott, "Cuts Hurt NASA's Safety," *Washington Times,* March 5, 1986.

29. Directors at each center have traditionally been given flexibility to set R&QA staffing and funding for projects under their control. Before *Challenger,* R&QA officials at NASA Headquarters could make recommendations about center staffing but had no direct control over this process.

30. Figures on reliability and quality assurance manpower were calculated from numbers provided to Congress by the chief engineer and by the Office of Safety and Mission Quality and the Office of Human Resources at NASA.

number and scope of their inspection activities.[31] Inasmuch as the agency was dependent on the Defense Department for political support for the shuttle program, NASA had little choice but to accept these limitations on the plant inspection efforts.[32]

NASA's R&QA function changed dramatically after *Challenger.* The Rogers commission castigated the space agency for its "silent safety program" and recommended that it revitalize its R&QA function. In response, NASA created the Office of Safety, Reliability, Maintainability, and Quality Assurance (later renamed the Office of Safety and Mission Quality). Established as a Level 1 organization, this office is headed by an associate administrator who reports directly to the NASA administrator. Staffing for the new NASA Headquarters office was immediately doubled and has since experienced more than 350 percent growth over its 1985 level. While NASA personnel levels have grown by 10 percent over the five years following *Challenger,* the R&QA function as a whole has increased by 123 percent during that time. As a result, R&QA as a percent of total NASA staff is back at 5.6 percent, similar to its position at the time of *Apollo 11* in 1969.[33] NASA made a strong and visible effort to restore the serial component at this level.

Within this office there exist several divisions, such as the Safety Division and the Space Station Safety and Product Assurance Division, which formulate office policy in their respective areas and provide some monitoring to ensure compliance. The real "teeth" of the office, however, are found in the Systems Assessment Division and the Programs Assurance Division. In Systems Assessment, top-level, senior engineers from a wide range of disciplines perform independent evaluation of technical problem areas and testing of systems readiness. The Programs Assurance Division also employs senior engineers to identify critical technical problems and to ensure that the office's concerns are properly addressed by the program organizations and field centers. Inasmuch as either of these two units has the ability to stop a launch

---

31. NASA normally seeks to "penetrate" its contractors to provide an adequate check on their work. Defense was concerned that technological secrets of military hardware constructed in the plant could be leaked out via the NASA inspectors from the field centers (Smith 1989, 230–31).

32. NASA certainly could not look to the contractors themselves for support on this issue. When asked about this issue, one NASA official said, "Contrary to popular belief, contractors have not always been our best allies . . . The fact that the same contractors do work for both NASA and Defense sometimes puts us in a spot. Let's face it, if a contractor has one set of contracts for $600 million and another for $6 billion, he'll always choose the bigger. When push comes to shove, contractors will go along with Defense" (Author interview, NASA Legislative Affairs, March 15, 1991).

33. Figures on reliability and quality assurance manpower were calculated from numbers provided to Congress by the chief engineer and by the Office of Safety and Mission Quality and the Office of Human Resources at NASA.

perceived to be unsafe, these two divisions work as serially independent linkages within the headquarters office. Creating two serial components within the larger serial component at headquarters increases the organization's reliability with regard to type I errors.

The R&QA function at the field center level was also resuscitated in the wake of the *Challenger* failure. Marshall, which had initiated the largest cuts in this area, has since increased its R&QA personnel by 178 percent over 1985 levels. R&QA staffing levels at the Kennedy Space Center and the Johnson Space Center also increased over 1985 levels by 175 percent and 56 percent, respectively.[34]

The agency further augmented its R&QA function through the development of the NASA Safety Reporting System (NSRS). Run by a contractor with no other NASA business, the NSRS provides employees with a confidential means of reporting problems that they believe have not been properly addressed. The system acts as an additional serially independent component in the NASA R&QA structure. Officials at the Office of Safety and Mission Quality state that there have been "no showstoppers" among the reports received by NSRS. Furthermore, the problems coming through NSRS have almost always been identified by the office first—evidence that its administrative structure is doing its job properly.

It is important to consider these organizational changes in the context of three-state reliability theory. In table 6.1 (Set A), I analyze the various R&QA structures first under the assumption that each component has a 20 percent chance of making type I and type II errors and the technology is not safe to operate 30 percent of the time (thus, the likelihood of any single component allowing a failure going unchecked is 6 percent and 14 percent for type I and type II failures, respectively). The original Project Apollo structure had three serial units, reducing the chance of a type I error to a remote 0.02 percent. The advantage of the Apollo structure can be clearly seen. Even if the individual components are not that reliable with regard to type I error and the technology is often susceptible to failure, the structure as a whole would guard against such a failure. As we noted earlier, the NASA structure in the shuttle era prior to *Challenger* was effectively reduced to a single unit. This shift resulted in a dramatic reduction of type II errors and lowered the probability of either form of system failure from 36.39 percent to 14.00 percent. The disadvantage is that a type I error, such as the *Challenger* accident, would be far more likely, rising in this case from 0.02 percent to 6.0 percent. Since then, NASA has made a concerted effort to restore the serial structure in R&QA and has even added an

---

34. Figures on reliability and quality assurance manpower were calculated from numbers provided to Congress by the chief engineer and by the Office of Safety and Mission Quality and the Office of Human Resources at NASA.

additional unit through the Office of Safety and Mission Quality. Adding the fourth component to the serial unit in this case lowers the probability of a type I error to less than 0.01 percent.

Some could argue that a change to a more streamlined structure would be acceptable if accompanied by an increase in component performance or technological advances. This is not necessarily the case. In Set B of table 6.1, I allow each component to lower its probability of error by half—from 20 percent to 10 percent. Under these circumstances, the pre-*Challenger* structure has a 3 percent chance of committing a type I error. In Set C, the technology is more reliable, but the components remain unchanged. In that case, likelihood of the pre-*Challenger* structure allowing a type I failure is also 3 percent. In contrast, the Apollo structure, even with less reliable components, had a less than 1 percent chance of committing such an error. In Set D, I consider when the technology becomes more complex and prone to failure (as is the case of the shuttle) and the structure is streamlined as it was before *Challenger.* The result is that the likelihood of a type I failure becomes even higher. This comparison makes it clear that: (1) these structural changes at NASA were consequential, and (2) streamlining the R&QA function increased the probability that a type I failure such as the *Challenger* accident would eventually occur.

TABLE 6.1.   Probabilities of Failure for NASA R&QA Structures (All Results Expressed as a Percentage)

Components and Structures	Set A	Set B	Set C	Set D
Technological failure	30.00	30.00	15.00	40.00
Component—Type I error	20.00	10.00	20.00	20.00
Component—Type II error	20.00	10.00	20.00	20.00
Apollo structure				
Type I failure	0.02	<0.01	<0.01	0.05
Type II failure	36.39	19.56	42.82	31.85
Shuttle structure before *Challenger*				
Type I failure	6.00	3.00	3.00	8.00
Type II failure	14.00	7.00	17.00	12.00
Shuttle structure after *Challenger*				
Type I failure	<0.01	<0.01	<0.01	<0.01
Type II failure	45.30	25.19	52.54	40.03

Note: A type I error for NASA would be a decision to launch an unsafe mission. A type II error would be a decision to abort a technically sound mission.

The figures for component and technological reliability, as well as the calculations that follow, are not empirically derived estimates but rather are assumptions made for the purpose of illustration.

Changes in the Launch Decision Structure

At the same time that the R&QA function at NASA was undergoing significant modifications, important changes in the launch decision process also occurred that exacerbated the problem of type I reliability at NASA. This section examines both the development and the impact of structural changes in the launch decision process prior to *Challenger.*

NASA's official launch decision structure is illustrated in figure 6.2. Designed originally in the Apollo era to limit type I errors, the system has a large number of serial components. Although the field centers are configured as parallel units in the diagram, this level of the structure actually operates as a serially independent system because the operating rule at the preflight readiness review is that if any center reports it is unready to fly, the mission is aborted. This is an example of a k-out-of-m network, where $k = m$. While most of this structure remained intact throughout the shuttle program, critical changes occurred at the Marshall Space Flight Center.

Marshall has responsibility for three aspects of the shuttle program: the main engines, the external tank, and the solid rocket boosters. At the center, there is a project manager and staff assigned to each section of the program. Before a launch, contractors for each element in the shuttle must certify in writing that their components have been examined and are ready to fly the specified mission. After this step, the Marshall staff responsible for that segment of the program must also verify that it is safe to fly under these conditions. This process is illustrated in figure 6.3.

This structure works well at preventing type I failures, but it is not as effective with regard to type II errors. Assume for a moment that the probability of each component in this system committing a type I error (incorporating both technical and administrative failure) is 5 percent and the chance of a type II error is 10 percent. In such a case, each subsystem (solid rocket boosters, main engine, and external tank) has only a 0.25 percent chance of committing a type I failure, but a 19 percent chance of allowing a type II error. This is certainly not good news for Marshall, which we noted earlier was under intense pressure to operate cost-effectively. Managers at the center sought to increase their type II reliability so as not have a launch stopped on account of a Marshall part.[35]

To achieve this objective, Marshall Center director William Lucas unofficially changed the organizational structure from a serial system to a parallel one as illustrated in figure 6.4. If either the contractor or the Marshall staff stated that a launch was justifiable, Lucas would insist that all parties agree to forward the necessary paperwork. Through his personal supervision of the

---

35. McConnell 1987, 109.

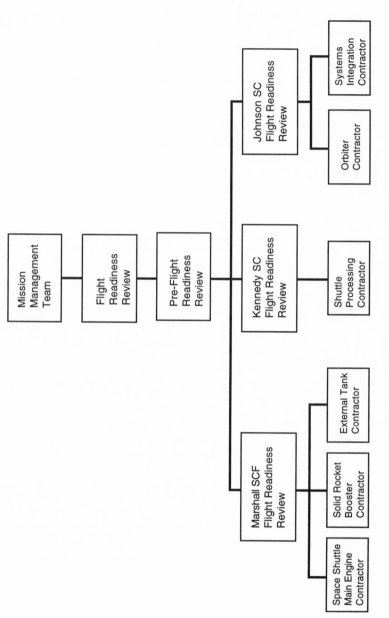

Fig. 6.2. NASA official launch structure, 1981–86

Onto Pre-Flight Readiness Review
(Level 2 Review)

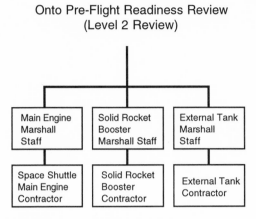

Fig. 6.3. Official structure of flight readiness review at Marshall Space Flight Center

launch decision process and his domineering style of management, Lucas was able to ensure that this unofficial structure prevailed.

Following the investigation of the *Challenger* accident, it was widely publicized that Marshall solid rocket booster managers had coerced engineers at Morton Thiokol into agreeing to a launch they opposed. Such pressure, however, has worked in both directions. In January 1985, solid rocket booster manager Larry Mulloy sent an urgent memo to Thiokol concerning O-ring erosion. A week later, in the review for shuttle mission 51-D, Thiokol's launch decision was to "accept risk."[36] Once this opinion was expressed, the ability of the Marshall staff to stop the launch was extremely limited. In sum, the launch decision structure at Marshall had been transformed from a serial system, which would require both parties to authorize the flight readiness of the equipment, into a parallel structure needing only one component to approve the launch.

It is also important to recognize that not only did the Marshall structure shift, but the interdependencies between the NASA program management staff and the contractors increased as well. This change occurred in large part due to the dwindling resources available at Marshall. As noted earlier and documented as well by McCurdy (1993), resources previously available for NASA employees to engage in "hands-on" work have been steadily declining since the 1970s. It is precisely this hands-on work that allows the program managers to make an independent assessment of system performance and

---

36. Presidential Commission, 1986, 136.

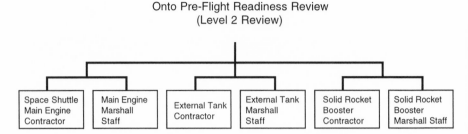

Fig. 6.4.   An unofficial change in the structure of flight readiness review at Marshall Space Flight Center

provide a serial check on the contractor's work. As resources declined, the NASA program management staff had to rely more heavily on contractors for information and technical data. As a result of this change, the level of interdependency between the units was increased and the two units were forced to move together (like the parallel system) rather than sequentially (as in a serial system).

In chapter 4 it was noted that such interdependency would be problematic if the less-reliable unit was the leader or cue giver. Was that the case for Marshall and the solid rocket booster program? Actually, because of the deeply held technical norms at NASA, in most cases the cue givers were the engineers at Thiokol. The program management staff at NASA often accepted the recommendations of the engineering staff at Thiokol, even if they did not full agree with them (as in the example of mission 51-D mentioned earlier). I would argue, however, that on the night that the decision was made to launch *Challenger,* the roles were reversed. NASA program managers were providing the cue for Thiokol—a cue that Thiokol managers recognized and took seriously. When Bob Lund of Thiokol was asked that evening to "take off his engineering hat and put on his management hat," he was essentially being asked to accept the role of cue taker rather than cue giver. The cues of the engineers, which had been accepted so often in the past, were rejected in favor of the cue coming from Marshall. Unfortunately, because the Thiokol engineers had more resources and better data, they were the more reliable cue givers. This fact was borne out in the aftermath of the tragedy.

Finally, it is important to look at the Marshall staff's assessments regarding the reliability of their technology. Throughout the investigation of the *Challenger* disaster, presidential commissioner and Nobel laureate Richard Feynman repeatedly castigated the NASA management in general and the Marshall personnel in particular for the inflated estimates of the reliability of their technology. In his assessment of the accident, Feynman wrote, "It appears that there are enormous differences of opinion as to the probability of failure with loss of vehicle and human life. The estimates range from 1 in 100 to 1 in 100,000. The higher figures come from working engineers and the very low figures from management." During the hearings, Feynman directly criticized Marshall's changing assessment of the O-ring problem when he said:

> It is a flight review, and so you decide what risks to accept. I read all of these reviews, and they agonize whether they can even go though they had some [O-ring erosion] . . . And they decide yes. Then it flies and nothing happens. Then it is suggested, therefore, that risk is no longer so high. For the next flight we can lower our standard a little bit because we got away with it last time . . . It is a kind of Russian roulette. You got away with it and it was a risk.[37]

It is true that NASA continually revised its assessment of the risk posed by O-ring erosion in the solid rocket boosters. However, as our discussion at the end of chapter 2 reveals, this type of behavior should not be surprising. Public agencies facing political uncertainty will continue to have an incentive to revise their failure probability estimates and shift scarce resources to meet other needs. The engineers may not have felt compelled to revise the probability of failure (as Feynman noted), but NASA managers certainly had strong incentives to do so.

Following the accident, the launch decision process at Marshall was restored to its previous status and new resources were provided to reduce interdependencies. In addition, the Office of Safety and Mission Quality was given a direct voice in the launch decision at the flight readiness review. This office was given the authority to stop any launch it believes is unsafe, linking it to the system in a serially independent manner as seen in figure 6.5. This authority has been exercised on previous launch attempts when the office was concerned with hydrogen leaks on the shuttle, defective door lug bolts, and other technical problems. On the whole, the launch decision system was structured to be more protective against type I failures and prevent another mishap like *Challenger.*

NASA Structure in the 1990s

Immediately following *Challenger,* pressures for cost-effectiveness had diminished and political incentives had once again favored greater type I reliability. This did not last, however. As we noted in chapter 3, concern over the federal budget deficit increased in the 1990s, causing politicians on both sides

---

37. Ibid., 148.

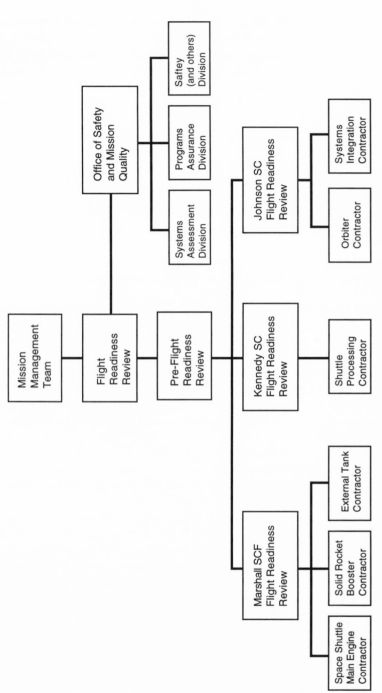

Fig. 6.5.   NASA official launch structure, 1986 to present

of the aisle to look at NASA as an expendable agency. After 1994, the Clinton administration began imposing sizable cuts in NASA's budget while some members of the Republican Congress were considering the privatizing substantial parts of the agency. The demand for type II reliability that the agency felt in the 1970s and 1980s has returned. Not surprisingly, NASA is considering a number of structural changes to adapt to the changes in its political environment.

Through the 1980s the agency sought to guard against type II errors in part by slashing into its R&QA function. In similar fashion, NASA is once again contemplating a substantial downsizing in the safety, reliability, and quality assurance (SR&QA) function of the shuttle management structure. A recent report by the Shuttle Management Independent Review Team argued that "restructuring and streamlining SR&QA throughout the shuttle program . . . must be accomplished to achieve significant cost reduction."[38] Whether this downsizing can occur without jeopardizing safety depends on whether shuttle operations are programmed tasks. The report answers this question by noting that although there have been sixty-five flights of the shuttle, constant hardware and software modifications and changing mission conditions prevent shuttle launch decisions from becoming more programmed. To overcome this obstacle, the independent review team recommended that NASA stop operating the shuttle in "quasi-research and development mode" and that the agency "freeze the current vehicle configuration, hardware and software, to stabilize the program and allow reductions in cost."[39] If that happens, then in time shuttle launches could become more programmed tasks and downsizing might be feasible. But if NASA were to institute the proposed cuts in SR&QA before that occurs, then the likelihood of another major shuttle failure increases noticeably.

It is clear that NASA is hoping it may be able to offset the impact of these structural changes through pursuit of a component strategy. In a press conference announcing these changes, one reporter asked of NASA administrator Daniel Goldin, "How many people will you have to hire back in the event that there's another major shuttle accident, as is predicted by NASA before the space station is half completed?" After the laughter died down, Goldin contended that the proposed downsizing would not adversely affect NASA's performance because, he said, "We're in a new way of thinking and it's very important to transform yourself into that mode."[40] Later in the press conference a second reporter asked Administrator Goldin again if NASA had

38. NASA Technical Memorandum 1995, ix.

39. Ibid., 14.

40. Press Briefing, March 27, 1995. Transcript from the White House, Office of the Press Secretary.

any contingency plans for hiring back employees in the event of another major failure. Once again, Goldin specifically rejected the idea that the space agency could enhance safety and reliability only by employing redundancy within the organization.

What the space agency seeks to do is to reduce personnel, eliminate redundancies, and then compensate for this loss by increasing the performance of the remaining members. Even with "new thinking" at the space agency, the analysis presented in chapter 5 clearly shows that NASA downsizing could hurt performance to the extent that the personnel reductions occur in areas where the agency is involved in nonprogrammed tasks. It is true that NASA is trying to make many of its functions more programmable and thus amenable to a component strategy. However, since a large portion of NASA missions remain novel and quite complex, it does seem likely that proposed downsizing will adversely affect the agency's ability to maintain performance.

Some policymakers have suggested that the shuttle program could eventually be privatized, and this sentiment was also echoed in the end of the independent review team's report. But as we noted in the previous chapter, our analysis is not strictly limited to public agencies. Thus, to the extent that shuttle missions would remain nonprogrammed tasks, simply shifting the burden to the private sector will not allow for substantial downsizing without affecting shuttle program safety and performance.

Pursuing Organizational Reliability at the FDA

NASA met the new demand for greater type II reliability by employing a systems strategy, which is what we expected given the amount of nonprogrammed decisions it faces. Agencies that rely on programmed decision making, on the other hand, should utilize a component strategy in order to achieve changes in organizational reliability. A review of the FDA's organizational behavior substantiates this contention. To demonstrate, I first provide a general overview of the procedure used by the agency in its review of new drugs. Following that, I discuss the organizational modifications that have occurred at the FDA in the wake of the changing political current. While there have been some cosmetic changes in the system, the substantive changes at the FDA show that the agency did indeed pursue a component strategy.

Before providing an overview of the drug approval process, there are a few misunderstandings that should be cleared up regarding the FDA's role in the licensing process for a new pharmaceutical. The most popular myth is that the FDA itself conducts the clinical testing of new drugs. The agency supervises the testing and evaluates its results, but it does not actually conduct the clinical trials. Preliminary trials may be run by the manufacturer itself. More advanced clinical trials are usually conducted by independent researchers and funded by the pharmaceutical company.

The second misconception is that the FDA has some authority over the price charged for the approved drug. After several new AIDS therapies were approved, many activists have returned to the FDA to complain about the high cost of the drugs. This issue also falls in the domain of the manufacturer. However, although the FDA has no direct authority to set prices, its actions can indirectly affect the final price of a new drug. The longer the FDA takes to review the drug, the greater the development costs are for the new pharmaceutical. These costs are passed on later to consumers in the form of higher prices. The FDA can also affect pricing by granting a new pharmaceutical "orphan drug" status, thereby increasing the manufacturer's monopoly and allowing for higher prices.[41] For the most part, however, the FDA's authority is limited after it approvals a new drug for marketing.

The new drug approval process begins with the pharmaceutical companies. A manufacturer develops a new chemical entity that it believes will successfully treat certain illnesses. The company conducts preliminary tests both in the test tube (in vitro) and on animals (in vivo) to verify this belief. These experiments are also important in that they demonstrate provisional measures of safety for later testing in humans.

At this point, the company submits to the FDA a form known as the "Notice of Claimed Investigational Exemption for a New Drug." Thereafter, the drug is referred to as an investigational new drug (IND). This form is used to acquire the agency's permission for clinical testing on humans. In the application, the sponsor tells the FDA the complete composition of the drug and how it is manufactured and reports the results of all animal studies to verify the safety of testing in humans. Additionally, the IND form provides a detailed outline of the proposed clinical testing. After receiving the application, the FDA has thirty days to review it before the clinical trials can commence.

Clinical testing is conducted in three stages, all of which are supervised by the agency. Phase I tests focus on the safety issues associated with the new drug. Factors addressed include the determination a safe dosage range for the drug, how it is absorbed into the body, and its possible levels of toxicity. These tests generally involve twenty to eighty subjects who are often in normal health. If more appropriate, the tests can be conducted with individuals who have contracted the disease. Effectiveness of the drug is considered at this stage, but researchers are primarily seeking evidence of

---

41. The reason for granting such status is to give manufacturers an incentive to create more therapies for the affliction. Several AIDS drugs have been classified as orphan drugs, resulting in high prices for these pharmaceuticals.

the drug's safety. For this reason, actual patients are not required at this stage. Assuming these tests are satisfactory, the company moves on to the next stage of the process.

Phase II testing involves a greater number of subjects than before; several hundred people are often enlisted. Researchers continue to test for safety but focus also on the efficacy of the new pharmaceutical. At this stage, scientists examine the drug's side effects, refine the dosage levels, and develop a dose schedule. Actual patients are incorporated into these trials to provide some evidence of the drug's effectiveness. These studies may or may not use randomized and blind testing with a placebo. If these trials prove successful, the researchers continue on to the third phase of clinical testing.

Phase III is the largest stage of the process and can involve hundreds of thousands of subjects. This phase usually demands the greatest rigor in the statistical methodology; placebo controls, "blinding," and randomization are standard elements. Researchers strive to ascertain with precision the drug's safety, its efficacy, and the most desirable dosage for treating patients. These studies generally pursue confirmation of earlier findings regarding safety and efficacy and provide the strongest comparative data on the experimental treatment versus other known therapies. When these tests are completed, the results are turned over to the FDA for review.

After completing three stages of clinical trials, approved and monitored by the FDA, pharmaceutical manufacturers begin the formal process of new drug review by submitting a new drug application (NDA) to the FDA. Among the materials included in this application are the drug's chemical structure, drug samples, and the proposed drug label. Additionally, the NDA reports all data gathered in the clinical trials for independent agency review. This requirement alone extends the typical NDA to several thousands of pages in length.

The NDA is turned over to one of eight divisions within the FDA's Center for Drug Evaluation and Research for review.[42] A review team is assigned to the NDA and consists of the following specialists:

a physician to evaluate the results of the clinical trials and review data on the drug's therapeutic and adverse effects

a chemist to focus on how the drug is put together and investigate the manufacturing controls of the drugs

a pharmacologist to study the effects of the drug on laboratory animals in short-term and long-term studies

---

42. These divisions are Cardio-Renal, Gastrointestinal and Coagulation, Neuropharmacological, Oncology and Pulmonary, Anti-Infective, Anti-Viral, Metabolism and Endocrine, and Medical Imaging, Surgical and Dental Drugs.

a biostatistician to evaluate the designs for each controlled study, the validity of statistical analyses, and the conclusions of safety and effectiveness based on the study data

additional staff to review the drug's labeling, packaging, and other special concerns raised by the clinical trials

The team performs an extensive review of the application and reports its findings to the next level of the agency.

The law allows the FDA 180 days to review an NDA from the time it is received and complete. During that time, the review team can, and usually does, contact the sponsor about perceived problems in the application. The team often orders the manufacturer to conduct additional tests to resolve specific concerns about the new drug. As a result, the average NDA review takes approximately twenty-eight months to complete.

If the agency finds an application particularly difficult or controversial, it can be referred to one of the FDA's seventeen standing advisory committees. These committees consist of nine to fifteen outside experts and have been used by the FDA since 1964. These experts briefly review the evidence gathered to date, debate the scientific merits of the new drug, and provide recommendations for the agency. The FDA is not bound to follow the counsel of the advisory committee, although the two groups are in agreement more often than not.

After the review team approves the drug application, the NDA moves up the chain of command for final approval. Routine applications can be signed off by the Division Director, where nearly half of all NDAs are decided. More difficult or controversial decisions are forwarded to upper management. The Director of the Center of Drug Evaluation and Research approves all significant new entities and combination drugs. Particularly controversial NDAs are sent to the commissioner for final approval.

The most salient feature of the FDA's drug approval process is the extremely serial nature of the system. Beginning in the manufacturer's lab, progressing through several stages of clinical trials, and contingent to final review at the FDA, the structure accommodates the agency's desire to protect against the possibility of type I failures. As illustrated in figure 6.6, 80 percent of all proposed drugs fail to make it through the entire approval process. The serial nature of the system prevents many harmful drugs from getting onto the market, but it no doubt has allowed some good drugs to be eliminated in the process.

Even within the FDA itself, the basic decision structure is serial. The review team essentially operates as a serially independent system. After its analysis is completed, the NDA is passed up to at least one more level for approval. One should be careful, however, not to assign too much weight to the performance of these upper-level components. For example, advisory

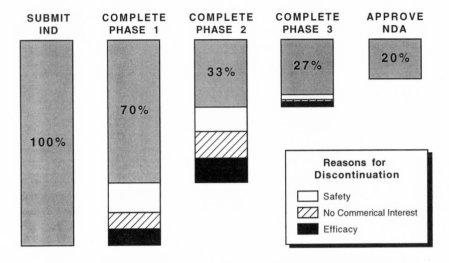

Fig. 6.6. Success rate of drugs in each stage of the FDA approval process and reasons for discontinuation, for INDs initially submitted between 1976 and 1978. (Data provided to Congress by the FDA. See U.S. House 1988, 388.)

committees face major time and resource constraints that limit their ability to review and critique the NDAs in a comprehensive manner. Their role, as well as the commissioner's approval, more often serves as political validation for potentially controversial decisions. While both these factors could halt the approval process, in actuality it is a rare occurrence.

A Systems Strategy for the FDA?

On the whole, the serial nature of the FDA's drug approval process seems to have met the agency's earlier objective of minimizing type I error. Since the mid-1980s, however, political factors have caused the FDA to shift its concern from type I to type II reliability. In no small part, this shift is due to the pressure the AIDS lobby has exerted against the agency and its congressional supporters. Since there is no cure and few treatments for AIDS, activists generally believe that the risks of taking a potentially dangerous drug are outweighed by the terminal nature of the disease and the possibility of some medical relief. In response, the FDA has instituted a number of organizational changes in response to these changing political demands.

One of the most publicized changes in the approval process occurring in the past few years has been the creation of the "treatment IND." The idea behind the treatment IND is to make a new drug under investigation available earlier in the process for those individuals who suffer from either "immediately life threatening" or "serious" illnesses. An immediately life-threatening disease has been defined as "one in which there is a reasonable likelihood that death will occur with a matter of months or in which premature death is likely without early treatment." Serious illnesses, on the other hand, have not been defined but are considered strictly on a case-by-case basis.[43]

As can be seen in figure 6.7, treatment INDs can make new pharmaceuticals available to patients toward the end of Phase II testing for life-threatening illnesses and midway through Phase III trials for serious illnesses. To obtain a treatment IND, physicians must contact the drug sponsor to gather the materials necessary for FDA consideration, including all data collected in the ongoing clinical trials. The agency is still cautious in its review of such applications, strongly considering safety issues and weighing other factors, such as the availability of alternative therapies and the impact of the exemption on clinical trials. Because of the proprietary nature of the information in a treatment IND application, the FDA does not make known the exact reasons for rejecting a particular request. Officials at the FDA indicate, however, that approximately half the treatment IND applications have been denied.

Additionally, the FDA has recently adopted a change in the approval process known as "parallel track" or "expanded access." While a drug is in Phase III of its clinical trials, parallel track allows patients access to the medication as part of a concurrent study without a control group. The parallel-track study differs from clinical trials in two important ways. First, individual physicians supervise administration of the drug and then send in quarterly reports of the results to both the FDA and the drug sponsor's research team. The quality of the data returned is considered more suspect than the clinical trial results. Consequently, this information is limited primarily to detecting major safety problems that might be uncovered by a larger sample size. Second, patients enrolled in the parallel-track studies are guaranteed to get the drug, while those in clinical trials may receive a placebo as part of the control group—which has proven to be a major disincentive for patients to enroll in clinical trials. Indeed, according to FDA statistics, the clinical trials for dideoxyinosine (ddI) had only ninety volunteers while more than twenty-seven hundred AIDS patients had signed up for the drug's expanded access studies. Because of the potential difficulties it can inflict on clinical research, use of the parallel-track policy has been somewhat limited to date.

Additionally, the FDA has instituted several changes in its internal structure. As a response to the AIDS crisis, the FDA has created two new offices.

---

43. FDA officials have been willing to cite Alzheimer's disease and certain forms of epilepsy as examples of serious illnesses.

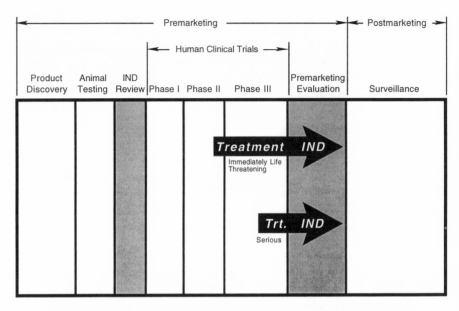

Fig. 6.7. Periods when experimental drugs can be made available through treatment INDs. Shaded areas represent stages involving FDA analysis. The FDA is regularly consulted, however, at other stages of the drug approval process. (Reprinted from Young et al. 1988, 2269.)

The first is the Anti-viral Drugs Division within the Center for Drug Evaluation and Research. This division is primarily responsible for reviewing all applications for the approval of AIDS drugs. The second new office is that of the AIDS Coordination Staff. Located in the Office of the Commissioner, this staff has two major functions. First, it monitors and coordinates internal activities on AIDS therapies to prevent questions of administrative authority from delaying the approval process.[44] Second, this staff communicates regularly with AIDS activists and presents the FDA's position on new AIDS policy recommendations.

Although these changes in organizational structure make it appear as if the FDA were following a systems strategy, the question that must be answered is how much of a difference these policies have made in the reliability

---

44. For example, the AIDS Coordination Staff intervened in an internal controversy over in-vitro AIDS diagnostic kits. The Center for Medical Devices had jurisdiction because the kit was essentially a medical device. At the same time, the Center for Biologics had responsibility because of its authority to license blood products. The AIDS Coordination Staff refereed the dispute and finally ordered all responsibility to be shifted to the Center of Biologics based on its greater experience in AIDS matters.

of the approval process. Consider for a moment the emergence of the treatment IND policy. In practice, treatment INDs come late in the process. While some drugs are eliminated in phase III trials, it was noted earlier that the primary purpose of this stage is to confirm earlier findings regarding safety and efficacy and ascertain these qualities with greater precision. Figure 6.6 also illustrates the reasons for discontinuation at each stage of clinical testing, demonstrating the low level of rejection in the final phase. Even FDA Commissioner Young admitted under congressional questioning that "90 percent of the drugs that are going to fail have already failed before we consider something for a treatment IND."[45] Furthermore, the agency has been very restrictive in its issuing criteria for treatment INDs, so the new policy is rarely invoked. These two factors combine to minimize the impact of the policy on organizational reliability.

Contrary to popular belief, the authority for treatment INDs and expanded access has existed for quite a while. A number of FDA officials have been quick to note that the agency has allowed exemptions in the past, prior to the AIDS epidemic.[46] Pharmaceutical companies agree. In an article by Dr. David Barry, a vice president of research development and medical affairs at Burroughs Wellcome, stated that "what is referred to as 'parallel track' reflects more a change in philosophy than in regulatory control . . . our experience has been that, other than minor paperwork changes which amount to 'i dotting' and 't crossing,' there has been little difference over the last three decades in the medical requirements necessary to make these drugs available before approval."[47] What has really happened, for the most part, is that past regulations have been repackaged in order to provide the agency with a more positive AIDS record. As one official said, "The AIDS lobby likes to think that these changes are all because of them. It's not true, but the perception certainly hasn't hurt us."[48]

Furthermore, the creation of the Anti-viral Drugs Division and the AIDS Coordination Staff have not resulted in major changes in structural reliability. The AIDS Coordination Staff has been helpful in resolving some controversies within the FDA, but as one staff member admitted, "the biggest part of our job is to be a buffer. Activists deal with us and that takes the heat off our medical officers so they can be more effective. In the long run, that's better for

---

45. U.S. House 1988, 364.

46. According to the Office of Legislative Affairs, the FDA has historically granted the early release of experimental drugs when legislators petition the agency on behalf of constituents. Although the FDA applies the same standards to these special releases as it does in deciding treatment INDs today, the agency tries as much as possible to accommodate these casework requests.

47. Barry 1990, 347.

48. Author interview, FDA AIDS Coordination Staff, June 18, 1991.

[the activists]."[49] Anti-viral Drugs is a new office for the FDA, but from the sponsor's perspective, it does not add to or subtract from the process. Rather, the new office is just a different component located in the same place along the system.

All in all, the FDA's use of structural modifications to satisfy changing political demands has been minimal. Changes have been more for publicity than anything else. As a director at the Center for Drug Evaluation and Research said, "[W]e've made some cosmetic changes in the past five years . . . but the structure itself has remained pretty constant."[50] The question then is, if FDA is not following a systems strategy, how is it meeting the political demand for greater type II reliability?

Increasing Component Reliability at the FDA

To comply with the demands for greater type II reliability, the FDA has clearly adopted a component strategy. It is most evident in the agency's approach toward new AIDS drugs. In response to this crisis, the agency has relaxed many of its rigorous standards. Dr. Ellen Cooper, director of the Anti-Viral Drug Division, wrote that one reason for the expedited approval of AIDS drugs was, "More risk is tolerated at every decision point."[51] The agency has lowered its acceptance criteria for the safety and efficacy of AIDS therapies and has reduced the statistical confidence levels it requires from clinical testing of these drugs. Such changes in component reliability have been possible for the agency precisely because of its reliance on programmed decision making.

FDA program standards will face further adjustment with the adoption of the "accelerated approval initiative." Under this initiative, preliminary approval for "breakthrough" drugs may be granted earlier based on gate end-points—physical signs that indirectly indicate patients are improving. While full approval is dependent on the final results of the clinical trials, using these leading indicators as proxies in FDA decision making is yet another way in which the agency can adjust its programmed operating procedures so as to raise type II reliability. Some medical officers at the FDA warn that using these indicators, precisely because they are preliminary and not definitive, may lead to the temporary approval of unsafe drugs. As noted earlier, gains in type II reliability often come at the expense of type I reliability. Such may well be the case with the accelerated approval initiative.

The creation of the Anti-viral Drugs Division has significantly affected the FDA's reliability insofar as it represents an increase in component re-

---

49. Author interview, FDA AIDS Coordination Staff, March 14, 1991.
50. Author interview, FDA Center for Drugs, June 17, 1991.
51. Cooper 1990, 331.

liability. Routing AIDS drugs through the new division boosted the reliability of the decisions made at this stage because of the greater AIDS expertise located in this office. Additionally, the Anti-viral Drugs Division has been able to dramatically reduce the time needed for FDA review of a completed NDA from twenty-eight months to just six. The FDA has established a number of policies to expedite these reviews, including a special classification for AIDS-related drugs. However, when directly asked how this feat was accomplished, several high-level officials responded that the increased staffing for AIDS drug reviews was a crucial element. As one manager stated, "We just staff the hell out of it."[52] Increasing personnel levels does not mean that there are more reviewers assigned to an individual case. Rather, the purpose of increased staffing is to reduce the workload of each reviewer and allow him or her to operate more quickly on the remaining projects.

Beyond its AIDS activities, the FDA has also adopted additional policies designed to alter its components' type II reliability in general. One proposal to decrease the processing time of a completed NDA was to order medical officers to rely more on summaries of the application during their review. The NDA summary is approximately two hundred pages long while the application itself often reaches several thousand pages in length. Except for drugs that demonstrated anomalous clinical results, FDA policy was changed in 1982 to limit the review to the contents of summary. This change was adopted at behest of OMB following its critique of FDA procedures in the early 1980s.

Some officials at the FDA have been concerned about the impact of this policy. Nearly everyone agrees that the policy allows officers to review an NDA more quickly and has thus accelerated the review process inside the FDA. The result has been lower amounts of type II error that might occur because of unneeded delay. At the same time, officials worry that more type I failures may develop because of the limited review. The summary statements of clinical trials, produced by the researchers in charge, tend to concentrate on the favorable aspects of the drug and its testing. Without getting into an independent and comprehensive analysis of the data, officers are concerned that potential type I errors may be overlooked. It is clear, however, that all these changes in the standard practices and procedures of agency officials have been effective in the FDA's quest for greater type II reliability.

To limit this concern for type I failures while still maintaining faster processing of NDAs, the agency is attempting to integrate its work through the use of computer systems. In the early 1980s, the FDA established a management information system that tracks NDAs and their review status within the agency. In 1985, the agency began experimenting with computer-assisted NDAs (CANDAs) to further lessen the review time. CANDAs contain all the

---

52. Author interview, FDA Center for Drugs, June 17, 1991.

data from clinical trials on magnetic disks, allowing the medical officers to perform their analysis more quickly on the computer. The review time has been cut from the average of twenty-eight months to seventeen months using CANDAs. This system currently has experimental status and has only seen limited use to date.[53] Managers at the FDA, however, believe that this technique will be enacted on full-time basis soon. The advantage of computer-assisted NDAs is that they allow the review team to maintain its type I reliability standards while reducing the type II errors associated with the delay of potentially valuable pharmaceuticals.

As a final note, the FDA is presently modifying its component reliability by developing a closer relationship with both pharmaceutical companies and clinical researchers. In the past, the FDA has set standards for acceptable testing but resisted pressures to collaborate with drug sponsors on the actual design and implementation of clinical trials. The agency has changed that policy with regard to AIDS drugs. To minimize delay caused by the need for additional testing, FDA officials are becoming actively involved in designing clinical trials for new AIDS pharmaceuticals. In an interview, an official outside the Anti-viral Drugs Division expressed concern over this policy, stating:

> Some medical officers [working with AIDS drugs] are now involved in helping the companies design their clinical trials. I think that's a mistake. It could easily prejudice the supervising officer. If the officer helps design a test which later gives vague and inconclusive results, will he be as inclined to order more? Speaking for myself, I think it'd be hard for me to do that. I wouldn't want to admit it wasn't good, especially because the companies are probably going to point out that this was my idea in the first place. I think we're better off sticking to our traditional role as supervisors.[54]

This policy was established to minimize delay and the type II errors associated with it. As an unintended consequence, it could plausibly reduce the component reliability with regard to type I failures. The full impact of this policy change, however, remains uncertain at this time because the tests in question have not yet been completed.

The pressure to achieve greater type II reliability will most likely expand beyond AIDS drugs in the near future. As the Republican majority in Con-

---

53. The FDA needs more resources to utilize this technique on a full-time basis. Furthermore, the agency has to deal with the concerns raised about the security of proprietary data available on the computer.

54. Author interview, FDA AIDS Coordination Staff, June 18, 1991.

gress finishes its initial work with the "Contract for America," some legislators and the interests they represent have suggested that Congress begin reviewing and revising the authority of the FDA to regulate new pharmaceuticals. The concern of these conservative legislators and interest groups is that the FDA's concern for type I reliability has hurt too many citizens through the denial or delay of new drug therapies. An advertisement by the Washington Legal Foundation, which routinely takes legal action against government regulations, proclaims: "If a murderer kills you, it's homicide. If a drunk driver kills you, it's manslaughter. If the FDA kills you, it's just being cautious."[55] In addition to the concern over lost lives, congressional Republicans also fret over the costs that FDA policy inflicts on industry. Speaker of the House Newt Gingrich once stated succinctly, the FDA is "the leading job-killer in America."[56] Although some reform bills have been moving in Congress, FDA reform has generated less political enthusiasm than the broader election-year issues of budget deficits and entitlement reforms. If the Republican Congress begins to seriously focus on the possible type II errors by the FDA, however, the agency will most likely make further efforts to comply with these new political demands.

If these new political forces concentrate their energies on the FDA, how would we expect the agency to respond? It is most likely that the FDA will pursue further type II reliability via a component strategy. Because it is engaged in more programmable tasks than NASA, the FDA has a greater opportunity to seek gains in administrative reliability through a component strategy. Since, as noted in chapter 5, component strategies offer certain advantages over systems strategies, we would expect to see an agency pursue that option first. Some agency defenders argue that the FDA has already begun to do so for all pharmaceuticals through the "user fee program" established in October 1992. The user fee program gave the FDA additional resources in order to reduce the approval time for new drug therapies by 1997. With the extra funds, the agency was expected to increase staff size and reduce the workloads of individual medical officers. The program did not change the structure of the FDA, but it was expected to enhance component performance and allow the medical officers and staff to meet the goal of faster reviews for new pharmaceuticals.

The FDA has also proposed a three-year experiment that would allow agency-approved outside contractors to conduct reviews for medical devices that do not directly affect life and death. If approved, this proposal will keep

---

55. This advertisement appears in a number of news outlets and was documented in Philip J. Hilts, "FDA Becomes Target of Empowered Groups," *New York Times,* February 12, 1995, A12.

56. Philip J. Hilts, "FDA Becomes Target of Empowered Groups," *New York Times,* February 12, 1995, A12.

the basic flow of the approval process intact while allowing the agency to tap into greater expertise from the private sector in order to make better decisions. Hence, it is primarily a component strategy. The FDA's plans are less ambitious than some Republican reformers who have suggested not only expanding that experiment (and making it permanent), but also eliminating some of the serial elements in the current review process. Such structural changes have been opposed by the FDA, which has argued that the same practical effect can be made through its own proposed changes without risking public health. True to form, the FDA prefers to gain greater type II reliability via a component strategy rather than embrace a riskier systems strategy. Of course, while pursuing a component strategy now does not preclude the possibility of structural changes at a later time, we should continue to expect to see further efforts by the FDA to boost the performance of components as political pressure for type II reliability continues to grow.

Conclusions

In looking at the administrative behavior of NASA and the FDA, both of these agencies behaved as we anticipated in the theoretical section. NASA, dominated by nonprogrammed tasks, used a systems strategy to meet the political demands to guard against type II errors in the 1970s and 1980s. At the same time, the FDA faced similar pressure regarding AIDS therapies but relied instead on a component strategy to meet this demand. Both agencies were successful in achieving results that were consistent with the political incentives they faced, even if all the consequences (such as the *Challenger* disaster) were not generally desirable.

It is not surprising that fairly sophisticated agencies like NASA and the FDA followed these strategies; as we have noted earlier, taking these avenues would maximize each agency's ability to achieve the desired results. Other bureaucracies, of course, may not follow this pattern because they are either unaware of these principles of organizational reliability or they simply do not care about the impact of agency failure. In the case of the latter, greater accountability of the agency needs to be established by political superiors; even nontechnical agencies must contend with the issue of policy failure and its political consequences. In the case of the former, as the concepts developed here are disseminated within public administration circles, we should expect to see a greater degree of agencies following the examples of NASA and the FDA in choosing strategies to minimize the possibility of organizational failures.

CHAPTER 7

Acceptable Risks

At the beginning of this book, concern was expressed over a single, dramatic incident: the destruction of the space shuttle *Challenger.* Given NASA's long history of reliable performance, such a dramatic failure seemed almost inconceivable. Further, as evidence following the accident revealed major technical problems with the shuttle, it was seemingly irrational for the agency to accept such a large risk. In the process of developing general theories of organizational reliability and agency behavior, we have been able to answer the specific questions of how and why the *Challenger* accident could have occurred.

To understand why NASA could have allowed this event to take place, one needs only to look at the political circumstances the agency was mired in. Beginning in the 1970s, the agency faced increased pressure to ensure that its operations were cost-effective—moving the agency from type I to type II reliability. Through the 1980s, the Reagan administration increased the pressure on NASA to pursue greater type II reliability. In an era of tighter federal budgets and ballooning deficits, Congress was more than willing to support the administration's demand for more cost-effective policy. That type II errors had become almost as visible as type I failures only accelerated this shift in policy. NASA clearly had enough political incentives to change its emphasis from a dominance of type I reliability to one where the two forms of reliability were more balanced.

The agency accomplished this shift through adjustments to its organizational structure. In the 1960s, NASA adopted a strongly serial process in order to limit the risk that a type I failure would occur. This structure is consistent with political incentives the agency faced at that time. As the agency faced greater pressure to achieve more type II reliability, it made a number of structural changes. First, it reduced the number of serial components within its reliability and quality assurance function. Second, it formed a number of parallel linkages at key locations within its launch decision structure. Both of these changes helped the agency avoid many unnecessary delays in launching shuttle missions, but they increased the probability that it would allow the launch of an unsafe mission. The chilling result of this transformation was the destruction of *Challenger.* Without a doubt, the actions NASA took led to results that were undesirable. However, remembering the political environment in which they operated, it is also clear that the decisions made by the space agency were not necessarily irrational.

Defining Acceptable Risks

NASA officials readily admit that the launching of *Challenger* was a mistake, but they also add that it was considered an "acceptable risk" at the time. In fact, when discussing the agency mission at NASA, one often hears mention of the term *acceptable risks*. This is a necessary concept inasmuch as the agency is unable to eliminate risk altogether. NASA must often carry out its mission while lacking information about the technology employed and the environment in which it operates. If officials could not act until all uncertainty was eliminated, then NASA would be hard-pressed to accomplish its mission of space exploration.

Consideration of acceptable risks plays an important role in the decisions of the FDA as well. The amount of testing the agency needs to conclusively prove that a new drug is safe would be so costly that it would discourage further pharmaceutical development. Although relevant to all drugs, the notion of acceptable risks is particularly salient to the testing and review of AIDS drugs. Because AIDS is an infectious and terminal disease that is spreading across the United States and other parts of the world, FDA officials recognize that they must be willing to allow for greater risks than the agency has traditionally accepted. Risk is an inescapable part of the FDA's drug approval process. Determining acceptable bounds for these risks is as important to the FDA as it is to NASA.

Many other agencies need to determine levels of acceptable risks when making policy decisions. For example, the Environmental Protection Agency needs to establish acceptable levels for numerous toxins in the environment. Likewise, the U.S. Forest Service needs to consider the risks of fire damage and other hazards when deciding on levels of tree harvesting from federal lands. Even in nontechnical agencies like the Social Security Administration, officials establishing eligibility procedures for disability compensation must weigh the potential risks of wasting resources on fraudulent claims against the possibility of denying benefits to truly needy people. It is clear that the issue of acceptable risks affects the decisions of a wide variety of public agencies. But this in turn raises an important question: What exactly constitutes an acceptable risk?

It is interesting to note that despite the pervasiveness of acceptable risks in policy-making, many public officials are reluctant to specify exactly what is meant by an "acceptable risk." When asked in interviews to define *acceptable risk* more precisely, NASA and FDA officials generally declined to comment for the record. Most offered instead examples of what the agency would consider clearly acceptable and unacceptable risks. Identifying these extreme points, however, is relatively easy. The more difficult part is to define the transition point between acceptable and unacceptable risks. As a manager at the FDA's Center for Drug Evaluation and Research stated, "It's the middle ground where [our decision to approve or reject new drug applications] is most difficult. We don't hesitate to approve drugs that are clearly safe or reject those which are clearly dangerous."[1] Despite the rhetoric, the concept of acceptable risks is one that these agencies are reluctant to define more accurately.

This hesitancy is understandable considering the political quandary in which this notion places each agency. In determining acceptable risks, agencies must consider trade-offs between two types of error. As we have noted earlier, policies designed to limit the risk of one type of failure often have the unintended consequence of increasing the probability that the other type of error occurs. Moreover, any decision that sets levels of acceptable risks will create groups of winners and losers. People who are aware of agency decisions and can expect to lose from such a policy typically rebel against such actions; they often seek to reverse the policy decision through their activity in the political process. Thus, explicitly announcing the point at which risks move from acceptable to unacceptable would encourage these people to attempt overturning policies that the agency believes is in the best interest of the public.

Publicly defining acceptable risks does more than interfere with the agency's ability to enact policy—it can jeopardize the survival of an agency. Most agencies have a small group of politicians and interests that supports their activities, another small group that opposes agency efforts, and a large segment that is indifferent. Adversaries may be able to use information of risk priorities as a device for swaying the indifferent to support their efforts to eliminate or reconsider the agency mission. When talking about this issue, officials at both NASA and the FDA often noted that they did not want to give their opponents any tool that could be used to pummel their respective agencies. Of course, even political supporters might use the controversy generated by a clearer identification of acceptable risks to strengthen their control over agency policy. In general, releasing more specific information on this point is contrary to the survival mode of thinking that exists in many bureaucracies.

Some officials at NASA and the FDA deny outright that they work in a "political agency," while many others are scornful of the role that politics plays in agency policy-making. It is not hard to understand why this attitude exists. Both agencies are dominated by professionals who view the need for expertise in highly technical policy decisions as their raison d'être. As profes-

---

1. Author interview, FDA Center for Drugs, March 13, 1991.

sionals, they know that they are better informed on the specific policy issues than the general public and most political leaders. To the extent that politics enters into the decision-making process, then, it is often seen as interfering with good decisions and undermining the value of agency expertise. It has been shown time and again that the concept of risk is not well understood by the public. Some people, believing in the value of neutral expertise, argue that society as a whole would be better off if unbiased professionals were allowed to make appropriate decisions regarding acceptable risks unfettered by political demands. This viewpoint, held by many scientific and technical professionals in public agencies, provides yet another reason for bureaucrats to be cautious in identifying what constitutes an acceptable risk.

This leads us to another important question: When it comes to determining acceptable risks, is it necessarily wrong that politics influences these decisions? There are several reasons why the answer to this question must be an emphatic *no*. First of all, we need to recognize that the decision over what is an acceptable risk is inescapably political. It is often said that politics is about who gets what, when, and how much. Politics is the process by which scarce resources are allocated to various interests. As we have seen so many times before, agencies endowed with limited resources must make trade-offs between each form of reliability. The existence of such trade-offs means that decisions about acceptable risks have inherent political consequences and are influenced by political factors. Public administration scholars have known for a long time that there is no such thing as neutral expertise, as appealing as that concept may be. Bureaucrats—no matter how knowledgeable they may be— are making political decisions when they determine which risks are tolerable and which are not.

If decisions about acceptable risks are inherently political, then it is important to have some measure of accountability over those decisions. Actions that attempt to exclude elected leaders and the interests they represent from influencing outcomes cause us to lose a measure of accountability over our system of government. Moreover, what makes the political values of agency experts superior to those of the general public? As we noted in chapter 2, the economic or physical costs of failure are borne primarily by constituents, not the agency itself—another compelling reason to allow for broader input on the definition of acceptable risks. On the whole, subjecting questions of acceptable risk to political scrutiny is a necessary exercise for responsible government.

If accountability is important in this area, then we need to have clear information about agency priorities. Many agencies, for reasons we have noted earlier, have plenty of incentives to be vague and nebulous when publicly discussing acceptable risks. Certainly this can be seen in the case of NASA. Even as the space agency was eliminating personnel and dismantling offices in its reliability and safety division, officials still made numerous public statements regarding the importance of safety in the space program. In general, because of the concern for catastrophic failure, most bureaucrats are sure to publicly state that safety and reliability are the agency's top priorities when asked by inquiring political superiors. More detailed information beyond these general pronouncements, however, is often hard to come by. If knowledge about what is considered an acceptable risk is necessary, but such information is difficult to obtain, then how is it possible to hold these agencies accountable?

This is one of the major benefits of this work: it gives us greater insights on the priorities of the agency. Although agencies avoid publicly identifying the point at which risks become unacceptable, this does not mean that they have not identified them at all. As we have just noted, many agencies cannot function without a clear idea of what risks are tolerated and which are not acceptable. While agencies might not be forthcoming with this information, the theoretical framework developed in this book can help us recognize agency preferences. Rather than rely only on the public testimony of agency leaders, we can look at organizational changes to get a better idea of what the agency hopes to accomplish and what risks it considers acceptable. If the agency is primarily engaged in nonprogrammed tasks, then we should look at its organizational structure for these insights. For example, to the extent that agency reorganization has added parallel units or deleted serial components, we know that a shift is occurring toward greater type II reliability. Likewise, if the agency is dominated by more programmed tasks, then it is more important to look at the efforts the organization has made to alter the behavior of individual components. By studying these organizational changes, we can independently assess the direction of the agency with regard to the two forms of reliability.

The value of this study of organizational change is illustrated well in the case of NASA. Throughout the 1970s and 1980s, agency leaders reiterated their commitment and concern for safety and type I reliability all the way up to the *Challenger* disaster. Knowing that NASA is an agency engaged in nonprogrammed tasks, we could have looked at structural changes that were occurring within the organization to confirm this commitment. In the Apollo era, we clearly see that the agency did pursue greater type I reliability. To do so, it developed large serial structures in both the reliability and quality assurance function and in the launch decision process. Over time there was greater demand for type II reliability, which NASA met through a series of structural changes in the agency that both reduced the number of serial components and added parallel ones. The intense criticism following *Challenger* led NASA to radically shift its structure to a system that was even more effective against type I errors. That structural changes mirrored the shifting demands for each form of reliability does not surprise us. As Alfred Chandler, the eminent management historian, once put it, structure follows strategy (Chandler 1962). In this case, by looking at the structural modifications within the space agency and understanding how these changes influence organizational reliability, we can gain some insight into NASA's true preferences and priorities with regard to different types of reliability.

Returning to the issue of accountability, if the truth be known, most bureaucracies are very receptive to political incentives. As we have seen in some detail, NASA and the FDA responded to political stimuli in their environments. Oftentimes, there are small groups of people who are fully aware of what the agency is doing, and consequently the agency tailors its efforts to please these groups. Those who are only able to follow agency policy on the margins—but still have a stake in the outcomes—are often left to rely on the public statements coming from agency leadership to give them some knowledge of what is going on. Rather than depending on rhetoric and waiting for visible accidents to occur, these groups would be able to hold agencies accountable to their interests as well if they had some other way to determine agency priorities. Applying the lessons learned here can empower these marginally interested groups and improve the responsiveness of agency decision making.

Cycles of Failure

If what constitutes an acceptable risk is a political decision, then it must be subject to the oscillation that naturally occurs within the American political system. Our analysis of NASA and the FDA seems to suggest this is the case. I would argue that these cases are not exceptions; agency failures cycle regularly between type I and type II errors, with major accidents occurring periodically. Let us see how this cycle is typically played out.

The initial concern for most new agencies is how to minimize the probability of a type I failure. The reason for this concern can be seen in the circumstances of the agency's creation. It is difficult to establish a new agency in our political system. Oftentimes it takes a major mishap or controversy to overcome the political inertia that naturally works to suppress the creation of a new agency. Having been created as a consequence of a major failure, it is understandable that the agency's initial focus is primarily on increasing type I reliability.

Over time, however, pressures arise that cause the agency to shift resources toward more type II reliability. One reason for this shift is that new policy issues inevitably arise, which demand attention and government resources. To have more money to fund these new programs, political leaders often demand that existing agencies operate more cost-effectively. Of course, the rhetoric still reflects some concern for maintaining safety while achieving these cost savings. But because the agency has been successful in preventing a major accident, political leaders discount the potential for such failure and thus do not see how this requirement for greater efficiency may conflict with the agency's ability to maintain safety. As we have noted throughout this book, this demand for cost-effectiveness translates into a greater need for type II reliability.

Furthermore, the agency faces increased pressure to seek greater type II reliability as the available information changes. Early on, the number of experts in a particular policy area is limited, and information regarding agency failures is generally restricted to the existence of type I errors. Over time, the agency's near monopoly of expertise is loosened, and consequently the public becomes more aware of type II failures. This information, combined with the natural desire to shift resources to other policy areas, leads the agency to show far more concern over type II failures than in the past.

Ultimately, we see that a cycle between greater type I and type II reliability occurs within an agency. The agency begins with concern for type I reliability but shifts to type II reliability in due time. This shift does not last, however. Given limited resources, this shift toward type II reliability comes at the expense of type I reliability. Eventually, that means that a major accident or near-failure will occur and refocus public attention on the potential hazards of the technology. The political dictum of "be seen doing no harm" then prevails and pushes the agency to seek greater reliability against type I errors. The pressure for cost-effectiveness, suppressed for a while as a result of the accident or near-failure, reemerges as the memory of the incident dims. The oscillation between type I and type II reliability continues as the agency now renews efforts to reduce the likelihood of a type II failure.

This picture of agency cycling seems a bit pessimistic on the surface. Is this cycle inevitable, or is it possible to redirect the agency onto a more stable course? I would argue that the oscillating behavior of the agency is in part a result of deeper conflicting political values widely held by the public. Most Americans hold to four fundamental political values: individualism, liberty, equality, and civic duty. Although each of these values is important, they are often in conflict with each other. For example, greater equality among the populace often comes through restrictions on the liberty of individuals. Enhancing civic duty often demands that the self-interest of individualism be throttled back. The proper balance between these conflicting values is the subject of endless political debate. At times, our society has shown more concern for equality; at other times, liberty and individualism were the paramount issues; at still other times, appeals were made to civic duty as the preeminent value. As certain values become more important and others less so, public policy inevitably shifts to accommodate these changes.

These conflicting values spill over into our expectations of public agencies. When asked to describe the perfect bureaucracy, some of the items people mention are as follows:

the agency should treat everyone equitably
the agency ought to be less rigid and more responsive to needs of individual cases
the agency should always be financially and politically accountable
the agency ought to be able to take the initiative to enact policies that are in the public interest

We would find few people disagreeing with the items on this list; in an ideal world, we would like the bureaucracy to be or do all these things all the time. Each of these elements reflects one or more of the political values that Americans cherish. But as such, the items listed here also lead the agency in opposite directions. For example, the desire for equity encourages the agency to strictly adhere to formal rules to ensure that no preferential treatment occurs. Responsiveness, on the other hand, requires that bureaucrats reduce their reliance on such rules and consider the individual merits of a case. Unable to fully resolve the contradictions within these demands, agency policy shifts as the political winds change.

These conflicting signals carry over into the debate that goes on between those pushing for greater efficiency (type II reliability) and those concerned with agency effectiveness (type I reliability). As the balance tilts toward equality or civic duty, we are more accepting of government intervention to accomplish the desired ends. Because we are focused on the output and effectiveness of the agency, type I reliability becomes the overriding concern at such a time. In contrast, when society expresses greater interest in values like liberty and individualism, government intrusion becomes less tolerated by the public. To the extent that government has to be involved in some policy, we push for greater cost-effectiveness in agency operations so as to minimize both the bureaucracy's ability to act and the costs to individuals for those actions. As the equilibrium between these political values readjusts from time to time, our preferences for either type I or type II reliability will change as well.

It is these shifting changes that lead to the political uncertainty mentioned at the end of chapter 2. In that chapter I argued that agencies are often driven by political uncertainty to revise their estimates of failure and shift resources toward other objectives. Over time, agency estimates of reliability are so high and resources allocated to guarding against failure so low that it is almost inevitable that a failure occurs. The only way to stop this pattern is to eliminate the political uncertainty that fuels this behavior. But since this uncertainty is at its core the result of incompatible but deeply cherished political values, this option is simply not possible. Again, it appears inevitable that most public agencies will experience cycles of failures in their efforts to manage risky technologies.

In the beginning of this book we also discussed the debate that existed between traditionalists, who pushed for greater administrative efficiency, and Landau and his students, who advocated greater emphasis on organizational reliability. The debate has often been conducted in either-or terms, with little tolerance for the opposing position. For example, in a critique of traditionalist thought, Landau and Chisholm state, "The most pernicious doctrine ever laid on the public administration is the doctrine of efficiency, a doctrine that appears to be so much a matter of common-sense as to be beyond debate."[2] Because of variations in the attention cycle and as a result of tensions in our fundamental political values, there will always be movement from type I to type II reliability and back again. Consequently, both groups of scholars will be able to find some evidence that their concern is important and yet neglected. But as we have seen again and again in the course of this work, the real issue is not reliability versus efficiency, as often discussed in the literature, but reliability *and* efficiency—striking an appropriate balance between two interconnected qualities of an administrative system.

Revisiting the High Reliability–Normal Accident Debate

In the first chapter of this book we also reviewed the ongoing debate between high reliability theorists and normal accident scholars. Although we have mentioned this issue in subsequent chapters, it is time for us to reexamine the controversy in a more systematic fashion.

The first major tenet of high reliability theory is the need for a commitment by political and organizational leaders to make safety a very high priority. These scholars are correct that such a commitment by leadership to safety will significantly enhance agency performance in this area. As we have seen, public agencies are sensitive to their political environment and will respond to the incentives provided by political superiors. To the extent that political leaders are able to maintain such a commitment, this can be an important step in the reliable management of risky technologies. Likewise, we know that if political and organizational elites shift their concerns from safety to cost-effectiveness, agencies will soon follow and the likelihood of a type I failure will rise.

Normal accident proponents, however, are undoubtedly right in their critique of this point. These scholars claim that safety may be a major objec-

---

2. Landau and Chisholm 1988, 1.

tive, but it is only one of many competing goals that agencies seek to satisfy. As we just discussed in the previous section, there are a number of factors within our political system that cause leaders to oscillate between the importance of type I and type II reliability. Political and organizational leaders may be able to maintain a commitment to safety for a while, but there is too much resistance for them to maintain this position indefinitely. The inconsistencies within our basic political values makes such change inevitable; when we also consider the variations in the attention cycle and the inherent political uncertainty that elected officials face, it is beyond a doubt that a commitment to safety by political elites cannot endure. While high reliability theorists are correct in identifying this factor as influential, the argument of normal accident scholars regarding the transitory nature of this commitment wins the day.

The second element of high reliability theory is the need for redundancy within and between organizations. Even though individuals within an organization are less than perfect, when operating in a redundant organizational structure, the system as a whole can limit the failings of the people within it. Thus, high reliability theorists have held that utilizing redundant organizational designs is an appropriate means toward reducing the likelihood of agency failure. Normal accident theorists rebut this by claiming that redundancy increases the likelihood of failure insofar as common mode failures such as shirking and cue taking are more likely to occur in human organizations than in mechanical systems.

What have we learned about organizational redundancy in the course of this work? Redundancy can be a very effective means for an agency to reduce the probability of an error. Of course, there are different types of errors and thus different types of redundancies that need to be employed. For example, adding a parallel unit to the administrative system will reduce the likelihood of a type II error, but it also increases the chances that a type I failure occurs. What we really see is that organizational redundancy is a two-edged sword— appropriate redundancies can limit certain types of errors, but generally at the cost of making other forms of error more prevalent. While redundancy can effectively reduce the likelihood of failure, it is no cure-all for the problem of organizational reliability.

We also recognize, however, that every agency does not need to rely on administrative redundancy to protect against the possibility of major failures. Agencies that primarily engage in nonprogrammed tasks will find it advantageous to utilize appropriate structural redundancies to minimize the probabilities of certain types of failure. Organizations that are dominated by programmed tasks can choose instead to alter the reliability of their performance through a component strategy. Therefore, while redundancy may not be a cure-all, it is also not necessary to employ redundancy in every case.

On the surface, it is hard to argue with the normal accident theorists' critique that human organizations are different from mechanical systems. People are self-aware and cognizant of how their behavior influences the larger world in a way that electrons and machine parts will never be. Furthermore, it is true that this difference can lead people within an organization to engage in shirking or cue-taking behavior, actions that violate the assumption of independence, which in turn can lead to common mode failures. While granting these potential difficulties, does it necessarily follow that redundancy cannot be an effective tool in reducing the likelihood of catastrophic failure? As we have seen in chapter 4, to the extent that the cue giver is the more reliable unit, it can actually help increase the reliability of the cue taker. Under such circumstances, the cue taker can decrease his or her probability of failure by following the lead of a more expert colleague. Of course, if the cue giver was the less reliable unit, then the probability of failure rises. That will also be the case when two or more units are shirking their responsibilities. But contrary to the claims of normal accident theorists, human factors do not completely negate the benefits of redundancy, and there are even certain circumstances in which organizational reliability may actually be improved by diminished independence.

The third element in high reliability theory is the development of a "culture of reliability" within an organization. High reliability scholars argue that this culture of reliability would boost safety by creating uniform and appropriate responses by field-level operators. Certainly, this approach seeks to increase the degree to which agency tasks are programmable. Normal accident proponents claim that this type of culture can be achieved only in military-style agencies and is antithetical to the democratic values of civilian-sector organizations. But as we have noted here, the real strength of the culture of reliability is that it may serve to discourage shirking behavior or encourage cue takers to take their cues from more reliable members of the organization. As we just mentioned, these factors can enhance the value of redundancy and improve the overall performance of the agency. While promoting any positive bureaucratic culture is aided by strong and committed leadership, this definition of a culture of reliability does not require the intense military-style discipline that is sometimes mentioned by both high reliability and normal accident theorists. Thus, it is possible for this type of culture to be established in both civilian and military organizations.

The final element in high reliability theory is the value of organizational learning. By running controlled simulations of potential failures, studying small-scale failures, and conducting extensive testing, an agency may engage in a learning process of "sophisticated trial and error." Normal accident theorists state that it can be hard for agencies to learn in these cases because of intense desire to avoid blame. We need to be a little careful here. Avoiding blame is an activity that primarily occurs after a publicized failure or near miss. Although we would hope that agencies would always learn from mistakes, the propensity to avoid blame can in some cases interfere with that function. But learning from small-scale failures is only one element of this learning; given that we are trying to avoid failure altogether, it is probably the least important part of this learning process. A good deal of organizational learning does come from training, simulations, and testing. In the course of this book, we have uncovered some insights that are germane to this discussion of learning. When agencies are dealing with nonprogrammed tasks, the data needed for such learning is limited; it is difficult and expensive to acquire large amounts of information in these cases. Organizational learning can occur with nonprogrammed tasks, but because of its limitations, the agency must employ additional strategies to ensure reliable performance. As tasks become increasingly programmed, there are far greater opportunities for the agency to rely on organizational learning as a means of preventing a catastrophic failure.

In looking over our discussion, it seems pretty clear that both groups have uncovered some important elements of truth. Two questions now stand out. First, which side, if any, has won the debate? Second, what has led to both sides uncovering part, but not all, of the truth? The latter question is easiest to answer. In this debate, each side has a fundamental flaw in its research design: insufficient variance in the dependent variable. High reliability theorists have generally studied organizations that have operated without any major failure in order to discover why they are so successful. Normal accident theorists analyze examples of failure and near misses to find out why these organizations failed. By limiting their cases in this way, there is too little variance in the dependent variables used by either side. Without such variance, it is difficult to claim with any reasonable degree of certainty that changes in independent variables have led to changes in the dependent variables. Thus, methodological limitations on both sides prevent these scholars from reaching definitive conclusions.

We could look at this problem another way. It is as if we had two blindfolded people each touching part of an elephant. One person touches the trunk and the other touches a leg and each person describes what she or he feels. Because they are touching different parts and cannot see the rest, they enter into a dispute over the true nature of the object they are describing. Each side is accurately describing her or his own section, but since neither sees the larger picture, their conclusions are at best only partially correct. This book has lifted the "blindfold" a bit and helped us see the elephant more completely. Through the use of formal models and empirical analysis of NASA and the FDA, we have moved closer to developing a more comprehensive theory of organizational reliability. Using this integrated framework, we recognize that both of these schools of thought offer important insights that are more complementary than contradictory.

If both sides have operated with such a fundamental flaw in their research design, it is difficult to say that either side has really won the debate. But there is a bottom-line question that must be asked: Can risky technologies be managed so as to achieve error-free operations for extended periods of time? Normal accident theorists claim the answer is no—major system failures are inevitable, according to these scholars. Ultimately, they are correct, and the reason why is straightforward. Of the four principles mentioned by high reliability theorists, the last three—redundancy, culture, and learning—tell us how agencies can go about improving reliability. The first element—a commitment by political and organizational leaders—speaks more to why an agency pursues such an objective and the motivation underlying it. Of course, if the steadfast motivation to pursue a course of action is missing, the tools that help reach these ends are of considerably less value. Unfortunately, as I have shown at length in this chapter, political variation and the uncertainty it causes will make the needed long-term commitment impossible. Thus, we are left to conclude that major accidents will periodically occur despite our best efforts.

Such a conclusion does not mean that high reliability scholarship is without value. Failures may periodically occur, but exactly how long are these periods? Perhaps the real goal ought to be to reduce the frequency of accidents to as low a level as possible. The principles enumerated in this book and confirmed in the high reliability literature can be very useful in lengthening the period between major accidents and reducing their overall frequency. Political variability may ensure that some form of failure will eventually occur in even the most diligent agencies, but it is possible to limit the potential level of failure an organization experiences.

Concluding Thoughts: Lessons for Political Leaders

Recognizing that there are inherent tensions in managing risky technologies, does this study provide any practical lessons for policymakers who are responsible for operating or regulating these technologies? The answer is clearly yes. Because agencies are sensitive to political incentives and these incentives shift over time, simplistic advice would be to insulate agencies dealing with hazardous technologies from the political process. As we noted earlier, however, taking such action—if it were possible—would be undesirable inasmuch as it removes accountability from agency decisions. But the truth of the matter is that such insulation is not possible. As Herbert Kaufman (1977) has stated, for better or for worse, we usually get the bureaucracy we want. Kaufman points out that we decry the evils of "red tape" but then make demands on an agency that make such excessive paperwork necessary. In the same way, agencies will vacillate between type I and type II reliability as our societal values waver over time. Knowing that political stimuli affect agency decision making, there are several things government leaders should keep in mind. First, political superiors should be aware that their rhetoric and other proddings can lead to unintended consequences. Pushing an agency to reduce one type of error increases the chances of failure in other areas. Second, leaders can use their public pulpits to remind us of past failings so that lessons learned from these incidents are not so quickly forgotten. Political superiors can undoubtedly influence agency decision making—the key is to use this power in a constructive manner.

The second major lesson for political and organizational leaders is that structure does affect the ability of agencies to perform reliably. For that reason, agency reorganizations should be carefully considered before implementation. Sometimes these reorganization efforts are politically motivated endeavors to limit the authority of career bureaucrats. Other times reorganizations occur simply as a result of a new presidential administration coming to power or a new director taking over the reins of an agency. But since structure affects decision making, it could be that these changes will have consequences that political superiors have not fully considered and may ultimately find undesirable.

A third lesson for political leaders is that reliance on a component strategy for increasing performance is limited. As we noted in chapter 5, the "reinventing government" effort and the introduction of total quality management are attempts to improve component performance. The advantage of such improvements is that we could reduce agency personnel and cut government expenses without jeopardizing agency reliability. As we have seen, this approach will have greater success in cases where agencies are engaged in more programmed tasks. Unfortunately, managing and regulating many hazardous technologies often present agencies with nonprogrammed situations. Relying on components, rather than structure, to ensure safety in these cases can lead to disastrous results. The short-term gains that come from reduced agency budgets can be easily outweighed by the long-term losses that a major systems failure would bring.

In the final analysis, we must recognize that risks are an inevitable part of the technologies that have supercharged our economy and raised our standard of living. Understanding these risks and all the consequences associated with them is necessary to make informed decisions regarding the management of new technologies. The purpose of this work was to provide greater insights on the nature and source of these risks, as well as strategies that can be employed to minimize them. The theory of organizational reliability developed in this book cannot eliminate the dangers associated with hazardous technologies altogether, but it can help ensure that future technical problems are not compounded by managerial mistakes.

References

Aggarwal, K. K., K. B. Misra, and J. S. Gupta. 1975. "Reliability Evaluation: A Comparative Study of Different Techniques." *Microelectronics and Reliability* 14 (1): 49–56.

Aberbach, Joel D., and Bert A. Rockman. 1976. "Clashing Beliefs within the Executive Branch: The Nixon Administration Bureaucracy." *American Political Science Review* 70:456–68.

Anthony, Robert N. 1965. *Planning and Control Systems: A Framework for Analysis.* Boston, MA: Harvard University Graduate School of Business Administration.

Arnold, Peri E. 1986. *Making the Managerial Presidency: Comprehensive Reorganization Planning 1905–1980.* Princeton, NJ: Princeton University Press.

Asch, Solomon E. 1952. *Social Psychology.* Englewood Cliffs, NJ: Prentice-Hall.

Barlow, Richard E., and Frank Proschan. 1965. *Mathematical Theory of Reliability.* New York: John Wiley & Sons.

Barry, David W. 1990. "A Perspective on Compassionate Parallel Category C Treatment Track IND Procedures." *Food, Drug, and Cosmetic Law Journal* 45:347–55.

Bendor, Jonathan B. 1985. *Parallel Systems: Redundancy in Government.* Berkeley and Los Angeles: University of California Press.

Bilstein, Roger G. 1989. *Orders of Magnitude: A History of the NACA and NASA, 1915–1990.* NASA SP-4406. Washington, DC: U.S. Government Printing Office.

Braybrooke, D., and C. Lindblom. 1963. *A Strategy of Decision.* New York: Free Press.

Brehm, John, and Scott Gates. 1993. "Donut Shops and Speed Traps: Evaluating Models of Supervision on Police Behavior." *American Journal of Political Science* 37:555–81.

Butler, Stuart M. 1985. *Privatizing Federal Spending.* New York: Universe Books.

Casamayou, Maureen. 1993. *Bureaucracy in Crisis: Three Mile Island, the Shuttle Challenger, and Risk Assessment.* Boulder, CO: Westview Press.

Chandler, Alfred. 1962. *Strategy and Structure: Chapters in the History of Industrial Enterprise.* Cambridge: MIT Press.

Chapman, Richard A. 1982. "Strategies for Reducing Government Activities." In *Strategies for Administrative Reform,* ed. Gerald E. Caiden and Heinrich Siedentopf. Lexington, MA: Lexington Books.

Chisholm, Donald W. 1989. *Coordination without Hierarchy: Informal Structures in Multiorganizational Systems.* Berkeley and Los Angeles: University of California Press.

Citrin, Jack. 1979. "Do People Want Something for Nothing?" *National Tax Journal* 32:113–29.

Cooper, Ellen C. 1990. "Changes in Normal Drug Approval Process in Response to the AIDS Crisis." *Food, Drug, and Cosmetic Law Journal* 45:329–38.

Cyert, Richard, and Morris DeGroot. 1987. *Bayesian Analysis and Uncertainty in Economic Theory.* Totowa, NJ: Rowman & Littlefield.

Cyert, Richard, and James March. 1963. *A Behavioral Theory of the Firm.* Englewood Cliffs, NJ: Prentice-Hall.

DeHaven-Smith, Lance. 1985. "Ideology and the Tax Revolt: Florida's Amendment 1." *Public Opinion Quarterly* 49 (fall): 300–309.

Deutch, John. 1991 "Mismanaging Science." *Technology Review* 94 (February/March): 73.

Dhillon, Balbir S. 1983. *Reliability Engineering in Systems Design and Operation.* New York: Van Nostrand Reinhold.

Dodge, Christopher B. 1979. *Food and Drug Administration: Reorganization and Historical Perspectives.* Congressional Research Service. Issue Briefing IB77003, January 31. Washington, DC: U.S. Government Printing Office.

Downs, George W., and Patrick D. Larkey. 1986. *The Search for Government Efficiency: From Hubris to Helplessness.* Philadelphia: Temple University Press.

Eads, George C., and Michael Fix. 1984. *Relief or Reform? Reagan's Regulatory Dilemma.* Washington, DC: Urban Institute Press.

Emme, Eugene M. 1981. "Presidents and Space." In *Between Sputnik and the Shuttle: New Perspectives on American Astronautics,* ed. F. C. Durant. San Diego: American Astronautical Society Publication.

Fink, Donald E. 1987. "The Space Leadership Void." *Aviation Week & Space Technology* 127 (July 27): 9.

Foreman, Christopher H. 1988. *Signals from the Hill: Congressional Oversight and the Challenge of Social Regulation.* New Haven: Yale University Press.

———. 1991. "The Fast Track: Federal Agencies and the Political Demand." *The Brookings Review* 9 (spring): 31–37.

Goodsell, Charles T. 1985. *The Case for Bureaucracy: A Public Administration Polemic.* 2d ed. Chatham, NJ: Chatham House Publishers.

Grabowski, Henry G. 1976. *Drug Regulation and Innovation: Empirical Evidence and Policy Options.* Washington, DC: American Enterprise Institute for Public Policy Research.

Grace, J. Peter. 1984. *Burning Money.* New York: Macmillan.

Green, Constance M., and Milton Lomask. 1970. *Vanguard: A History.* NASA SP-4202. Washington, DC: U.S. Government Printing Office.

Hayes, Michael T. 1992. *Incrementalism and Public Policy.* New York: Longman.

Heckman, James J., and Robert J. Willis. 1977. "A Beta-logistic Model for the Analysis of Sequential Labor Force Participation by Married Women." *Journal of Political Economy* 85:27–58.

Hey, John D. 1983. *Data in Doubt: An Introduction to Bayesian Statistical Inference for Economists.* Oxford, England: Martin Robertson & Co.

Hoff, Joan. 1993. "The Presidency, Congress, and the Deceleration of the U.S. Space

Program in the 1970s." Paper presented at the NASA–American University Conference on Presidential Leadership, Congress, and the U.S. Space Program, 25–26 March, Washington, D.C.

Jones, Charles O. 1984. *An Introduction to the Study of Public Policy.* 3d ed. Monterey, CA: Brooks, Cole.

Juran, J. M. 1944. *Bureaucracy: A Challenge to Better Management.* New York: Harper & Brothers.

Kahan, Jonathan S., and David T. Read. 1990. "Expedited Availability of New Drugs," *Food, Drug, and Cosmetic Law Journal* 45:81–94.

Kaufman, Herbert. 1977. *Red Tape.* Washington, DC: Brookings Institution.

Kaufmann, A., D. Grouchko, and R. Cruon. 1977. *Mathematical Models for the Study of the Reliability of Systems.* New York: Academic Press

Kettl, Donald F. 1992. *Deficit Politics: Public Budgeting in Its Institutional and Historical Context.* New York: Macmillan.

Kosterlitz, Julie. 1985. "Reagan is Leaving His Mark on the Food and Drug Administration." *National Journal* 17 (July 6): 1568–72.

Kuttner, Robert. 1980. *Revolt of the Haves: Tax Rebellions and Hard Times.* New York: Simon and Schuster.

Ladd, Everett C. 1979. "The Polls: Taxing and Spending." *Public Opinion Quarterly* 43 (Spring): 126–35.

Landau, Martin. 1969. "Redundancy, Rationality and the Problem of Duplication and Overlap." *Public Administration Review* 29, no. 4 (July–August): 346–58.

———. 1973. "Federalism, Redundancy, and System Reliability." *Publius* 3, no. 2 (fall): 173–96.

———. 1991. "On Multiorganizational Systems in Public Administration." *Journal of Public Administration Research and Theory* 1, no. 1 (January): 5–18.

Landau, Martin, and Donald Chisholm. 1988. "The Arrogance of Optimism." Paper presented at the annual meeting of the American Political Science Association, 1–4 September, Washington, D.C.

LaPorte, Todd R. 1994. "A Strawman Speaks Up: Comments on Limits of Safety." *Journal of Contingencies and Crisis Management* 2:207–11.

LaPorte, Todd R., and Paula M. Consolini. 1991. "Working in Practice but Not in Theory: Theoretical Challenges of High-Reliability Organizations." *Journal of Public Administration Research and Theory.* 1, no. 1 (January): 19–47.

Lerner, Allan W. 1986. "There Is More than One Way to be Redundant." *Administration and Society* 18, no. 3 (November): 334–59.

Lester, James. 1989. *Environmental Politics and Policy.* Durham, NC: Duke University Press.

Levine, Arnold S. 1982. *Managing NASA in the Apollo Era.* NASA SP-4102. Washington, DC: U.S. Government Printing Office.

Levine, Charles H. 1990. "Human Resource Erosion and the Uncertain Future of the U.S. Civil Service." In *Current Issues in Public Administration,* ed. F. S. Lane. New York: St. Martin's Press.

Lindblom, Charles. 1959. "The Science of 'Muddling Through.'" *Public Administration Review* 19:79–88.

Logsdon, John M. 1970. *The Decision to Go to the Moon.* Cambridge: MIT Press.

————. 1986. "The Space Shuttle Program: A Policy Failure?" *Science* 232 (May 30): 1099–1105.

March, James, and Herbert Simon. 1958. *Organizations.* New York: John Wiley & Sons.

McConnell, Malcolm. 1987. *Challenger: A Major Malfunction.* Garden City, NY: Doubleday.

McCubbins, Mathew D., and Thomas Schwartz. 1984. "Congressional Oversight Overlooked: Police Patrols Versus Fire Alarms." *American Journal of Political Science* 2:165–79.

McCurdy, Howard E. 1990. *The Space Station Decision: Incremental Politics and Technological Choice.* Baltimore, MD: Johns Hopkins University Press.

————. 1993. *Inside NASA: High Technology and Organizational Change in the U.S. Space Program.* Baltimore, MD: Johns Hopkins University Press.

McDougall, Walter A. 1985. *. . . the Heavens and the Earth: A Political History of the Space Age.* New York: Basic Books.

Meier, Kenneth J. 1980. "Executive Reorganization of Government: Impact on Employment and Expenditures." *American Journal of Political Science* 24:396–412.

Milgram, Stanley. 1974. *Obedience to Authority: An Experimental View.* New York: Harper & Row.

Miller, Gary J. 1992. *Managerial Dilemmas: The Political Economy of Hierarchy.* New York: Cambridge University Press.

Moe, Terry M. 1990. "The Politics of Structural Choice: Toward a Theory of Public Bureaucracy." In *Organization Theory: From Chester Barnard to the Present and Beyond,* ed. Oliver E. Williamson. New York: Oxford University Press.

Morone, Joseph G., and Edward J. Woodhouse. 1986. *Averting Catastrophe: Strategies for Regulating Risky Technologies.* Berkeley and Los Angeles: University of California Press.

Mullen, John D., and Byron M. Roth. 1991. *Decision-Making: Its Logic and Practice.* Savage, MD: Rowman & Littlefield.

NASA Technical Memorandum. 1990. *Report of the Advisory Committee on the Future of the U.S. Space Program.* Report no. 104952. Washington, DC: U.S. Government Printing Office.

Niskanen, William. 1975. "Bureaucrats and Politicians." *Journal of Law and Economics* 18:617–44.

Nixon, Richard M. 1970. *Setting the Course, the First Year: Major Policy Statements of President Nixon.* New York: Funk & Wagnalls.

————. 1972. *A New Road for America: Major Policy Statements of President Nixon.* Garden City, NJ: Doubleday.

Olson, Mancur. 1965. *The Logic of Collective Action.* Cambridge: Harvard University Press.

————. 1982. *The Rise and Decline of Nations.* New Haven, CT: Yale University Press.

Osborne, David, and Ted Gaebler. 1992. *Reinventing Government: How the Entrepreneurial Spirit is Transforming the Public Sector.* Reading, MA: Addison-Wesley.

Perrow, Charles. 1984. *Normal Accidents: Living with High-Risk Technologies.* New York: Basic Books.

———. 1994. "A Review of Sagan's Limits of Safety." *Journal of Contingencies and Crisis Management* 2:212–20.

Peters, Thomas J., and Robert H. Waterman, Jr. 1982. *In Search of Excellence: Lessons from America's Best Run-Companies.* New York: Warner Books.

Peterson, Paul E. 1985. "The New Politics of Deficits." In *The New Directions in American Politics,* ed. John E. Chubb and Paul E. Peterson. Washington, DC: Brookings Institution.

Peterson, Peter G., and Neil Howe. 1988. *On Borrowed Time: How the Growth in Entitlement Spending Threatens America's Future.* New York: Touchstone.

Presidential Commission on the Space Shuttle Challenger Accident. 1986. *Report of the Presidential Commission on the Space Shuttle Challenger Accident.* Vol. 1. Washington, DC: U.S. Government Printing Office.

Pressman, Jeffrey L., and Aaron Wildavsky. 1973. *Implementation.* Berkeley and Los Angeles: University of California Press.

Quirk, Paul J. 1980. "Food and Drug Administration." In *The Politics of Regulation,* ed. James Q. Wilson. New York: Basic Books.

Raiffa, Howard. 1968. *Decision Analysis: Introductory Lectures on Choices under Uncertainty.* New York: Random House.

Ripley, Randall B., and Grace A. Franklin. 1976. *Congress, the Bureaucracy, and Public Policy.* Homewood, IL: Dorsey Press.

Roberts, Karlene H. 1989. "The Significance of Perrow's Normal Accidents." *Academy of Management Review* 14:285–89.

———. 1990. "Some Characteristics of One Type of High Reliability Organization." *Organization Science* 1:160–76.

Robinson, Enders A. 1985. *Probability Theory and Applications.* Boston: International Human Resources Development Corporation.

Rochlin, Gene I., Todd R. LaPorte, and Karla H. Roberts. 1987. "The Self-Designing High-Reliability Organization: Aircraft Carrier Flight Operations at Sea." *Naval War College Review* (autumn): 76–90.

Rosholt, Robert L. 1966. *An Administrative History of NASA, 1958–1963.* NASA SP-4101. Washington, DC: U.S. Government Printing Office.

Sagan, Scott D. 1993. *The Limits of Safety: Organizations, Accidents, and Nuclear Weapons.* Princeton, NJ: Princeton University Press.

———. 1994. "Toward a Political Theory of Organizational Safety." *Journal of Contingencies and Crisis Management* 2:228–40.

Savas, E. S. 1982. *Privatizing the Public Sector: How to Shrink Government.* Chatham, NJ: Chatham House Publishers.

Schein, Edgar H. 1985. *Organizational Culture and Leadership.* San Francisco, CA: Jossey-Bass.

Schichtle, Cass. 1983. *The National Space Program: From the Fifties into the Eighties.*

National Security Affairs Monograph Series 83-6. Washington, DC: National Defense University Press.

Schick, Allan. 1983. "Incremental Budgeting in a Decremental Age." *Policy Sciences* 16:1–25.

Schiesl, Martin J. 1977. *The Politics of Efficiency.* Berkeley and Los Angeles: University of California Press.

Schlesinger, Arthur. 1958. *The Coming of the New Deal.* Boston: Houghton Mifflin.

Schultze, Charles L. 1977. *The Public Use of Private Interest.* Washington, DC: Brookings Institution.

Sears, David O., and Jack Citrin. 1982. *Tax Revolt: Something for Nothing in California.* Cambridge: Harvard University Press.

Shapiro, Joseph P., and Joanne Silberner. 1987. "An Experimental Wonder Drug Awaits Approval." *U.S. News and World Report* 103 (September 21): 68.

Simon, Herbert A. 1965. *The Shape of Automation for Men and Management.* New York: Harper & Row.

Smith, Robert W. 1989. *The Space Telescope.* Cambridge: Cambridge University Press.

Steinbruner, John D. 1974. *The Cybernetic Theory of Decision.* Princeton, NJ: Princeton University Press.

Stockman, David. 1986. *The Triumph of Politics: The Inside Story of the Reagan Revolution.* New York: Avon Books.

Stokey, Edith, and Richard Zeckhauser. 1978. *A Primer for Policy Analysis.* New York: W. W. Norton.

Tillman, Frank, Ching-Lai Hwang, and Way Kuo. 1980. *Optimization of Systems Reliability.* New York: Marcel Dekker.

U.S. Congressional Budget Office and General Accounting Office. 1984. *Analysis of the Grace Commission's Major Proposals for Cost Control,* February 28. Washington, DC: U.S. Government Printing Office.

———. 1989. *FDA Resources: A Comprehensive Assessment of Staffing, Facilities and Equipment Needed.* GAO/HRD-89-142, September. Washington, DC: U.S. Government Printing Office.

———. 1990. *Funding for NASA's Safety Organizations Should Be Centralized.* GAO/NSIAD-90-187, August. Washington, DC: U.S. Government Printing Office.

U.S. House. 1961. Committee on Science and Astronautics. *Discussion of the Soviet Man-in-Space Shot.* 87th Cong., 1st sess.

———. 1981. Committee on Science and Technology, Subcommittee on Natural Resources, Agricultural Research, and Environment. *Drug Lag.* 97th Cong., 1st sess.

———. 1983. Committee on Science, Space and Technology, Subcommittee on Space Science and Applications. *Review of the National Aeronautics and Space Act of 1958.* 98th Cong., 1st sess.

———. 1985. Committee on Science, Space and Technology, Subcommittee on Space Science and Applications. *Centaur Cost, Schedule and Performance Review.* 99th Cong., 1st sess.

———. 1986a. Committee on Science, Space and Technology. *Investigation of the* Challenger *Accident,* vol. 1. 99th Cong., 2d sess.

———. 1986b. Committee on Science, Space and Technology. *NASA's Quality Assurance Program.* 99th Cong., 2d sess.

———. 1987. Committee on Energy and Commerce, Subcommittee on Health and the Environment. *AIDS Issues,* pt. 3. 100th Cong., 1st sess.

———. 1988. Committee on Government Operations, Subcommittee on Human Resources and Intergovernmental Relations. *Therapeutic Drugs for AIDS: Development, Testing, and Availability.* 100th Cong., 2d sess.

———. 1990. Committee on Science, Space and Technology, Subcommittee on Space Science and Applications. *Hubble Space Telescope Flaw.* 101st Cong., 2d sess. H. Doc. 156.

U.S. Office of Technology Assessment. 1990. *Access to Space: The Future of U.S. Space Transportation Systems.* OTA-ISC-415, April. Washington, DC: U.S. Government Printing Office.

Vaughan, Diane. 1990. "Autonomy, Interdependence, and Social Control: NASA and the Space Shuttle *Challenger.*" *Administrative Science Quarterly* 35:225–57.

———. 1996. *The* Challenger *Launch Decision.* Chicago: University of Chicago Press.

Weick, Karl E. 1987. "Organizational Culture as a Source of High Reliability." *California Management Review* 29:115–28.

Weimer, David L. 1982. "Safe—and Available—Drugs." In *Instead of Regulation,* ed. Robert W. Poole. Lexington, MA: Lexington Books.

Weiss, Howard M. 1971. "NASA's Quality Program—Achievements and Forecast." Paper presented at the twenty-fifth annual ASQC Technical Conference, 21 May, Chicago.

Welch, Susan. 1985. "The 'More for Less' Paradox: Public Attitudes on Taxing and Spending." *Public Opinion Quarterly* 49:301–16.

Wildavsky, Aaron. 1984. *The Politics of the Budgetary Process.* Boston: Little, Brown and Company.

———. 1988. *Searching for Safety.* New Brunswick, NJ: Transaction Books.

Wilensky, Harold. 1969. *Organizational Intelligence.* New York: Basic Books.

Wilson, James Q. 1967. "The Bureaucracy Problem." *Public Interest* 6:3–9.

Winston, Wayne L. 1995. *Introduction to Mathematical Programming.* Belmont, CA: Duxbury Press.

Woodhouse, Edward J. 1988. "Sophisticated Trial and Error in Decision Making About Risk." In *Technology and Politics,* ed. Michael E. Kraft and Norman J. Vig. Durham, NC: Duke University Press.

Wynne, Brian. 1988. "Unruly Technology: Practical Rules, Impractical Discourses, and Public Understanding." *Social Studies of Science* 18:147–67.

Young, Frank, John Norris, Joseph Levitt, and Stuart Nightingale. 1988. "The FDA's New Procedures for the Use of Investigational Drugs in Treatment." *Journal of the American Medical Association* 259:2267–70.

Index

accelerated approval initiative, 158
acceptable risks, 164–68
accountability, 166–68
aerospace industry, 46–47
Agriculture, Department of, 57, 59
AIDS/HIV, 66–69, 154–55, 164
AIDS lobby, 67, 154, 157
American Medical Association, 57
Apollo missions
  Apollo 1 fire, 43–44, 136
  Apollo 11, 44–45
  See also Project Apollo
Army Ballistic Missile Agency, 38
Asch, Solomon, 91
Astro mission, 6, 51–52
AZT, 15

Bayesian decision making, 31, 33, 116
Beggs, James, 48
Bendor, Jon, 2, 4, 9, 77, 103
beta distribution, 113, 115, 117–18,
  127–28
biased information, 126
budget deficit, 102, 123, 124
bureaucratic culture, 9, 11, 21, 65, 95,
  173
bureaucratic growth, 101–2

Carter, James, 47, 102
Casamayou, Maureen, 52
Challenger, 1, 4, 6, 17, 51–55, 135,
  140–43, 145–47, 163–64, 167
Chisholm, Donald, 4, 171
clinical testing, 151–52, 160
Clinton, Bill, 55, 68, 102, 149
common mode failures, 94–96, 172

component performance, 72, 74, 80–81,
  98, 125, 129, 131, 134, 167
components, defined, 71
component strategy, 103–4, 106–8,
  127–28, 131, 133, 149–50, 161–
  62, 172
Consolini, Paula, 4, 8
consumer and health groups , 63, 68
context, 106, 117–18
contractors, 138–39, 140n, 143. *See
  also* aerospace industry
cost-effectiveness. *See* efficiency
cost of failure
  economic, 17, 19, 166
  political, 17–19
costs, administrative, 104, 110, 112
cue-taking/giving, 92–94, 146, 172–73
cybernetic decision making, 31, 33
cycles of failure, 34, 168–71

decompositional methods, 74, 88–89
Defense, Department of, 39, 46, 48–51,
  103, 139–40
dideoxyinosine (ddI), 155
downsizing, 123–24, 149–50
drug
  efficacy, 60, 152–53, 158
  labelling, 57–58, 153
  pricing, 59, 151, 158
  safety, 59–60, 151–53, 155, 158

efficiency, 3, 101–3, 124–26, 163, 168–
  69
  at FDA, 61
  at NASA, 42–43, 48–49, 51, 53, 55–
  56, 138, 147, 149